E-COMMERCE MARKETING

Kleindl and Burrow

Australia • Brazil • Japan • Korea • Mexico • Singapore • Spain • United Kingdom • United States

E-Commerce Marketing
Brad Alan Kleindl, James L. Burrow

VP/Editorial Director:
Jack W. Calhoun

VP/Editor-in-Chief:
Dave Shaut

Senior Publisher:
Karen Schmohe

Executive Editor:
Eve Lewis

Project Manager:
Penny Shank

Consulting Editor:
Leslie Kauffman

VP/Director of Marketing:
Carol Volz

Senior Marketing Manager:
Nancy A. Long

Marketing Coordinator:
Yvonne Patton-Beard

Production Editor:
Martha Conway

Production Manager:
Tricia Boies

Manufacturing Coordinator:
Kevin Kluck

Design Project Manager:
Tippy McIntosh

Photography Manager:
Darren Wright

Permissions Editor:
Linda Ellis

Production House:
Navta Associates, Inc.

Cover and Internal Design:
Tippy McIntosh

Cover Images:
© PhotoDisc and © Corbis

Printer:
China Translation & Printing Services Ltd.

Printed in China

6 7 8 9 10 16 15 14 13 12

10-digit ISBN: 0-538-43808-8
13-digit ISBN: 978-0-538-43808-7

For more information contact South-Western, 5191 Natorp Boulevard, Mason, Ohio, 45040.
Or you can visit our Internet site at school.cengage.com

PHOTO CREDITS
Page i: © PhotoDisc and © Corbis
Pages iv–vii: Airplane photo © THINKSTOCK; all other photos © GETTY IMAGES/PHOTODISC

E-COMMERCE MARKETING

CONTENTS

http://w
BUY IT!
FRAGILE
handle with care
Select Payment Method
Credit Card Type
Credit Card Number
Exp. Date

.com
Secure Site

REVIEWERS

Sandra Bell-Duckworth
Westerville, OH

Mike Closner
Grandview, WA

Shelly Devos
Auburn, IL

Michael Foley
Manassas, VA

Thomas D. Griffin
Maple Heights, OH

Laura Hilzendeger
Tacoma, WA

Keri Holter
Salem, WI

Atkins D. (Trey) Michael, III
Raleigh, NC

Sherry Ponds
Pensacola, FL

James Rademacher
Daytona Beach, FL

TO THE STUDENT

WELCOME TO E-COMMERCE MARKETING!

The field of e-commerce marketing is rapidly growing. Many universities, colleges, and high schools now offer specializations in e-commerce marketing. The general principles of marketing that are presented throughout this book are intended to be a guide in taking your first career step into the exciting world of e-commerce. Learn how to plan and market electronic business products and online services in a flash.

Functions of Marketing

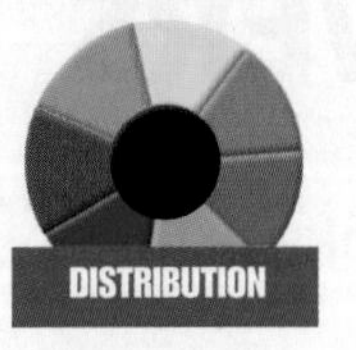

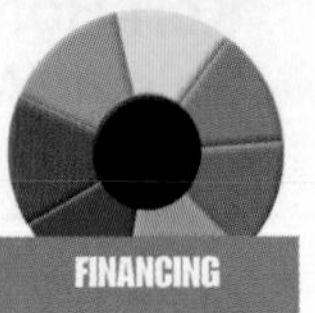

The basic **functions of marketing** are visually identified by icons throughout the text.

Winning Strategies presents successful real-world strategies used in e-commerce marketing.

Logging On begins each lesson and encourages you to explore the material in the upcoming lesson. Logging On also gives you opportunities to work with other students in your class.

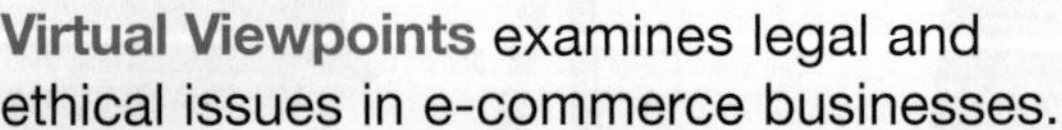

Internet Intelligence investigates e-commerce on the Internet.

Virtual Viewpoints examines legal and ethical issues in e-commerce businesses.

E-Marketing Myths explores some common myths about e-commerce marketing functions.

Project Dot.com provides you with projects to improve your skills in planning an e-commerce business.

Cyber Check provides you with an opportunity to assess your comprehension at key points in each lesson. Ongoing review and assessment helps you understand the material.

Working Online acquaints you with various careers in e-commerce marketing.

Time Out introduces you to interesting facts and statistics about e-commerce marketing.

DECA Prep prepares you for competitive events with a Case Study and Event Prep in every chapter.

ecommkt.swlearning.com includes Internet activities and crossword puzzles for every chapter.

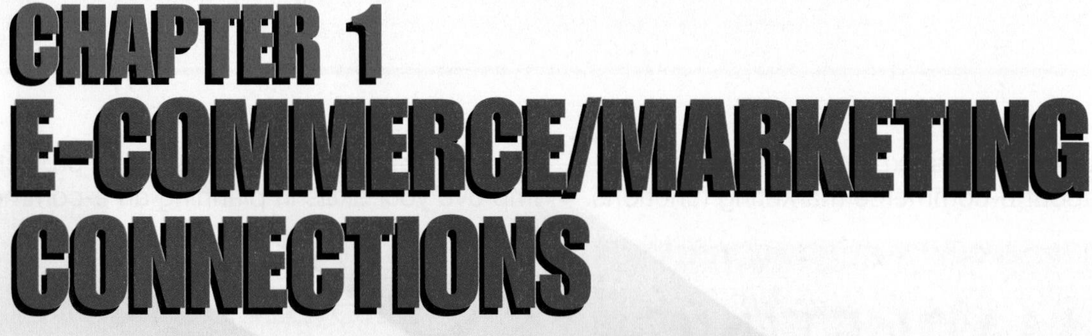

CHAPTER 1
E-COMMERCE/MARKETING CONNECTIONS

1.1 Marketing Foundations
1.2 The Changing Nature of Business and Marketing
1.3 Improving Business—Customer Exchanges
1.4 Advantages and Challenges of E-Marketing

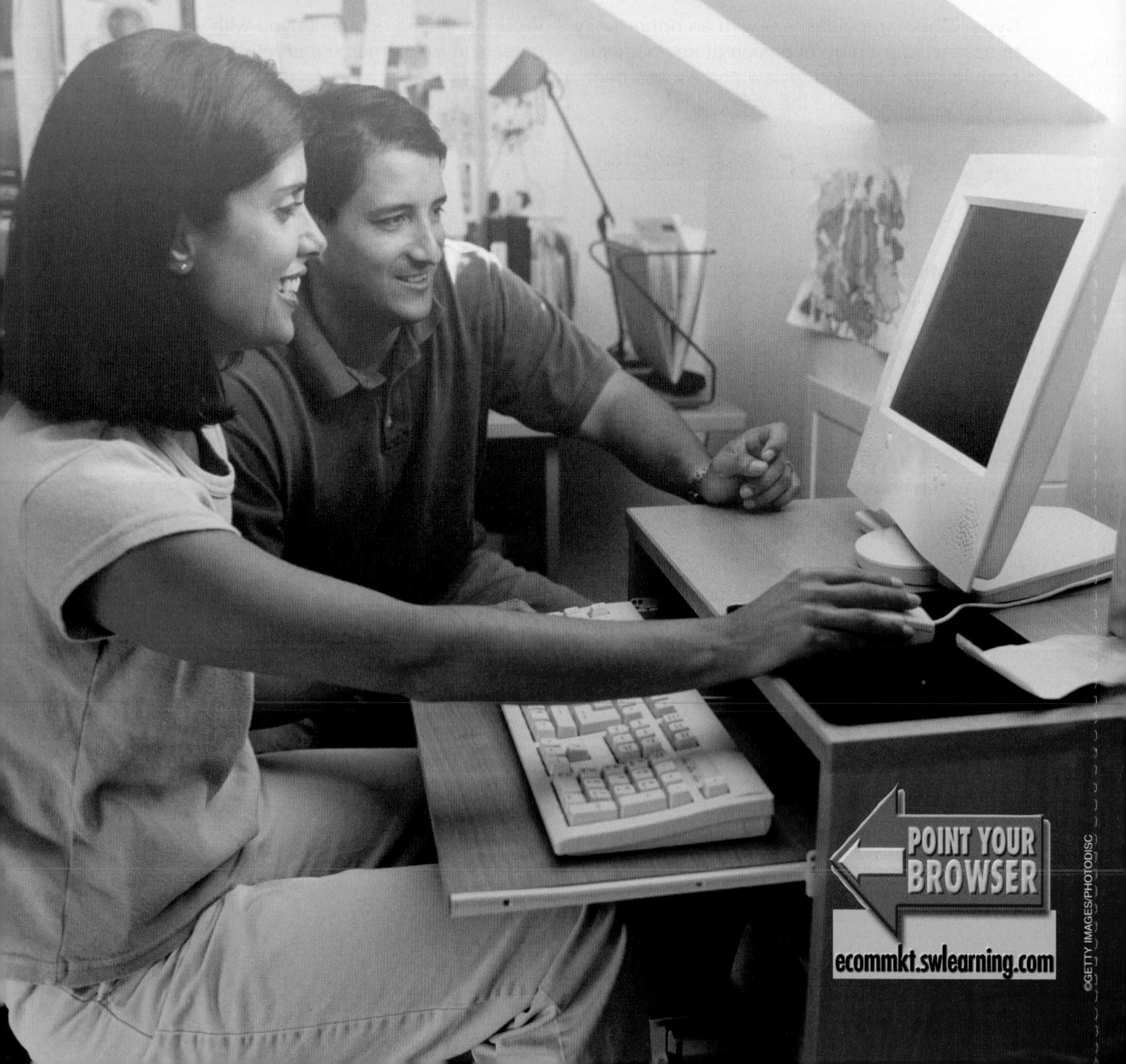

POINT YOUR BROWSER
ecommkt.swlearning.com

ONLINE PLANE DESIGN

Would you purchase a 250-passenger airplane from a web site? Most major airlines wouldn't, especially a model that won't be available for several years. So why did Boeing Company begin advertising the new 7E7 airliner on its web site in 2003 when it will not be available until 2008?

Boeing is one of the world's leading companies in the use of the Internet for business-to-business marketing. However, Boeing's Internet marketing effort for the new 7E7 is directed toward consumers rather than business customers. Investing in the development of a major new airplane design is a huge risk. In order to sell 3,000 airplanes over a 20-year period, Boeing wants to build excitement and name recognition for the new model among air travelers. It wants the 7E7 to be viewed as both passenger-friendly and environment-friendly.

Boeing has developed an alliance with AOL Time Warner. AOL subscribers may participate in the 7E7's development and watch it being designed and ultimately built. If you are an AOL subscriber, you will have exclusive access to pictures of the new model. Boeing will ask you to participate in surveys that will help name the airplane and design it to meet consumer needs. Survey participants who submit their e-mail addresses and age brackets have the chance to win a trip to Seattle. While there, the winner will be able to operate the flight simulator used to train Boeing's pilots.

THINK CRITICALLY

1. Since the average Internet user cannot buy the new 7E7 airplane, what value will this advertising initiative have for Boeing?
2. What name would you recommend for the airplane? How would that name help sell the airplane?

MARKETING FOUNDATIONS

LESSON 1.1

Describe the role marketing plays in business.

Define the seven functions of marketing.

LOGGING ON

Do you have a "buddy list"? If so, you are one of over 60 million people who use instant messaging (IM) on your computer. IM services are available from AOL, Yahoo!, MSN, and many other companies. With these services, you can instantly engage friends, family, and co-workers in conversation. IM allows you to check who is online and talk to one person or dozens of people at the same time.

Instant messaging is used for communicating both at work and at home. It is estimated that over five billion minutes of work time and 14 billion minutes of leisure time were used for IM in a recent year. So many people use IM that companies are now using instant messaging to promote their products. Capitol Records uses IM to introduce new recordings and to promote music groups and tours. Fans can get advance information and answers to questions. ELLEgirl.com introduced an IM tool directed at teenage girls. IM increased the number of people viewing ELLEgirl's web site by 83 percent.

Work with a partner to discuss why instant messaging is so popular both at work and at home. What problems might a business encounter when using IM to promote its products?

THE ROLE OF MARKETING

The American Marketing Association developed a comprehensive definition of marketing. *Marketing* is the process of planning and executing the conception, pricing, promotion, and distribution of ideas, goods, and services to create exchanges that satisfy individual and organizational objectives. Those words describe a complicated but important part of every business. Marketing includes a variety of activities and a number of businesses in our economy. A simpler definition emphasizes the important role of marketing. **Marketing** is the development and maintenance of satisfying exchange relationships between businesses and consumers.

MARKETING ACTIVITIES

Marketing activities occur around you all the time. Some marketing activities are obvious. You see or hear advertisements for products when watching television, listening to the radio, or waiting for a movie to begin at the theater. You even see signs of marketing on the clothing that you and your friends wear. When you visit a store, the displays, product packaging, and salesperson assistance are all examples of marketing.

Less obvious but equally important marketing activities include the movement of goods by trucks, trains, ships, and airplanes from distant locations to your city. A great deal of marketing is not even directed at final consumers. Businesses market products and services to other businesses that, in turn, use those products and services in their own business operations or sell them to final consumers. Banks lend money to retailers so that they can purchase products from manufacturers to sell to their customers. Insurance companies sell policies to businesses in order to reduce the financial risk that might result from accidents, product damage, or theft.

MARKETING ON THE INTERNET

Many traditional marketing activities continue today. However, the Internet is changing the way those activities are completed. The Internet also is opening up new marketing opportunities. Using the Internet and related technologies to complete significant marketing activities is known as **e-marketing** or *electronic marketing*.

Log on to the Internet and you are immediately bombarded with advertisements for products and services targeted at typical viewers of the web sites that you are visiting. You can qualify for a credit card, compare prices of products, or talk with a customer service representative via e-mail or a live "chat" session. An airline may deliver an e-ticket to you for an upcoming trip. You can even purchase and print postage from the U.S. Postal Service.

Businesses use the Internet to conduct research, process customer orders, transfer funds to a supplier's bank, and provide access to customer service representatives 24 hours a day, seven days a week. When used properly, e-marketing increases the effectiveness of exchanges between businesses and consumers. When consumers and businesses misuse the Internet, it often results in problems, complaints, and dissatisfaction.

INTERNET INTELLIGENCE

With today's technology, newly released movies, live concerts, and entire editions of newspapers and magazines can be viewed on a home computer. This technology eliminates the need for consumers to go to cinemas, purchase concert seats, or have newspapers delivered to their homes.

THINK CRITICALLY

1. **Use the Internet to find ten examples of movies, music, books, newspapers, and magazines that are accessible online.**
2. **For both businesses and consumers, discuss the advantages and disadvantages of Internet access for these types of products.**

The volume of Internet business is growing rapidly each year. It is estimated that annual consumer purchases on the Internet now top $50 billion. That amount is small compared to business-to-business Internet sales that exceed $2 trillion a year. Internet sales are increasing dramatically as more people become comfortable with online purchasing and more businesses move or expand to the World Wide Web.

Do men and women visit different web sites? Surprisingly, the top three sites visited by men and women are the same—Amazon.com, BarnesandNoble.com, and CDNow.com. Men are drawn to BestBuy.com while women prefer to shop online at JCPenney.com.

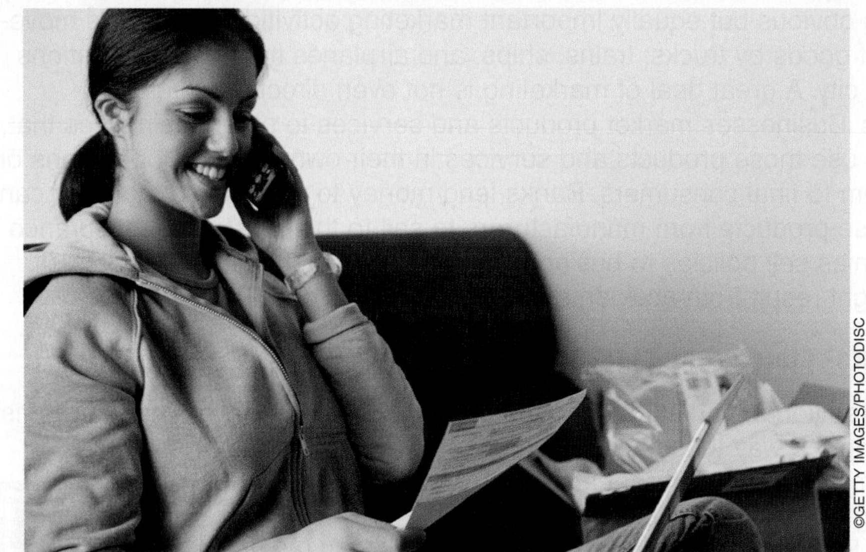
©GETTY IMAGES/PHOTODISC

cyber check

Describe several ways that marketing activities are completed using the Internet.

you can qualify for a credit card, compare prices of products, or talk with a customer service representative via e-mail or live chat session

MARKETING FUNCTIONS

Marketing activities occur around us every day. While many of the activities are important to us, we often don't recognize them as a part of marketing. When you hear the term "marketing," you may have visions of advertisements or salespeople. Marketing is much more complex than that. Marketing activities can be organized into seven functions. Each function occurs every time a product or service is developed and sold. Businesses provide many of the marketing functions. Consumers often are responsible for one or more of the marketing functions when they make purchases.

Product/service management is designing, developing, maintaining, improving, and acquiring products and services so that they meet consumer needs. Producers and manufacturers develop new products, but other businesses also are involved in product/service management when they obtain the products for resale.

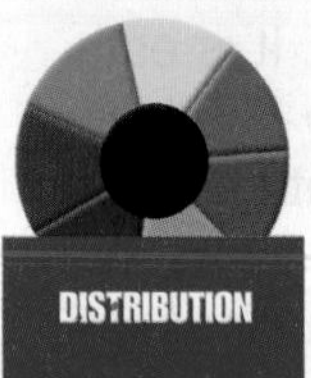

Distribution involves determining the best methods and procedures to allow customers to locate, obtain, and use the products and services of an organization. Careful shipping, handling, and storing of products are needed for effective distribution.

Selling is communicating directly with prospective customers to assess and satisfy their needs. Selling can be face to face, such as when a customer visits a business or when a salesperson goes to the home or business of a prospective customer. Selling is also performed using a telephone or other technology, including Internet tools such as instant messaging or videoconferencing.

Marketing-information management is obtaining, managing, and using market information to improve business decision making and the performance of marketing activities. This function includes marketing research and the development of databases with information about products, customers, and competitors.

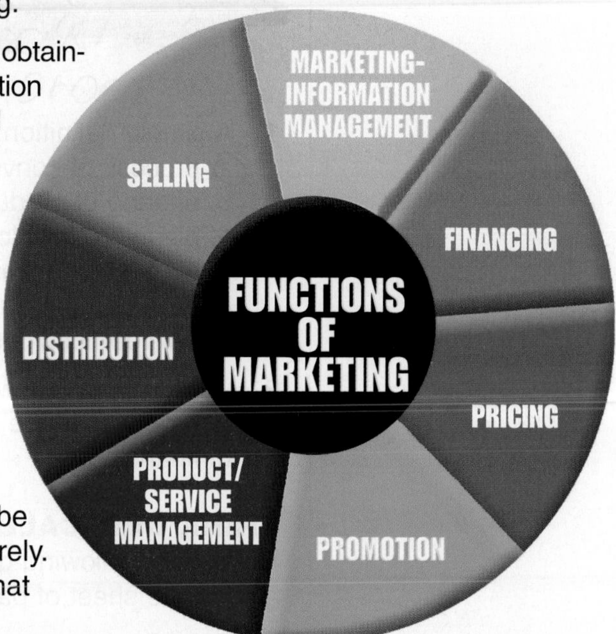

©2000, MARKETING EDUCATION RESOURCE CENTER, COLUMBUS, OHIO

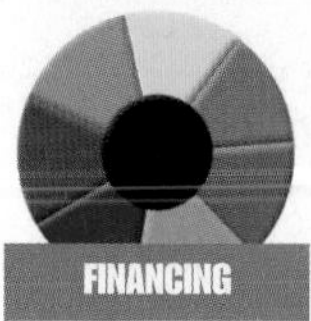

Financing is budgeting for marketing activities, obtaining the necessary funds needed for operations, and providing assistance to customers in purchasing the business's products and services. E-commerce customers must be able to make payments easily and securely. E-commerce businesses must ensure that they receive the payments.

Pricing is establishing and communicating the value of products and services to prospective customers. Customers must be able to readily identify the price of each item in which they are interested or they will move on. Consumers want to know that they are getting a fair value for the money they are spending. Prices must be set low enough that customers are willing to pay but high enough that a profit is generated for the business.

Promotion is communicating information about products and services to prospective customers through advertising and other promotional methods to encourage them to buy. Advertising may be accomplished through a variety of media—television, newspapers, magazines, radio, direct mail, and the Internet. Other promotional methods include contests, product displays, sponsorships, and public relations activities.

List the seven marketing functions.

•products/service mangagmet •Distribution •Selling
•Marketing-information •Financing •pricing •Promotion

LOGGING OFF

UNDERSTAND MARKETING CONCEPTS

Circle the best answer for each of the following questions.

1. A simple definition of marketing is the
   a. process of convincing customers to buy.
   b. offering of products for sale that are superior to the competition.
   c. planning, development, and distribution of services to consumers and other businesses.
   d. development and maintenance of satisfying exchange relationships between businesses and consumers.
2. Which of the following is *not* one of the seven marketing functions?
   a. product/service management
   b. financing
   c. selling
   d. buying

THINK CRITICALLY

Answer the following questions as completely as possible. If necessary, use a separate sheet of paper.

3. Describe how an e-commerce business might complete each of the seven marketing functions.

____

____

____

____

____

4. **Communication** A veterinarian in your neighborhood has asked for your advice on using the Internet to promote her business. Write a two-paragraph memo to Dr. Alvarez describing how her business could benefit from using the Internet.

____

____

____

____

____

THE CHANGING NATURE OF BUSINESS AND MARKETING

LOGGING ON

EBay has brought one the oldest forms of marketing to the Internet—negotiating through an auction to establish the selling price of a product. eBay describes itself as "the world's largest online community of buyers and sellers. It's a place to buy what you want, sell what you have, and make a few friends while you're at it."

One reason for eBay's success is that it provides a convenient place and method for consumers to buy unique products. eBay has created thousands of entrepreneurs who have found a new way to start and run a small business. These entrepreneurs list products for sale online. Sometimes the products are the sellers' own creations. More often, they are new or used products the seller has purchased from another source and hopes to resell on eBay at a profit.

Work with a partner. Discuss why eBay is one of the few e-commerce businesses that has been profitable from the beginning. What makes participation in eBay auctions so attractive to both buyers and sellers? Visit the eBay site. What unique products did you find for auction there?

Discuss how the Internet has changed the nature of business.

Identify the steps in developing a marketing strategy.

BUSINESS AND OUR ECONOMY

Businesses are an important part of our economy and lives. Often, you are not aware of the many businesses that provide the products and services you use. Even in small communities, you see many examples of companies that produce products, provide transportation, and supply electricity. You see other companies that offer entertainment, provide healthcare, and sell the products and services that you and other community members want and need. In addition, businesses provide employment opportunities. They also pay taxes and support the growth and development of the communities in which they operate.

There are many types of businesses that provide goods and services. *Producers* and *manufacturers* convert raw materials into consumable products. Channel members, including wholesalers and retailers, complete a variety of business activities to sell and distribute products from producers to consumers. *Service businesses* do not provide tangible products. They provide complete activities that benefit their customers. Service providers can range from barbers, travel agents, and florists to accountants, airlines, and musicians.

BUSINESS IS CHANGING

Business is quite different today than it was just 15 to 20 years ago. Companies compete on a global scale. They buy and sell products and services from other companies around the world. They face competition from businesses located on other continents. Environmental concerns require companies to conserve resources, reduce pollution, and provide a healthy work environment for employees. New technology often reduces the number of employees required to complete a task. At the same time, it increases the knowledge and skill requirements of the people who work for the company.

IMPACT OF THE INTERNET

Few things have dramatically and immediately impacted our lives and the way many businesses operate more than the development of the Internet. Consumers can now sit down in front of their computers and in just minutes locate several businesses. They can visit the businesses' web sites, compare products and prices, and make purchases without leaving home. If a problem arises with a product after business hours, customers are often able to contact the company online for immediate help.

Businesses benefit from the Internet in many ways. Employees traveling around the world can now stay in contact with their companies. They can access needed information through an Internet connection. A manufacturer can track a customer's order at any time as it is being shipped. The Internet gives businesses quick access to research findings provided by the federal government or universities. Companies can instantly order the raw materials, supplies, or other goods they need by using the web sites of their suppliers. A company's use of the Internet to support or complete business transactions is known as **e-commerce**. The Internet has increased competition and the speed of business.

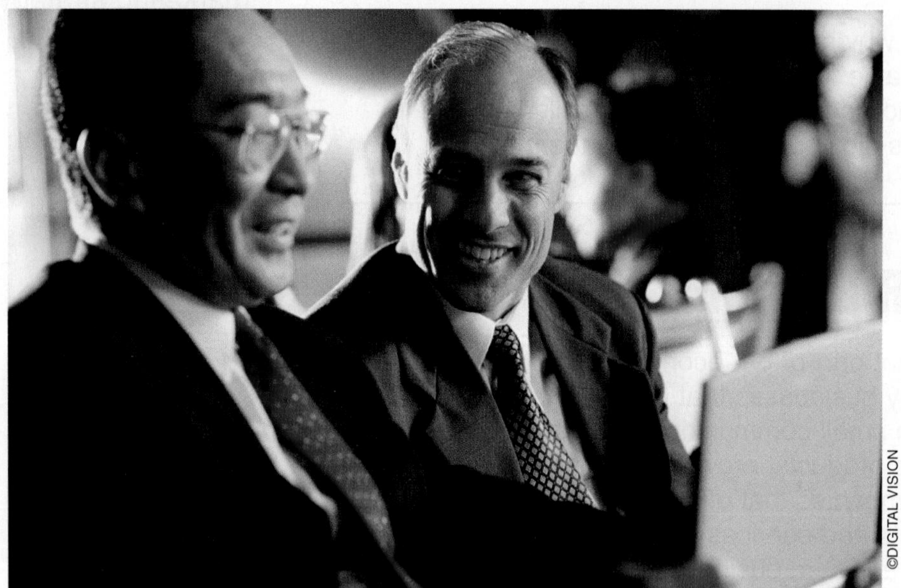

List three ways that the Internet has changed business.

visit the businesses web sits, compare products and prices and make purchases without leaving home

MARKETING BASICS

The ways that some marketing activities are performed have changed as businesses have turned to e-commerce. However, the basic principles of marketing still apply. E-commerce businesses must understand marketing basics and use them effectively in order to be successful and profitable.

Education makes a difference in Internet use. Only 5 percent of non-high school graduates use the Internet, while 23 percent of high school graduates are online. Almost 40 percent of college graduates use the Internet regularly.

MARKETING PLANNING

Successful marketing results in satisfying exchanges between businesses and consumers. Businesses offer products and services that satisfy their customers' needs. Customers pay for those products and services, providing the businesses with revenue. Businesses must plan carefully in order to identify the products and services that satisfy customer needs and that can be produced and sold at a profit. A company's plan that identifies how it will use marketing to achieve its goals is called a **marketing strategy**. A successful business thinks first of customers' wants and needs as it makes marketing decisions.

DEVELOPING A MARKETING STRATEGY

Development of a marketing strategy is a two-step process. The first step is to identify a target market. A **target market** is a specific group of consumers that have similar wants and needs. Many companies attempt to promote their products to a wide audience whose wants and needs are quite varied. It is difficult for the company to meet all of those needs. The result is that many people will not want the company's products or will be dissatisfied with them. Focusing on a target market with specific needs makes it easier to develop products and services that the customers want.

The second step in the development of a marketing strategy is to create a marketing mix. A **marketing mix** is the blending of four marketing elements—product, distribution, price, and promotion. A successful marketing mix satisfies the wants and needs of the target market and produces a profit for the company.

eToys.com is an example of an e-commerce business that has developed a successful marketing strategy. The web site sells a variety of toys and makes it easy for customers with different needs to find what they want. Web site visitors can search by categories, such as learning toys, collectibles, or video games. Each category appeals to a different target market with specific needs. Customers can even find toys categorized by age groups.

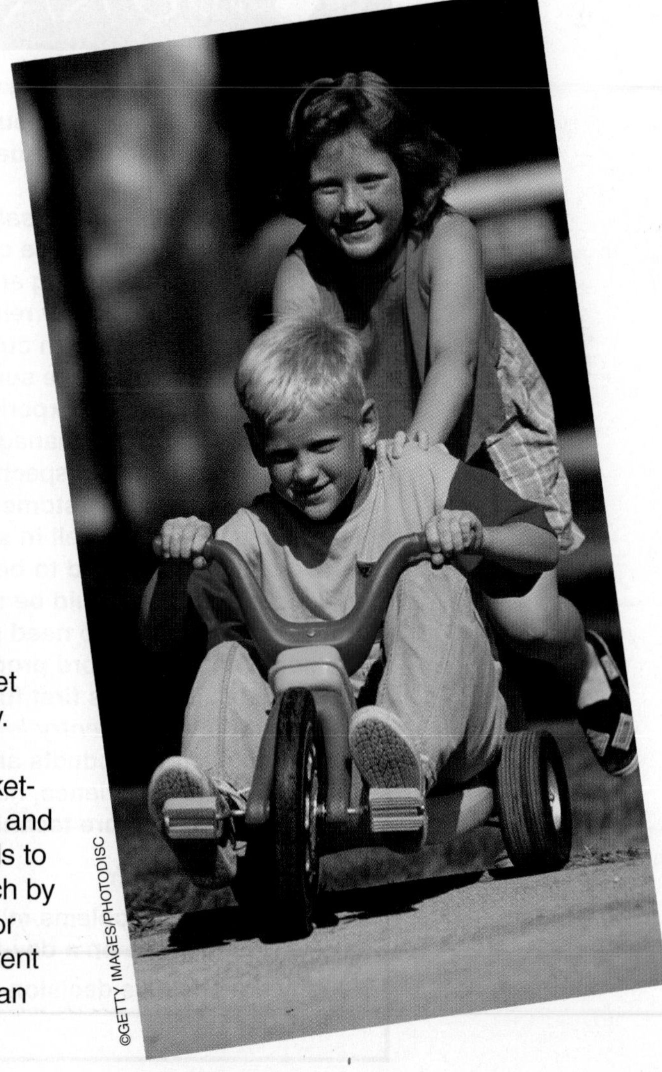
©GETTY IMAGES/PHOTODISC

The marketing mix of eToys starts with the *product.* A variety of name-brand toys are available for sale. *Distribution* is provided through direct shipment to the customer's home. Shipping policies are explained and the cost of shipping is calculated when an order is placed. For some purchases, free shipping is offered as an incentive to buy. *Prices* are clearly shown for each product. Consumers can even select the amount they want to spend for a toy when beginning their search. *Promotion* is accomplished through clear descriptions and attractive pictures of the toys.

What are the two steps in the development of a marketing strategy?

• target market

• marketing mix

WORKING ONLINE

Doug, a recent graduate, has strong human relations and communications skills. Doug wants to put these skills to use in his first full-time job. He has decided to pursue a customer service position with a local e-commerce business.

A *customer relationship sales specialist* is an important career position in e-commerce. E-commerce companies want customers to feel comfortable with online purchasing and to receive support if they have questions or problems. The customer relationship sales specialist monitors customer orders, communicates with customers by e-mail and telephone, and follows up on orders to make sure that customers are satisfied with their purchases and purchasing experiences. The specialist recommends to the e-commerce marketing manager ways that ordering procedures can be improved and ways that specific customer needs and requests can be met.

To be an effective customer relationship sales specialist, you must be able to communicate well in short, written messages and in telephone conversations. You need to be a problem solver with effective decision-making skills. You should be motivated to provide a high level of customer service. You also need proficiency in basic computer usage, including database, word processing, and communications software.

Since this is Doug's first full-time job, his customer relationship sales specialist position is *entry level,* meaning that he is responsible for a limited number of products and less complex customer support issues. As Doug gains experience, he will be able to provide extensive customer service related to more technical products.

THINK CRITICALLY

1. **What types of problems might a customer relationship sales specialist like Doug handle on a day-to-day basis?**
2. **Why are effective decision-making skills an important requirement of this position?**

LOGGING OFF

UNDERSTAND MARKETING CONCEPTS

Circle the best answer for each of the following questions.

1. The primary responsibility of a manufacturer is to
   a. distribute products to consumers.
   b. offer services to its customers.
   c. convert raw materials into consumable products.
   d. use promotion to attract customers.
2. The two steps in the development of a marketing strategy are
   a. developing a product and creating advertising.
   b. choosing customers and identifying competitors.
   c. identifying a target market and developing a marketing mix.
   d. selecting marketing functions and communicating with customers.

THINK CRITICALLY

Answer the following questions as completely as possible. If necessary, use a separate sheet of paper.

3. Consider each of the major types of businesses (manufacturers and producers, channel members, and service businesses). Use a business directory, telephone book, or the Internet. For each type of business, identify one local company and one national or international company as examples.

4. **Communication** Locate a business web site that effectively identifies a target market the business serves. Describe in as much detail as possible who the target market is and the wants and needs of the target market. Explain how the business is trying to satisfy those wants and needs with its products and services.

IMPROVING BUSINESS–CUSTOMER EXCHANGES

Describe the marketing concept.

Explain how marketing can increase customer and business satisfaction.

LOGGING ON

Security measures in airports make travel more time-consuming and difficult. Long check-in lines have become the norm as travelers obtain seat assignments and boarding passes. The savvy traveler can streamline this process. Some airlines offer seat selection on the Internet. Using a web site, you can enter your flight number and view the interior of your airplane with available seats identified. You can point and click to select the seat you want. You can then print your boarding pass on your home printer. At the airport, you may bypass the long lines and go straight to your departure gate. At the gate, you will present a picture identification card and have your preprinted boarding pass scanned.

Work with a partner. Identify and discuss other ways that the Internet can be used to reduce some of the problems people experience when traveling. What are the risks of buying an airline ticket online?

THE NEED FOR EFFECTIVE MARKETING

Marketing plays an increasingly important role in business. Yet, many business people and customers do not understand how marketing is used effectively. Some believe that marketing is nothing more than advertising and sales. They believe that a persuasive advertisement or a high-pressure salesperson can influence consumers to buy things they really don't want or need.

©GETTY IMAGES/PHOTODISC

To be successful, businesses must make a profit. Customers generating the most profits are those satisfied with a business and its products. These customers return to purchase again and again. Dissatisfied customers are not likely to make additional purchases. They also will likely tell others about their dissatisfaction. Businesses must work hard to satisfy their customers. Effective marketing is an important part of that effort.

THE MARKETING CONCEPT

Many companies think only of their product when making business decisions. They believe they know what consumers want without seeking consumer input. They distribute the product to a location where customers can buy it. They make sure it is well advertised to catch customers' attention. As long as companies complete these activities, they believe that consumers will purchase whatever they produce. This philosophy has proven false, and many products sit on store shelves unsold. Others are purchased and then returned for a refund because they don't meet customer needs.

A new approach to product planning and marketing is the marketing concept. The **marketing concept** is the focus on the needs of customers during the planning, production, distribution, and promotion of a product or service. Successful businesses think first of customers and their needs rather than of the products they want to sell. When using the marketing concept, businesses

- identify their customers and their customers' needs.
- develop and market products and services that their customers consider better than other choices.
- operate profitably.

THE MARKETING CONCEPT AND E-COMMERCE

The owners of the first Internet businesses often knew very little about marketing or the marketing concept. The owners believed that the new technology would easily put their products in front of a large number of prospective customers. These customers would find it convenient to place orders using the Internet. One famous example was Pets.com. The company planned to sell pet food and other pet supplies from an Internet site. There was adequate money to start the company, a recognizable name, and a large number of pet owners as potential customers. The company even had a cute promotional image—a talking dog sock puppet. Pets.com created excitement when it decided to spend over $3 million on a 30-second television advertisement that was aired during the 2000 NFL Super Bowl. After two years of operation with no profits, the company closed.

©GETTY IMAGES/PHOTODISC

A major reason that Pets.com failed is that it didn't apply the marketing concept. While there are many pet owners who purchase pet food and other supplies, these customers weren't comfortable ordering on the Internet. They didn't want to wait several days for delivery. Also, customers had many other places where they could purchase pet food and supplies in their local communities. These businesses often offered prices that were equal to or lower than Pets.com's prices.

To succeed, an e-commerce business must identify customers who want its product and are willing to purchase online. The business must provide adequate information to help the customer decide to buy. Customers should be able to ask questions and have them answered. The ordering process must be easy and safe. The company must be able to deliver the product to the customer, provide customer service, and resolve problems if they occur. It must be able to do all of these things and still make a profit. You can see that e-commerce is not easy. It requires managers and other employees who understand business and marketing.

On what must businesses focus when using the marketing concept?

• Identify their costomers and their needs
• develop and market products and services
• operate profitchly

SATISFYING EXCHANGES

Marketing is a process of exchange. Businesses produce and sell products and services to consumers in exchange for money. The goal is to cover business costs and show a profit from the sales. Consumers have wants and needs that the businesses attempt to satisfy. Consumers exchange money for the products and services that they believe will provide the most satisfaction for the money spent. If businesses cannot produce and sell products at a profit, they will not be satisfied. If customers find that the products and services they purchase do not meet their needs, or that they could have made the purchases at a lower cost, they will not be satisfied.

ECONOMIC UTILITY

A principle from economics describes how businesses can increase customer satisfaction. **Economic utility** is the amount of satisfaction received from using a product or service. A product providing great satisfaction has high economic utility. A product providing little satisfaction has low economic utility. Businesses can improve economic utility and customer satisfaction by changing the form, time, place, or possession of a product.

Form Utility Making a product better or easier to use increases form utility. Customers will be more satisfied if the product is durable, has important features, or is sold in the size or quantity desired. Making CDs that can be recorded and erased is a significant form improvement over those that just have recorded music or video content.

Time Utility Consumers expect to be able to purchase a product when they need it. If they have to wait for delivery or if the product is not available at a convenient time, customers will not be satisfied.

E-MARKETING MYTHS

Many companies that use the Internet to market their goods and services employ misleading tactics to attract customers' attention. The companies believe that these tactics benefit the business, when in fact they often alienate customers. Pop-up advertisements announce that consumers have won a contest. The ads state that the consumers can redeem the prize by clicking on the link to the company's web page. E-mail messages tell consumers that they are selected to be members of a research panel. The online research questions are actually disguised promotional messages.

THINK CRITICALLY

1. **How would you feel about receiving misleading messages from an e-commerce company?**
2. **How might misleading tactics harm a company?**

Place Utility Consumers may expect products and services to be available at a particular location. If customers must search for a product, must drive a long distance, or are unable to purchase several related items at the same location, their dissatisfaction will increase.

Possession Utility If consumers cannot afford to purchase (possess) a product, their need for the product will be impossible to satisfy. There are several ways a business can increase possession utility. The business can extend credit, allowing the customer to make several payments for the purchase over a period of time. Customers may be able to obtain a home or an automobile by leasing rather than purchasing in order to reduce the monthly payments. Video stores and cable television services rent movies to consumers for one-time viewing at a much lower cost than purchasing the movies.

ECONOMIC UTILITY AND E-COMMERCE

The Internet provides many opportunities for companies to increase economic utility and, therefore, customer satisfaction. The most obvious forms of improved utility are time and place. Information can be accessed and products can be purchased any time of the day or night. Purchasing can be completed from the consumer's home.

PRODUCT/ SERVICE MANAGEMENT

The form of some products is modified with the use of the Internet. Electronic books, e-tickets, digital photographs, and online bill paying are examples of changes in the form of traditional products. Some consumers find the new forms more satisfying while others prefer the products in their original forms.

One aspect of place utility that is difficult for Internet businesses to perform better than local businesses is the distribution of the product to the customer. Assume that a commonly used product is available at a local store for a reasonable price. Although it may be convenient to purchase the product online, there is little value in doing so if you must travel to a business to pick it up or wait several days for delivery.

Possession utility may be somewhat hampered with e-commerce. Forms of payment are almost solely limited to credit cards. Some customers may be concerned about the security of entering their credit card numbers online. Internet companies that allow customers to easily compare the prices of products from competing businesses or to calculate the difference between owning and leasing a product are possibly increasing possession utility.

What are the four ways that businesses can improve economic utility?

• Form Utility • Time Utility

• Place Utility • Possession Utility

The top U.S. cities in terms of Internet use in 2003 were Seattle (with 81 percent of all homes having access), Boston (with 79 percent), and San Diego (with 78 percent). Those cities were followed by San Francisco, Hartford, Portland, Washington D.C., and Kansas City.

LOGGING OFF

UNDERSTAND MARKETING CONCEPTS

Circle the best answer for each of the following questions.

1. When using the marketing concept, successful businesses are most concerned about
   a. customers and their needs.
   b. competitors.
   c. profits.
   d. the products they plan to sell.
2. The four types of economic utility are
   a. planning, producing, promoting, and selling.
   b. form, time, place, and possession.
   c. electricity, natural gas, water, and sewer.
   d. none of the above

THINK CRITICALLY

Answer the following questions as completely as possible. If necessary, use a separate sheet of paper.

3. Think of a product you have purchased that was satisfying. Describe how each of the four types of economic utility was provided. Which type of utility contributed most to your satisfaction?

____

____

____

____

____

4. **Communication** You are trying to determine the needs of potential customers for a new restaurant. Develop a five-question survey that would help determine how the restaurant could satisfy customers' needs.

____

____

____

____

ADVANTAGES AND CHALLENGES OF E-MARKETING

LOGGING ON

Many people believe that the most profitable customer groups for e-commerce businesses are teenagers and young adults. These groups have grown up with computers and the Internet, and they are technologically savvy. However, older adults age 50 and above are increasingly becoming online shoppers and are the type of customers e-businesses want to reach. Older adults tend to have more money to spend on luxury items. They are more likely to use credit cards for purchases. The average older shopper buys expensive electronic items, new automobiles, and travel services more frequently than younger shoppers do. Because they have more flexible time, older adults spend an average of over six more days per month online than 18- to 24-year-olds, and they stay logged on over 40 hours more per month.

Work with a partner to discuss why it is often believed that older adults are not good potential customers for e-commerce businesses. Assume that you own a new e-commerce business. If you wanted to attract older adults, what types of products would you emphasize? What types of promotional appeals would you use?

Recognize ways that e-commerce has changed how marketing is performed.

Describe challenges that companies may encounter with e-marketing.

CHANGES IN MARKETING

Marketing is equally important for e-commerce businesses and traditional businesses. Many marketing processes change when companies use the Internet to conduct business. Not all marketing activities can be completed online. Activities that are not Internet-based may be performed differently when they are a component of e-marketing. Some areas of marketing that have changed with the advent of e-commerce are competition, customer relationships, data management, and promotion and communications.

E-COMMERCE COMPETITION

For businesses engaged in traditional marketing, most competition comes from other businesses located nearby. Most often, businesses of similar size compete with each other. With e-commerce, anyone with access to a computer and the Internet becomes a potential customer. Any business offering similar products and services over the Internet becomes a competitor. Geography or size of the business no longer limits the number of competitors.

In 2003, the average web user in the United States spent over 100 hours each month on the Internet. In comparison, average users in England and Australia spent between 11 and 13 hours per month online.

CUSTOMER RELATIONSHIPS

Businesses want to develop long, successful relationships with their best customers. They want customers to be satisfied and return to purchase again and again. With the Internet, customers can contact businesses at any time. They expect to receive information, have questions answered, and have problems solved. E-marketing requires that businesses understand when and how customers want to be contacted and the information they expect to receive. Further, businesses need to know the amount of time customers are willing to spend gathering information, ordering products and services, and working with customer service personnel. Some customers will want to complete all of their activities with a business online. Others will want to use the phone or visit the business for face-to-face meetings.

DATA MANAGEMENT

Effective marketing requires information. Businesses need to know who their customers are. They need to know customers' mail and e-mail addresses and telephone numbers. It is important to maintain records of customers' previous purchases, methods of payment, and unique needs or preferences. It is also useful to know the types of information that helped customers make previous purchasing decisions.

Competitive information is also important. Businesses gather data on competitors' products, prices, strengths, and weaknesses. Businesses need to know which companies their customers consider the best alternatives and which companies are using e-commerce effectively.

Finally, businesses need knowledge of market conditions. This information includes the state of the economy, laws and regulations that affect business operations, new product research, and changes in technology.

E-commerce provides unique data collection opportunities. Customers supply a great deal of information as they interact with businesses online. Many Internet transactions ask consumers to supply identifying information. Orders are automatically recorded and entered into a computer database that stores the order processing, shipping, and customer service information. A great deal of competitor and market information is accessible via the World Wide Web. Most e-commerce businesses conduct a great deal of marketing research online.

PROMOTION AND COMMUNICATIONS

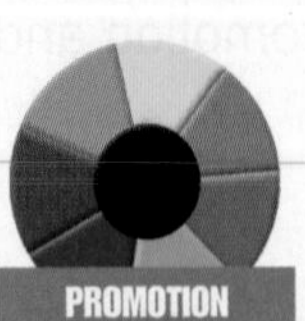

Perhaps the aspects of marketing most noticeably affected by the Internet are promotion and other marketing communications. The Internet provides direct access to and interaction with prospective customers. As consumers search for information on the Internet, their requests can trigger pop-up advertisements, links to company web sites, and other information. If an Internet user visits a company's web site and requests data or orders a product, the business can follow up with product information, personal contacts, and special offers. E-mail, instant messaging, and even live audio/video links provide opportunities for routine, effective communications over the Internet.

List four areas of marketing that have changed for e-commerce businesses.

• E-commerce competion • Customer Relationships

• Data managment • Promotion Commuication

E-MARKETING CHALLENGES

E-commerce offers new marketing challenges. Many Internet business failures in the 1990s resulted from a lack of understanding of the importance of marketing or how marketing needed to change.

Not all businesses using e-commerce are completely Internet-based. Some businesses continue to serve many customers and complete many activities in traditional ways. While marketing changes may not be as drastic, business operations become more complex. It is as if the company is operating two different businesses—the original business and the new Internet business.

Three major e-marketing challenges result from issues related to consumers, customer service, and technology.

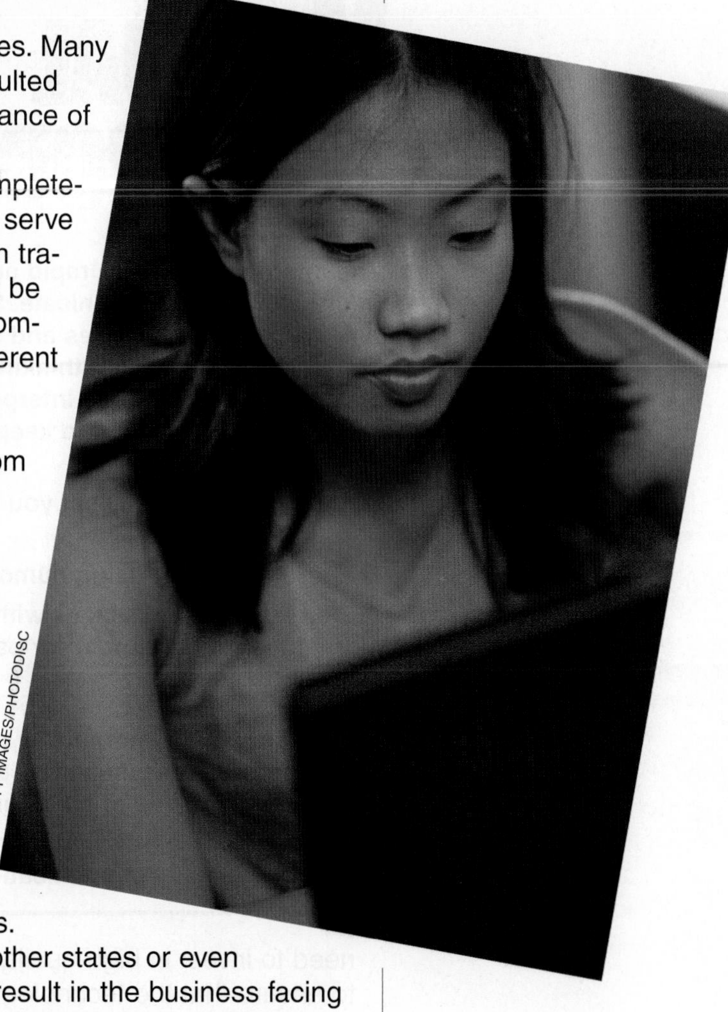

©GETTY IMAGES/PHOTODISC

THE NEW CONSUMER

Expanding to the Web opens the business to many potential customers. Internet customers often have needs and expectations different from those of traditional customers.

DISTRIBUTION

The business must decide if it will serve all new customers regardless of where they are located. Internet customers may create distribution challenges. Orders may require shipment to other states or even to other countries. A wider customer base may result in the business facing issues such as various state laws and tax rates. The business may face challenges of accepting payment in foreign currencies.

SELLING

While e-commerce may expand the reach of the business, it may also restrict access to some consumers. Many people are not yet comfortable using the Internet to make purchases and payments. A company may lose those customers if operations move completely online. For that reason, most companies that use the Internet continue to offer alternative methods of shopping that do not require online purchasing.

SERVING CUSTOMERS

Achieving effective customer service is one of the greatest marketing challenges facing e-commerce businesses. Customers expect to easily navigate web sites, obtain information needed to make purchasing decisions, and submit orders without worrying about security or lost information. They want quick delivery, access to technical help and product repairs if needed, and the capability to easily return merchandise.

High-quality web design is an important aspect of e-marketing. Information must be well organized and easy to find. Customers must be able to move easily among web pages. Product information and pictures should attract customers' attention.

A major challenge for e-businesses is making customer service and technical support personnel available to customers whenever needed. These personnel must be knowledgeable and have effective communications and human relations skills.

TECHNOLOGY

Above all, a web site must work efficiently if an e-business is going to be successful. The web site must be stable and not be slow or down from heavy customer usage. The coding of web pages cannot have bugs that result in lost order information or incorrect links to other pages. If the technology used on the site is too advanced to work properly with the average consumer's computer hardware and software, the business will not succeed. Companies that plan to participate in e-commerce need to invest in high-quality technology. They must have experts available to ensure that the technology works as planned and as customers expect.

VIRTUAL VIEWPOINTS

The Internet provides a rapid and often informal way to communicate. Sometimes a person composes and sends an e-mail message without thinking carefully about how it will be interpreted by the receiver. Guidelines to keep in mind when sending e-mail are

- **Be professional in what you say about others.**
- **Be careful when using humor.**
- **Don't forward messages without asking the original sender for permission.**

THINK CRITICALLY

1. **Why are people more likely to send inappropriate messages by e-mail than by other methods of communication?**
2. **What are some other important guidelines for e-mail communications?**

What are three major e-marketing challenges?

• The new consumer

• Serving costomers • technology

LOGGING OFF

UNDERSTAND MARKETING CONCEPTS

Circle the best answer for each of the following questions.

1. An important difference in marketing for e-commerce businesses is
   a. many customers may be far from the business geographically.
   b. there will be fewer competitors with similar products.
   c. all customer contacts will occur online.
   d. all of the above

2. E-commerce may restrict access to some customers because
   a. some states have laws that do not allow e-commerce.
   b. e-commerce costs more than traditional business operations.
   c. some customers are not comfortable using the Internet to make purchases.
   d. many products cannot be distributed using the Internet.

THINK CRITICALLY

Answer the following questions as completely as possible. If necessary, use a separate sheet of paper.

3. Identify two ways that customer service is different for an e-commerce business than for a traditional business. How should an e-commerce business ensure that customer service activities satisfy its customers?

____

____

____

____

____

4. **Communication** Locate one business web site that communicates effectively with consumers. Locate another web site that does not communicate well. Describe what makes one site effective and the other ineffective.

____

____

____

____

REVIEW E-COMMERCE MARKETING CONCEPTS

Write the letter of the term that matches each definition. Some terms will not be used.

- a. distribution
- b. e-commerce
- c. economic utility
- d. e-marketing
- e. financing
- f. marketing
- g. marketing concept
- h. marketing-information management
- i. marketing mix
- j. marketing strategy
- k. pricing
- l. product/service management
- m. promotion
- n. selling
- o. target market

B 1. A company's use of the Internet to support or complete business transactions

L 2. Designing, developing, maintaining, improving, and acquiring products and services so they meet consumer needs

C 3. The amount of satisfaction received from using a product or service

G 4. The focus on the needs of customers during the planning, production, distribution, and promotion of a product or service

D 5. Using the Internet and related technologies to complete significant marketing activities

J 6. A company's plan that identifies how it will use marketing to achieve its goals

K 7. Establishing and communicating the value of products and services to prospective customers

F 8. The development and maintenance of satisfying exchange relationships between businesses and consumers

A 9. Determining the best methods and procedures to allow customers to locate, obtain, and use the products and services of an organization

H 10. Communicating directly with prospective customers to assess and satisfy their needs

Circle the best answer.

11. To succeed, businesses must
    - a. find new customers to replace dissatisfied ones.
    - b. continually increase sales.
    - c. make a profit.
    - d. switch to e-commerce.

12. The four marketing elements that make up the marketing mix are
    - a. economy, technology, customers, and competition.
    - b. product, distribution, price, and promotion.
    - c. selling, advertising, public relations, and publicity.
    - d. e-commerce, e-marketing, the Internet, and secure ordering.

THINK CRITICALLY

13. Why must e-commerce businesses operate differently if they compete on a global scale rather than solely in their home country? Provide several examples of how business e-commerce activities might change with global operations.

14. Why are businesses less likely to succeed if they do not consider customer needs and wants before planning the products and services they will sell? Identify a company involved in e-commerce that you believe uses the marketing concept well. Provide two reasons to support your choice.

15. You are asked to advise a new e-commerce business on what it takes to be successful. List three suggestions you would make. Justify your answers.

16. What is meant by "effective customer relationships"? In what ways are customer relationships for e-commerce businesses different from customer relationships for traditional businesses?

MAKE CONNECTIONS

17. **MARKETING MATH** Jeffrey wants to purchase a new digital camera. His local camera shop offers the camera he wants at a price of $289. He will have to pay 6% sales tax as well. Jeffrey finds the same camera available through an online retailer for $254. There will be no sales tax for the online purchase, but he will have to pay $11 shipping and handling. Calculate the difference in the actual product cost and the total cost to Jeffrey from the two retailers. What is the percentage of savings for Jeffrey if he buys from the retailer with the lowest total cost?

18. **TECHNOLOGY** One of the advantages customers have in using the Internet is the easy access of information about companies that sell specific products. Identify a product about which you are interested in learning more. Using a search engine such as Google.com, identify three companies that sell the product using e-commerce. For each, list the name of the company, the address of its web site, and the geographic location including city, state, and country.

19. **COMMUNICATION** Some consumers are reluctant to purchase products using the Internet. Write a one-page letter to be sent to a business's customers encouraging them to try online shopping from the company's web site.

20. **COMMUNICATION** Use a word processing program to prepare two tables that compare the advantages and disadvantages of using the Internet for e-commerce. The first table should make comparisons for businesses selling products and services. The second table should make comparisons for consumers purchasing products and services.

Business ownership is the dream of many people. The Internet provides new opportunities for entrepreneurs to open and build businesses. However, e-commerce is risky, as evidenced by the hundreds of dot.com business failures in the past decade. Careful planning must be completed with an understanding of both the opportunities and risks of e-commerce.

Through Project Dot.com, you and a small group of classmates will make decisions about a new Internet business. At the end of each chapter, you will apply what you learned by completing a set of planning activities for your business.

Work with your team members to complete the following activities.

1. Team members should individually identify the main product or service each believes the business should sell. Write a one-paragraph description of the product or service and another paragraph discussing why you believe it is a good choice for an e-commerce business.
2. Each team member should present his or her recommendation to the group. After the presentations, discuss the choices and decide on one product or service that will be the focus for your team's dot.com project.
3. Make a list of several groups of customers that might be interested in purchasing your product or service. The groups may be final consumers or other businesses. From the list, select two groups as your target market. Write a detailed description of each group and a one-paragraph rationale for each choice.
4. Use a telephone or business directory to identify businesses from your community that offer the same product or service you have selected. Then use the Internet to locate several businesses that use e-commerce to sell the product or service. Develop a list of competitors, including the company name, mailing address, and Internet address (if available) for each.
5. Choose a name for your business. The name should help customers recognize and remember your company, as well as create a positive and unique image of your company and its products. Search the Internet to verify that no other company has the same name that you have chosen.

USING E-COMMERCE

Businesses use the Web to sell items ranging from toys to antiques. The Web also can be used successfully to sell complicated products and professional services to other businesses.

The Web can be an effective medium for business-to-business transactions. Success depends upon having "Internet-appropriate" methods of selling. Businesses must consider how they have traditionally sold products and services. Most businesses already practice the best techniques to sell their goods and services. Companies should not abandon what has worked in the past just because the selling medium has changed.

All You Can Eat

The sales pages of most business-to-business web sites are structured like salad bars. Everything is nicely presented in individual, unrelated displays. Customers depend upon past experience to find what they need and to finalize the sale, often with mediocre results. Organizing information into individual displays is not necessarily a bad strategy. However, a more positive message is sent to the customer who can access needed information within five minutes rather than wading through unrelated data for an hour.

Preserved Treescapes International is a company that has effectively incorporated e-commerce into its sales plan by designing the treescapes.com web site. Product categories are featured individually as well as in business settings so prospective customers can see how products can be combined and displayed. Treescapes.com goes beyond the typical "salad bar" approach with the use of photos and case studies that provide a wealth of ideas that will encourage sales.

Personalized Sales

There are many examples of companies selling products and services to other businesses through web sites. Early successes are ignited by customers who are acquainted with the companies and their products. Technically sophisticated programs are emerging that allow the business customer to interact at many points with another business's web site. The presentation then tailors itself to the needs of the customer. Technology will be counted on to move the sales process from a self-serve model of information gathering to a more personalized, user-friendly sales approach.

Think Critically

1. **What are the challenges of conducting business-to-business transactions using the Internet?**
2. **Describe a common mistake made by businesses when trying to sell to other businesses via the Internet.**
3. **Visit the treescapes.com web site. Evaluate this site for business-to-business sales possibilities as well as personal appeal.**

E-COMMERCE MARKETING MANAGEMENT TEAM DECISION MAKING

You are the marketing consultant for Eaton Garden Center. The owner wants your input on developing a web site for the business.

Eaton Garden Center has been in business for 70 years, selling high-quality wholesale and retail products. Family-owned and operated, the store sells trees, perennials, annuals, seeds, vegetable plants, bulbs, and cut flowers. Eaton also sells sod, mulch, soil, fertilizer, fountains, and garden art. For holidays, the store features unique plants, flowers, and related home decorations.

Eaton Garden Center is located in a rapidly-growing rural community. Locals know that Eaton has the finest quality at the best prices. Employees are friendly specialists who advise customers and answer questions. The store publishes tip sheets for gardening that are displayed throughout the store. Eaton also offers free weekly seminars covering gardening and landscaping topics.

Business at Eaton Garden Center is good, but the huge, national competitors will soon enter the local scene due to a growing population. There are few advertising media available in the area, and the owner feels that some people don't know about Eaton's high-quality plants and services. The owner thinks that a web site, with gardening tips and related information, as well as some products for sale, would inform customers about Eaton Garden Center. The owner realizes that selling all products online isn't feasible since the shipping costs of highly perishable items would drastically increase their costs.

You are to determine the content and look of a web site designed to encourage sales at Eaton Garden Center. Also determine which products should be sold on the site. You want to build a growing customer base before the national chain stores arrive in the community. You will present your ideas to the owner in a meeting to take place at Eaton.

Performance Indicators Evaluated

- Understand the opportunities and challenges faced by Eaton Garden Center.
- Explain the need to expand Eaton's target market with a web site.
- Explain the use of personalization strategies in e-commerce marketing activities.
- Describe the information that will be included on Eaton's web site.
- Describe how customers will learn about the web site.

Go to the DECA web site for more detailed information.

1. Why is it smart for a business in a small community to use e-commerce?
2. What large competitors will likely arrive soon in the community? What are their advantages over Eaton?
3. What unique characteristics of Eaton Garden Center should be emphasized on its web site?

www.deca.org/publications/HS_Guide/guidetoc.html

CHAPTER 2
E-COMMERCE AND E-RETAILING

POINT YOUR BROWSER

ecommkt.swlearning.com

AMAZON.COM

Jeff Bezos was well positioned to be the founder of Amazon.com. He graduated from Princeton in 1986, summa cum laude and Phi Beta Kappa. His degrees were in electrical engineering and computer science. Upon graduating, he worked for an investment firm evaluating computer-related businesses. He helped manage over $250 billion in assets and became the company's youngest vice president. In the early 1990s, Bezos learned that the Internet was growing at a rate of 2,300 percent per year. He realized that the Internet could be an ideal channel for commerce.

Bezos chose his product carefully. From a list of the top 20 mail-order products, he looked for one to which he could provide greater consumer satisfaction through the Internet by offering selection, convenience, and low prices. He believed that books were products that consumers were familiar with and could purchase without physically examining them. Bezos started Amazon.com in a garage with three workstations and desks made from wooden doors. Amazon.com went live on July 16, 1995, and soon became one of the fastest-growing companies in the history of U.S. business. By 2003, it had revenue of over $4 billion and was growing at 20 percent per year.

Amazon.com was not designed to replace more traditional booksellers or superstores such as Barnes & Noble. A customer shopping in a local retail bookstore is most likely looking for a different type of shopping experience. However, online sales have pressured a number of book retailers to follow Amazon.com's example. Barnes & Noble launched its own web site, offering many of the same advantages as Amazon.com.

THINK CRITICALLY

1. List as least three reasons why a buyer may want to use Amazon.com to purchase books.
2. Amazon.com has expanded the products it sells beyond books. Explain why this may be a good strategy.

LESSON 2.1

E-COMMERCE BASICS

List the different combinations of buyers and sellers engaged in e-commerce.

Explain why many online-only e-commerce companies failed and why traditional businesses have added e-commerce.

LOGGING ON

The process of buying and selling is continuously evolving and expanding. Commerce has moved from village squares to small stores, department and discount stores, malls, catalogs, and most recently the Internet. The introduction of e-commerce does not mean that traditional retail sales systems will disappear. Instead, most businesses are selling to their customers in a variety of ways. Department and discount stores sell in traditional stores and online. Catalog companies allow customers to order by phone or online. Even the village square market can be found online at sites such as eBay. It is vital that businesses engaged in buying and selling understand the role of e-commerce.

Work with a partner. Evaluate advantages and disadvantages of e-commerce for a traditional retail store.

E-COMMERCE CATEGORIES

The process of using the Internet to allow buyers and sellers to engage in trade is known as **e-commerce**. The buyers and sellers can be businesses or individuals. The online environment allows businesses to sell to the final consumers (*B-to-C*), consumers to sell to consumers (*C-to-C*), and businesses to sell to businesses (*B-to-B*).

Consumers are probably most familiar with B-to-C sales because of advertising and personal experiences searching for products and purchasing online. This type of online retail trade is a small percentage of the multibillion dollars spent online annually. Most online sales occur in the B-to-B market. The greatest number of consumer sales transactions is on C-to-C sites.

E-commerce is not just practiced by online-only companies. Most businesses use the Internet to support their traditional commerce process.

BUSINESS-TO-CONSUMER E-COMMERCE

Business-to-consumer sales is the most recognizable form of e-commerce. Businesses such as Amazon.com, Dell, and Orbitz are examples of online-only, B-to-C businesses that advertise heavily and own large shares of their markets. In contrast, traditional retail businesses operating out of buildings where customers come and shop are called **brick-and-mortar stores**. Many businesses that traditionally used stores or catalogs for sales have added e-commerce as part of a **multichannel strategy**. Businesses that offer both traditional and Internet sales are called **brick-and-click businesses**.

CONSUMER-TO-CONSUMER E-COMMERCE

©GETTY IMAGES/PHOTODISC

eBay is an example of a company that offers consumer-to-consumer e-commerce. eBay is an auction site where individuals electronically submit, or post, products. Buyers use search features to find products they want to buy. They then engage in an auction where individuals bid against each other for the product. The winning bidder must rely upon the seller to ship the product. eBay is the largest online C-to-C auction site. Many other e-commerce sites also use auctions to link buyers and sellers.

Other types of C-to-C e-commerce businesses include online exchanges. Best Sellers Exchange allows consumers to trade various products such as books, games, videos, and DVDs with other consumers.

BUSINESS-TO-BUSINESS E-COMMERCE

Business-to-business sales account for the largest total dollar volume of e-commerce. Online B-to-B sales may reach as high as $8 trillion worldwide by 2007.

Business markets are different from consumer markets. The average sales amount is much higher. Buyers are more demanding in their product specifications. Companies often want their inventory systems connected to suppliers' systems. The online environment aids this process by allowing information to move rapidly from business buyers to suppliers.

B-to-B e-commerce web sites offer many of the same features as B-to-C sites. These features include the ability to order, check inventory, and make payments online.

B-to-B e-commerce companies may use auctions to sell products. Buying companies may force suppliers to compete in **reverse auctions** where businesses bid against each other for customer orders.

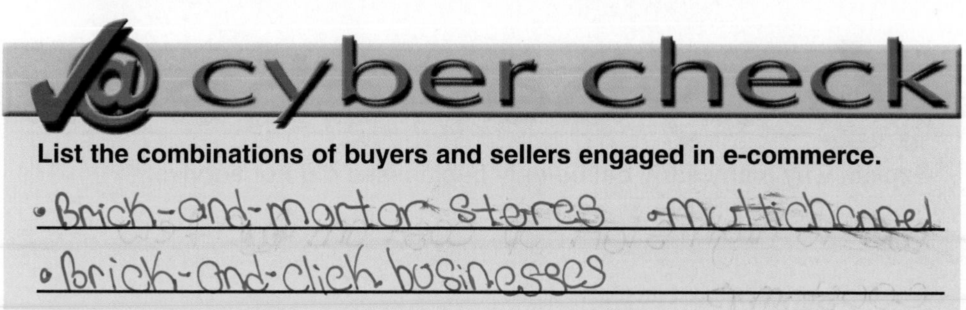

@ cyber check
List the combinations of buyers and sellers engaged in e-commerce.
• Brick-and-mortar stores • multichannel
• brick-and-click businesses

TIME OUT

Over 50 percent of consumers use multichannel shopping strategies. Stores have found that 45 percent of consumers use the Internet to browse for and review competing products before they decide to buy. This trend is forcing businesses to shift marketing efforts to the Internet.

ONLINE-ONLY TO BRICK-AND-CLICK

E-commerce is less than ten years old and still in its early stages of development. At first, many traditional businesses viewed e-commerce as an unproven and expensive way to reach customers. This left e-commerce open for individuals who were starting their own companies.

In the 1990s, online-only e-commerce businesses attempted to sell just about everything online, from groceries to homes. These online-only businesses had to develop all of the marketing functions for an online environment without the benefit of an established parent company or brand name. They had to build systems for warehousing and distribution in addition to the web sites for communication and ordering. They had to promote the sites and persuade customers to purchase products online. Many online-only Internet businesses attempted to serve the same markets, forcing strong price competition. Most early online-only businesses did not survive due to high start-up costs and few customers.

Traditional businesses gradually saw a strong and growing market acceptance of e-commerce. Most large businesses added Internet-based marketing functions to serve their markets. These multichannel businesses had advantages over the newer, online-only businesses because they had established distribution systems, expertise with their products, and existing relationships with their markets.

Success in traditional markets does not guarantee success online. Wal-Mart has redesigned its web site more than once to attract a market. Despite Wal-Mart's large customer base, the total number of users on its web site is much lower than that of Amazon.com, eBay, Yahoo! Shopping, or MSN Shopping.

Smaller businesses find it harder to implement e-commerce on their own. These businesses often use an *e-commerce service provider* to manage their e-commerce functions.

INTERNET INTELLIGENCE

Over 80 percent of adults with Internet access (which translates to almost half of all adults in the United States) have purchased products online. Traditional retailers are seeing these statistics and adding online sales to their business strategies.

THINK CRITICALLY

1. **Discuss why a traditional retailer would want to include e-commerce in its business strategy.**
2. **Explain what could happen to traditional retailers' ability to compete if they did not engage in e-commerce.**

Explain why many early online-only businesses did not survive.

due to high start-up cost and few coustomers

LOGGING OFF

UNDERSTAND MARKETING CONCEPTS

Circle the best answer for each of the following questions.

1. E-commerce allows buying and selling between
   a. businesses and consumers.
   b. consumers and consumers.
   c. businesses and businesses.
   d. all of the above

2. Multichannel businesses have succeeded because of
   a. established distribution systems.
   b. expertise with their products.
   c. existing relationships with their markets.
   d. all of the above

THINK CRITICALLY

Answer the following questions as completely as possible. If necessary, use a separate sheet of paper.

3. Create a list of 20 e-commerce companies. Determine which e-commerce category (B-to-C, C-to-C, or B-to-B) each business represents.

4. Why do you think Wal-Mart's web site is less popular than Amazon.com's site?

LESSON 2.2

ONLINE BUSINESS STRATEGIES

Describe the e-commerce functions adopted by online businesses.

List the different types of products sold online.

LOGGING ON

An e-commerce business must develop strategies to serve its markets better than its competitors. 1800CONTACTS is an example of an effective e-commerce business that has adopted a number of strategies to compete in the online marketplace. Its web site communicates well and allows for inventory searches and ordering. Its distribution system and large volume of sales made directly to consumers help keep costs down. Orders may be made by phone, Internet, mail, or fax. Customer service agents are available seven days a week to provide assistance by phone or e-mail. 1800CONTACTS processes orders within one day and delivers orders in one to seven days, depending on the customer's shipping preference. A customer's order information is stored for future reference so that the customer can repeat an order, making adjustments as necessary without rekeying all of the information.

Work with a partner and visit an e-commerce web site. Evaluate the site's design based on its search systems, ease of online shopping, and availability of customer service agents through e-mail contact.

E-COMMERCE FUNCTIONS

©GETTY IMAGES/PHOTODISC

Any business engaged in e-commerce must undertake the seven marketing functions in an online environment. E-commerce firms must design effective web sites that communicate well and allow for product searches and ordering. These businesses must be able to fill and deliver orders in a timely manner. They must also be able to meet the individual needs of their customers. In most cases, a business's web site acts as the point of contact for customers. The web site must allow the customer to find products or services, arrange for distribution, communicate benefits to promote and sell the product, collect information on the buyer, display prices, and allow for online payments.

E-COMMERCE SITE DESIGN

The decision process that consumers use to shop online is the same as in a brick-and-mortar store. Customers will most likely want to browse for products, compare prices, and evaluate service options before they buy. E-commerce sites must allow for the same types of activities.

E-commerce businesses have an advantage in their ability to use information technology such as web sites, search systems, databases, and e-mail to aid in the shopping process. An online environment enhances the ability to search for information and compare products and prices.

A typical business-to-consumer e-commerce transaction might consist of the following steps.

1. A buyer uses a web site as the main communication source for information on a company and its products.
2. A buyer uses the web site search feature to find products on the site. Web site search engines link to inventory databases. This link allows for word searches to locate products.
3. The buyer searches for the same or similar products available through other e-commerce businesses. The buyer compares products and prices.
4. The buyer uses a credit card to pay for the order. The credit card company acts as the financier for the purchase.
5. The business communicates with the buyer by sending an e-mail to confirm the sale.
6. As part of its service, the business sends an e-mail to notify the buyer when the product ships and when it should arrive.
7. The business's database collects the transaction information. This information is used to aid in future marketing to the buyer.

E-MARKETING MYTHS

Many e-commerce web sites collect customer information for future marketing purposes. Some sites sell this information to other companies that are looking for ways to generate new business. These practices can scare away potential customers. The two greatest concerns individuals have are that they may receive junk e-mail and that credit card information may not be secure.

The U.S. Federal Trade Commission requires that businesses post privacy statements if they collect customer data. In the United States, 70 percent of online customers say they are concerned about privacy, but only 40 percent have ever bothered to read a web site's posted privacy statement.

THINK CRITICALLY

1. **Develop a list of the advantages a business gains by collecting customer information. Develop a list of concerns an individual may have about a business's collection of information. Do you think the customer benefits in any way from this data collection? Explain your answer.**
2. **Visit an e-commerce web site to view its privacy statement. Do you feel this business is protecting your privacy? Why or why not?**

PERSONALIZATION

Understanding and meeting customers' needs fulfills the marketing concept. Knowing individual customers on a personal level is one of the advantages of a brick-and-mortar business. Databases are helping e-commerce businesses serve customers at the individual level. Firms such as Amazon.com customize their web sites for the individual based on past interaction and purchases at the site.

A web site provides **personalization** when it uses information collected from the customer to provide content that is specific to the individual. The web site may suggest products or provide information that would be of interest to the individual. Personalization can increase the chances of future sales. For example, if you are ordering an article of clothing, the site may pop up information regarding matching accessories. Amazon.com displays related products that other customers have purchased in addition to the product you are buying. When revisiting, the site initially displays and suggests products by the same author or in the same category as your previous orders.

The online collection of personal information has led to concerns about privacy. In the United States, the data a business collects belongs to that business. A business can sell this information. In the European community, the information belongs to the individual, and businesses cannot sell information without the customer's permission.

PORTALS

Some web sites act as "windows" to online content. A customer **portal**, such as AOL, MSN, or Yahoo!, designs its site to allow individuals to find a variety of online content on its and others' sites. These portals make money from advertising revenue and the sale of products.

Shopping portals such as Amazon.com and Buy.com allow consumers to find and purchase products online. *Specialized portals* allow individuals to find content in more narrowly defined areas. For example, Kelley Blue Book's site offers information on automobile prices, reviews, tips, and advice, and allows a buyer to find cars at local dealers.

©GETTY IMAGES/PHOTODISC

Many portals want to develop long-term relationships with customers. To aid in this process, they generate customized web sites based on the individuals' personalized profile information.

Business portals support B-to-B e-commerce. Covisint.com is a portal for the automotive industry. It allows major automotive companies to act as buyers and lets their suppliers engage in online commerce and inventory control.

FULFILLMENT

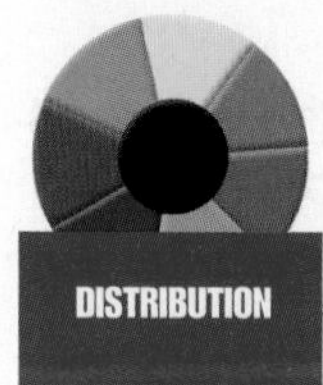

All businesses need to deliver place utility. Traditional businesses that have retail outlets allow you to purchase and receive a product immediately. Online businesses must also deliver products in a timely manner. This is especially true for B-to-B e-commerce companies. Businesses typically want their products or parts delivered *just in time*, or just before they are needed in the manufacturing process. Consequently, the business can delay payment and reduce the amount of space needed for parts in inventory.

Fulfillment, or the order delivery process, usually works the same for both individual and business buyers. The buyer uses online search systems to look for products in stock. An online order form, often called a **shopping cart**, is used to place an order. When the order is submitted, an e-mail notification confirming the order is sent to the buyer. Once the order is ready to be shipped, a second e-mail notification announces the expected delivery time. The shipment is automatically deducted from inventory records. As stock gets low, a purchase order is triggered to replenish the business's inventory. These fulfillment processes are cost effective but can be expensive to build and implement. Just one of Amazon.com's six warehouses has over 840,000 square feet dedicated to fulfillment.

VIRTUAL VIEWPOINTS

Many web sites see nothing wrong with providing tools for sharing and downloading files. Often, these files contain *copyrighted* materials owned by their original authors and not intended for free distribution.

The recording industry has tried a number of strategies to limit the illegal downloading of music. It sought to make MP3 players illegal, it sued companies such as Napster to limit file-sharing web sites, and it opened its own pay-for-play music sites.

These strategies have not stopped individuals from downloading music. In the United States alone, over 40 million people have downloaded music from file-sharing web sites. Consequently, record companies are having a difficult time selling music online. Up to 84 percent of those who download music say they are not willing to pay for it.

THINK CRITICALLY

1. **Do you think people should be allowed to download free music from the Internet? Why or why not?**
2. **Explain how current attitudes toward paying for online music may limit the development of other digital products, such as online movies.**

Explain the functions important for e-commerce success.

Digital services bank stock broker and schools

There is considerable resistance to paying for digital entertainment. Over 47 percent of individuals believe that most online content should be free. Even so, consumers spent close to $2 billion for online content in 2002.

E-COMMERCE PRODUCTS

Physical products sold over the Internet are the same as those found in any retail location. *Digital products* are sold and transferred directly over the Internet to the customer. Digital products include multimedia entertainment, online information services, published documents, games, music, and video. *Digital services* are sold and performed online. Many service businesses, such as banks, stockbrokers, and schools, are making their services available over the Internet for the convenience of their customers.

The Internet delivers digital products directly to the user, but copyright violations and the unwillingness of individuals to pay for digital content have slowed the growth of this market. Fewer than ten percent of individuals over age 12 have paid for music they have downloaded. Total music sales dropped by ten percent in 2001, largely as a result of online downloading.

Services such as online banking are growing around the world. Over 17 percent of bank customers in the United States use online banking. In some European countries, this percentage is even higher, with up to 40 percent of customers using online banking.

cyber check

List the categories of e-commerce products and identify which ones are selling well online.

____

____

©GETTY IMAGES/PHOTODISC

LOGGING OFF

UNDERSTAND MARKETING CONCEPTS

Circle the best answer for each of the following questions.

1. E-commerce businesses are concerned with the marketing function(s) of
   a. a site design that allows for effective communication, inventory searches, and ordering.
   b. personalization.
   c. fulfillment of customer orders.
   d. all of the above
2. Which of the following is *not* considered a digital product?
   a. multimedia entertainment
   b. music
   c. a car
   d. games

THINK CRITICALLY

Answer the following questions as completely as possible. If necessary, use a separate sheet of paper.

3. **Distribution Management** Develop a strategy to ensure that a company will be paid for delivering digital products.

4. **Technology** Assume you want to start an e-commerce business. What will you include on the web site? Determine if it is necessary to personalize content. Describe how you will achieve product fulfillment.

LESSON 2.3

E-RETAILING

Describe the role of e-commerce in retailing.

Identify the factors that aid and limit e-commerce around the world.

LOGGING ON

At one time, local travel agents sold almost all airline tickets. By 2002, almost all airline tickets were purchased through online sales. Travelers use portals such as Expedia.com to check ticket prices and travel times. In addition, airline companies have moved heavily into selling directly to the customer over the Internet. These companies provide search features, service, and online delivery of tickets. Customers are e-mailed if there is a change in a flight schedule.

Work with a partner to determine the advantages that an online travel site has over a local travel agent. Is it possible for a local travel agent to compete against companies such as Expedia.com or an airline's direct ticket sales? Explain your answer.

MULTICHANNELS

Total online retail sales for 2002 were more than $100 billion dollars. While this figure seems large, it was less than two percent of total retail sales. Online-only companies captured only 28 percent of e-commerce sales. Multichannel companies are obviously increasing their dominance in e-commerce.

The Internet's ability to provide information is important to shoppers. Forty-five percent of consumers use the Internet to search for information before they buy. Researchers have predicted that the Internet will influence up to 35 percent of all retail sales by 2007.

Even service businesses, such as colleges and universities, are adopting a multichannel approach. *Distance learning* is growing at college and university campuses around the world. Distance learning uses the Internet as a platform for delivering coursework. Lectures and assignments are given online. Students submit their homework by e-mail and take interactive quizzes that give immediate feedback. Professors interact with students through e-mail and chat rooms. Over 80 percent of college faculties in North America believe the Internet helps students achieve success.

©GETTY IMAGES/PHOTODISC

Airline tickets make up the largest dollar volume in online retail sales. The second highest category in online retail sales is apparel. The major online apparel companies are all multichannel and include Old Navy, GAP, Victoria's Secret, and Lands' End. Each of these companies has expanded from brick-and-mortar stores or a catalog business.

TRADITIONAL RETAILERS

Traditional retailers have always adapted to new environments. In the 1800s, Sears used the recently developed railroad system and catalogs to reach new customers. In the second half of the 1900s, Sears took advantage of improved roadway systems and built stores in suburbs to serve these newly developing markets. Today, Sears wants its customers to be able to shop in stores, by phone, or online. Up to 40 percent of Sears' online sales are picked up at a local store.

Traditional retailers have found that different sets of skills are required to develop and manage e-commerce businesses. Online retailers, or **e-retailers**, must catalog inventory into databases, design web sites, develop fulfillment systems, develop customer databases, and have expertise in direct marketing. Set-up costs can be high, delaying profitability. To avoid high start-up costs, some retailers, such as Target and Toys "R" Us, use Amazon.com or another established e-retailer as an e-commerce service provider. The managers of many traditional stores do not have expertise in e-commerce or technology. These traditional businesses often hire new management talent to run their e-commerce divisions.

Small retailers may be at the greatest disadvantage in a multichannel environment. Small retailers often lack the human and financial resources needed to develop an e-commerce site. If small retailers do expand to e-commerce, it is recommended that they serve narrow target markets.

CATALOG RETAILERS

Direct marketers sell directly to consumers through outlets such as catalogs or direct mail. These retailers are more familiar with e-commerce skills because they likely have already developed inventory and customer databases, fulfillment systems, and managerial expertise in direct marketing. Catalog retailers are finding that their print catalogs can generate mail-order, online, and store sales. They often use their customer databases to send e-mails to their customers about products known to be of interest to them.

©GETTY IMAGES/PHOTODISC

Web sites allow catalog companies to offer a variety of services and customized features. Lands' End has embraced e-commerce. It has web sites for the United States and six other countries. Its web sites allow for personalization, including personalized virtual models and personalized wardrobe-shopping consultants. Customers can use chat rooms to talk to service representatives and have clothing custom made.

ONLINE-ONLY E-RETAILING

An online-only retailer must support its entire business through online sales. This challenge requires having a large **unique audience**, or unduplicated visitors to a web site. Amazon.com and eBay have captured large unique audiences, with close to 16 million users each. Most online-only retailers focus on much smaller audiences. These companies have found success in markets that are not well served by large online-only or multichannel businesses.

List reasons that a business would want to adopt a multichannel retail strategy.

political and legal barriers

INTERNATIONAL E-COMMERCE

Currently, the United States is the leader in total e-commerce spending. However, the U.S. market accounts for less than half of global online spending. E-commerce spending is growing at a faster rate in other countries. Europe is catching up to the United States as spending per person closes in on U.S. averages.

This global growth does not mean that e-commerce is accepted everywhere around the world. A number of cultural, political, and legal factors limit e-commerce in many countries.

Sweden has the highest *e-readiness* rating. This means that Sweden is poised for rapid growth in e-commerce. This measure takes into consideration a country's Internet infrastructure, business environment, consumer and business adoption of e-commerce, cultural acceptance, and a supportive legal environment.

LIMITATIONS TO GLOBAL E-COMMERCE

The United States, Canada, Scandinavia, and Australia have the highest potential for e-commerce. This potential is largely due to high rates of Internet usage and people who readily accept new technology. Many other areas of the world do not have Internet access or the infrastructure necessary to fulfill online orders.

Many countries face political and legal barriers to developing e-commerce. In some countries, advertising is limited. Ads cannot target children, for example. Credit cards may not be common or trusted. Shipping systems needed for timely delivery of products to individuals' homes may not exist or may be extremely expensive. No-return policies may cause customers to feel uncomfortable about buying products without seeing them.

©GETTY IMAGES/PHOTODISC

What are some limitations to global e-commerce?

The United States, Canada, Scandinavia and Australia

©GETTY IMAGES/PHOTODISC

WORKING ONLINE

Jennifer will be graduating from college in one year and is planning a career in e-commerce. She has looked at a number of job openings. These positions stress that candidates must have skills in planning and organizing human and financial resources. These positions interface with a number of business units, so strong communication skills are required. Candidates also must be able to research consumer behavior on the Internet, review the technical construction of web sites, and write comprehensive strategy documents. Employers are looking for people who are highly motivated and focused, with a passion for the Internet and marketing.

Jennifer is interested in responding to the following advertisement:

Our company is looking for a motivated self-starter who is prepared to take responsibility for a variety of tasks, including web maintenance, database management, project marketing, PowerPoint presentations, company literature production, and communication with suppliers and channel partners. You will work closely with the Marketing Coordinator to plan and produce materials for a range of marketing programs. The role is suited to someone who has excellent computer literacy, an eye for detail, and strong initiative. You must be a team player who has a flexible, can-do attitude.

THINK CRITICALLY

1. **Why do you think e-commerce employers look for the skills mentioned in this advertisement?**
2. **Would the job requirements differ for a similar position with a brick-and-mortar business? Explain your answer.**

LOGGING OFF

UNDERSTAND MARKETING CONCEPTS

Circle the best answer for each of the following questions.

1. Which of the following is a reason that retailers are using a multichannel approach?
   a. Most retail sales are through online-only stores.
   b. Shoppers look for product information online before they buy.
   c. Many states require that retailers use more than one outlet.
   d. None of the above is a reason for using a multichannel approach.
2. Which of the following is true about international e-commerce?
   a. The United States accounts for less than half of global online spending.
   b. Online spending is growing most rapidly in the United States.
   c. Most countries around the world use e-commerce.
   d. China is the country most ready for e-commerce.

THINK CRITICALLY

Answer the following questions as completely as possible. If necessary, use a separate sheet of paper.

3. Give an example of a purchase made using multichannel systems. List the reasons that each channel is part of the buying process.

____

____

____

____

____

4. Assume that a local brick-and-mortar retailer has asked your advice about online selling. Determine all of the factors the retailer needs to consider before selling online.

____

____

____

____

____

REVIEW E-COMMERCE MARKETING CONCEPTS

Write the letter of the term that matches each definition. Some terms will not be used.

- a. brick-and-click businesses
- b. brick-and-mortar stores
- c. e-commerce
- d. e-retailers
- e. fulfillment
- f. multichannel strategy
- g. personalization
- h. portal
- i. reverse auctions
- j. shopping cart
- k. unique audience

B 1. Traditional retail businesses operating out of buildings where customers come and shop

C 2. The process of using the Internet to allow buyers and sellers to engage in trade

F 3. Adding e-commerce to store and/or catalog sales

A 4. Businesses that offer both traditional and Internet sales

G 5. When a web site uses information collected from the customer to provide content that is specific to the individual

H 6. A web site that allows individuals to find a variety of online content on its and others' sites

E 7. The order delivery process

J 8. An online order form

D 9. Online retailers

K 10. Unduplicated visitors to a web site

Circle the best answer.

11. When businesses bid against each other for customer orders, it is called
    a. an auction.
    (b.) a reverse auction.
    c. e-commerce.
    d. none of the above

12. A small business that is finding it difficult to implement e-commerce may want to use a(n)
    a. portal.
    (b.) e-commerce service provider.
    c. e-retailer.
    d. none of the above

13. E-commerce products include
    a. digital products.
    b. digital services.
    c. physical products.
    (d.) all of the above

THINK CRITICALLY

14. With another student, spend five minutes discussing the advantages of using a multichannel approach for retailing. Make a list of at least five advantages. Share the list with the class.

15. Make a list of local businesses in your area. Determine if these businesses offer B-to-B, B-to-C, or C-to-C sales. Specify which of these businesses would be good candidates for e-commerce. Justify your reasoning.

16. List the advantages that consumers and businesses gain by having e-commerce available in their country. Discuss what can happen to a country that does not develop or keep up with e-commerce technology.

MAKE CONNECTIONS

17. **MARKETING MATH** Your e-commerce business wants to determine the size of its unique audience. You have collected data that shows you have 140,000 hits on your site each year. Research shows that 10 percent of visitors have viewed your site three times during the year and 20 percent have viewed it twice. All other visitors viewed the site once. What is your audience size?

18. **RESEARCH** Use the Internet to visit an e-commerce site. Evaluate how this business fulfills e-commerce marketing functions through site design, personalization, and fulfillment. Compare and contrast your findings with others in your class.

19. **COMMUNICATION** You work for a local brick-and-mortar store. You are proposing to the owner that she develop a multichannel approach to retailing. List reasons that justify your recommendation. Be sure to cite material from this chapter.

20. **COMMUNICATION** Work with a group. Think of the web sites where you shop online. How many of these web sites recognize you when you revisit? Describe the ways they personalize their sites for you. How many of them send e-mails with information related to your interests? Do you enjoy getting these e-mails, or do you get annoyed? Do you have concerns regarding privacy? Discuss all of these questions within the group. Summarize your findings, and make general recommendations that web sites should follow regarding personalization and privacy.

This part of the project will focus on how you will deliver web content to your market.

Work with your team members to complete the following activities.

1. Your team identified a business in the Project Dot.com exercise in chapter 1. You now need to determine your e-commerce strategy. Write a one-page strategic summary. Describe your business's e-commerce category. Specify if you are recommending an online-only or multichannel approach. Justify your decision.
2. Use the Internet to evaluate your competition. Each team member should find a site in the same e-commerce category that sells the same product or service as your business. Print each home page. Identify the functions provided at these sites, such as personalization, search features, and fulfillment. Develop a list of features that your site will offer. Specify the role that e-mail will play in your e-commerce strategy.
3. Create a rough draft of how you want your site to look. Indicate how the design will give your business an advantage over its competition and will appeal to its target market.
4. Evaluate whether your business should target international markets. Develop a list of factors you need to consider before deciding to sell internationally. Justify your final decision.

FINDING CUSTOMERS WHO ARE LOOKING FOR YOU

Reaching the right customer at the right time is the key to selling. Chances for success increase greatly if you reach customers at the very moment that they are actively seeking what you sell.

Listing Your Company

Online search listings can provide the means to efficiently bring buyers and sellers together. Many of the top catalogs, chain stores, and national retailers use search listings effectively. Search listings allow businesses to reach customers at the moment they are most likely to purchase.

Listings are distributed to major portals where they show up in numerous, relevant online searches. Search listings are priced on a per-click basis, and companies only pay for the leads that come to their sites.

Nearly 40 percent of the 280 million Internet searches conducted in the United States every day are for products or services. Imagine the exposure that search listings can provide a business.

Yellow Pages listings grew when telephone service spread across the nation. Web search listings are projected to catch up with the huge growth of Internet usage. Purchases of search listings are growing at a rate of over 200 percent per year. Search listings are projected to become a $3-billion industry by 2005, according to LookSmart Research.

Paying for Listings

Businesses can choose between two types of search listings. *Pay-for-prominence* listings provide top-of-the-web-page visibility at premium prices. *Pay-for-inclusion* listings offer cost-effective promotional power across the Internet. Many companies choose both types of listings for their sites.

Major brands like Macy's and Banana Republic find it easy to sell clothing online, but may require pay-for-prominence listings or a special offer like free shipping in order to sell electronics. Multichannel retailers often use pay-for-inclusion listings to inexpensively extend their online presence by showing their entire inventories on major search engines. Businesses using search listings hope that the increased exposure will ultimately result in higher sales.

Think Critically

1. **What are online search listings?**
2. **Should online search listings locate businesses by store names, type of merchandise, or both? Why?**
3. **What types of businesses are good candidates for online search listings? Why?**
4. **How can a business notify potential customers that its web site is accessible through online search listings?**

E-COMMERCE MARKETING MANAGEMENT TEAM DECISION MAKING

You and a partner are marketing consultants for Unique Rugs. The owner wants your input to determine if and how the company should expand to the Internet.

Unique Rugs has one suburban location in the fourth largest city of the United States. The business offers more than 20 different styles of rugs, with a wide array of colors and sizes in each style. Prices range from $400 to $10,000 depending on the size, style, and manufacturer of the rug.

The target market for Unique Rugs consists of middle-class to upper-class households interested in high-quality interior decorating and located within a 50-mile radius of the store. Unique Rugs has a sales representative who will visit a home and recommend colors and styles. However, most customers hire their own interior decorators who make purchase decisions about rugs.

Unique Rugs has earned a reputation for quality and personalized customer service. Carpets can be custom made to fit a home's décor. Customers are allowed to try several different rugs in their homes to determine the best fit.

Unique Rugs is profitable but wants more national exposure and increased sales. The owner of Unique Rugs realizes the importance of e-commerce but needs your expertise.

You must analyze the business and determine how it can benefit from e-commerce. One part of your presentation should include an overview of e-commerce and its impact on a business. Other topics covered should include legal factors, costs, and competition from other web sites and retail outlets. The owner must be given enough information to make a sound business decision. You will present your recommendations to the owner in a meeting in the store's office.

Performance Indicators Evaluated

- Understand the opportunities and challenges faced by Unique Rugs.
- Explain the need to expand Unique Rug's target market with a web site.
- Describe the information that will be included on Unique Rug's web site.
- Describe how customers will learn about the web site.
- Explain the use of online search listings to reach more target customers.

Go to the DECA web site for more detailed information.

1. How can a company use the Internet to promote its business nationally?
2. What types of pictures should customers be able to access on the Unique Rug web site?
3. Would a virtual tour of the store be beneficial for the web site? Explain your answer.

www.deca.org/publications/HS_Guide/guidetoc.html

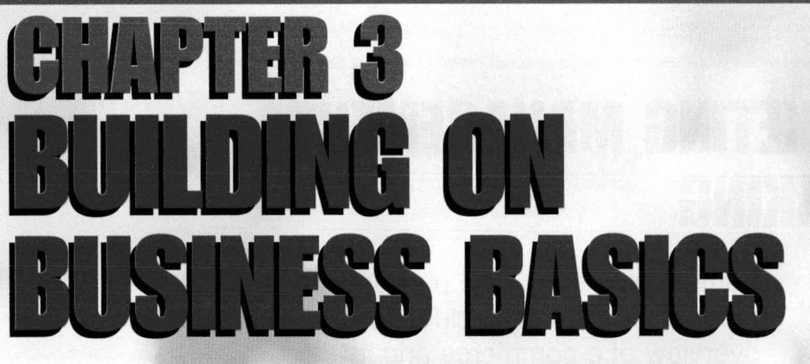

CHAPTER 3 BUILDING ON BUSINESS BASICS

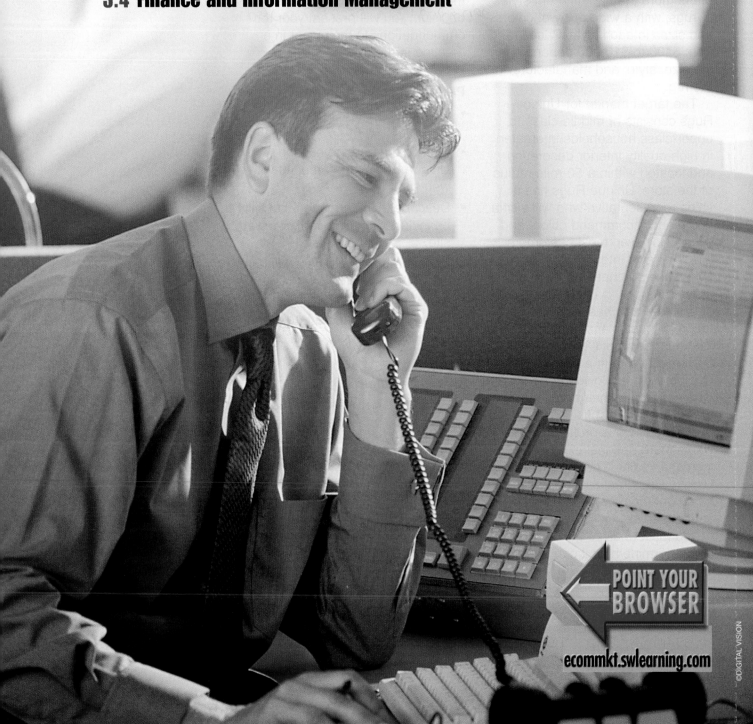

POINT YOUR BROWSER

ecommkt.swlearning.com

ANYTIME, ANYWHERE INTERNET

The Internet opens up access to information around the world. Until recently, access required that you have a wired computer connection to an Internet service provider (ISP). This connection was through a telephone line or a cable line.

The new technology that promises anytime, anywhere Internet access is called Wi-Fi (wireless fidelity). Rather than wired connections, computers use high-speed wireless cards. Businesses provide access points that transmit a wireless signal up to 500 feet away. Computer users with wireless technology can sit anywhere in these "hot spots" and access the Internet at extremely fast speeds. One access point may be all that is needed for a restaurant or café. Large organizations such as airports, colleges, and businesses with many buildings require several access points.

Where reliable Wi-Fi is available, business travelers have quick access to their networks. Students can open their computers anywhere on campus and connect to the library or an online assignment. Vacationers can sit around the pool at a hotel and send e-mails or shop online. Today, there are about 3,000 locations in the United States where consumers can access Wi-Fi. Up to two million hot spots will be available within the next ten years.

THINK CRITICALLY

1. If you owned a restaurant or a bookstore, would you offer Wi-Fi access to your customers? Why or why not?
2. What types of businesses other than those listed above might consider offering Wi-Fi for their customers? Explain your answer.

THE ECONOMICS OF BUSINESS

LESSON 3.1

Explain the role of supply and demand in our economy.

Describe the changing role of marketing.

LOGGING ON

WebVan is one of the dot-coms of the late 1990s that no longer exists. WebVan wanted to be the virtual supermarket of the future. From the company's web site, you could order all of your grocery items. They would conveniently be delivered to your home from one of the company's large warehouses. Creating a totally new business and relying only on Internet customers for sales didn't work for WebVan. The selling price for most grocery items allows for only a small percentage of profit. Supermarkets are mostly successful by selling large volumes. WebVan's costs of developing a brand new business, including warehouses and delivery services, were much higher than expected.

Despite WebVan's demise, several brick-and-mortar supermarkets are now expanding to the Internet. These businesses already have the necessary buildings and equipment in place. They can sell to traditional as well as Internet customers. Therefore, they have a chance to be profitable using a brick-and-click strategy.

Work with a partner. Find one or more supermarket web sites that offer Internet ordering. Discuss the advantages and disadvantages to customers of shopping for groceries online.

THE ROLE OF PRIVATE ENTERPRISE

The economic system of the United States is known as a private enterprise. A **private enterprise economy** recognizes that both consumers and businesses should have the freedom to make individual and independent decisions about what is produced and what is purchased. With private ownership of most resources, any person can open a business and produce and sell products and services. Similarly, people can use available money to purchase the products and services they need or want from any business that offers them for sale. In a private enterprise economy, government plays a limited role. The government's role is to safeguard natural resources, protect the safety and health of citizens, and prevent unfair business practices. An important economic concept that describes the relationship between businesses and consumers in a private enterprise is supply and demand.

©GETTY IMAGES/PHOTODISC

THE LAW OF SUPPLY

Businesses are free to decide what products and services they will produce and in what quantities. Businesses usually will offer products and services that they believe will make the most profit. If they predict a product will be quite profitable, they will produce a large quantity. If they believe the profit will be small, they will usually produce less of that product and increase production of more profitable ones. The relationship between price and production decisions is known as the **law of supply**. Whenever possible, businesses use their resources to provide products and services that command prices that will result in the greatest profits.

THE LAW OF DEMAND

Consumers have limited resources available to satisfy unlimited wants and needs. Therefore, they will try to spend their money in a way that brings the greatest satisfaction for the lowest cost. If the price of a needed product or service decreases, consumers buy a larger quantity, so demand increases. As the price goes up, demand decreases as consumers buy a smaller quantity of the product or service. When prices are high, consumers will try to find less expensive options. The relationship between price and purchase decisions is known as the **law of demand**. Consumers will usually pay the lowest possible prices for products and services to maximize the value of the money they have available to spend.

BALANCING SUPPLY AND DEMAND

There are thousands of consumers and businesses in a private enterprise economy. When all consumers wanting to buy a particular product or service are totaled, it determines how many of the products and services will be consumed. It also determines the price consumers are willing to pay. When the decisions of all the businesses offering the same product or service are totaled, it determines how many of those products and services will be for sale. It also determines the price the businesses can charge. If more products are available than consumers demand, businesses will lower the price in an effort to increase demand. If consumers want to purchase more products than are available, the product price will increase.

SUPPLY AND DEMAND ON THE INTERNET

The laws of supply and demand apply to online businesses as well as to brick-and-mortar businesses. However, the mix of suppliers and consumers is different on the Internet. The different mix causes different supply–demand relationships. Thus, an e-commerce business must be careful about the pricing of its products and services.

When shopping online, you can easily find several businesses that offer the same products. It is also a simple process to compare the prices charged for those products. There are Internet sites that will do the searching and price comparisons for you, such as mySimon and bottomdollar.com. As a result, consumers often have access to a much larger supply of a product than if they had to choose only from local businesses.

Yahoo! is the world's largest online business directory. It is a unique type of search site. Listings of both businesses and specific products are added to the Yahoo! directory by the company's employees. It currently costs a business $299 per year to have a listing reviewed and included in one of Yahoo!'s directories.

In the same way, using the Internet to sell products opens new customer markets for businesses. Companies now can market their products nationwide and worldwide if they choose. While the market is larger, the competition is in some ways tougher. Internet customers have more product choices and the capability for easier information searches and price comparisons.

Describe the law of supply and the law of demand.

law of supply the relationship between price and production. law of demand the relationship between pric and purchase

HOW MARKETING IS CHANGING

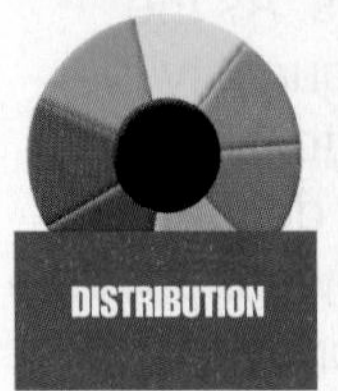

Marketing plays a different role in businesses today than it did in the past. At the start of the twentieth century, marketing was not even considered a part of business. The most important marketing function at that time was *distribution*. Because of a lack of good roads and transportation methods, businesses had a difficult time getting their products to customers. As railways and highways expanded and improved, businesses were able to reach more customers.

In the early twentieth century, most businesses did not have the same attitude toward customers as many do today. They believed that if they made a product, customers would want to buy it. There was less competition among businesses, and consumers had fewer choices. There was less of a necessity to meet consumer needs and wants. Consider how many variations of the same type of soft drink may have existed 60 years ago compared to today.

MARKETING AS PROMOTION

In the middle of the twentieth century, the standard of living was increasing. Consumers were spending more money on products and services. With improved distribution, businesses had access to more customers. Technology was improving both the quality and quantity of products produced. Businesses were competing with each other for consumer dollars. To attract customer attention and to convince customers that their products were the best, companies increased their use of salespeople and advertising. *Selling* and *promotion* were the most used marketing functions of that time.

With expanded competition, businesses could not always sell their products. There was pressure on marketers to promote the products. Sometimes salespeople and advertisements would not be honest and factual when trying to convince consumers to purchase a particular brand. Customers became distrustful of many companies. Marketing developed a poor reputation.

MEETING CUSTOMER NEEDS

Competition continued to increase, and consumers lost confidence in businesses. Unethical businesses tried to take advantage of customers with deceptive pricing, poor service, and reduced product quality. Other businesses recognized that to be profitable and successful, customer satisfaction was highly important. Marketing changed in response to that awareness.

In the 1960s and 1970s, the number of marketing activities began to increase. The way marketing activities were planned and managed changed. For years, businesses had first decided what to produce and then tried to convince customers to buy. Businesses began using marketing research to study customer needs and wants. They wanted to know what customers found satisfying and dissatisfying. They then developed the products and services that customers wanted. In addition, they provided effective customer service to ensure that consumers were satisfied.

The purchase of products directly over the Internet by consumers is growing each year. The amount of B-to-C online sales is projected to be over $105 billion by 2007. The Internet is projected to influence an additional $250 billion in offline spending by consumers.

THINK CRITICALLY

1. **Locate an Internet site that provides its amount of B-to-C and B-to-B sales for the current year. Which is greater?**
2. **Discuss why the Internet influences consumers to purchase offline in a greater amount than online purchases.**

Today, most businesses recognize the importance of the marketing concept. They use each of the seven marketing functions to satisfy customer needs at a profit. Regardless of the sales channel, marketing is critical to business success and customer satisfaction.

Describe how marketing has changed in the past century.

The belived that if they made a product customers would want to buy it

LOGGING OFF

UNDERSTAND MARKETING CONCEPTS
Circle the best answer for each of the following questions.

1. Which of the following statements is true regarding the law of supply?
   a. Businesses will increase production of products they believe will sell at high prices and provide high profits.
   b. Businesses will decrease production of products they believe will sell at low prices and provide small profits.
   c. The law of supply only works in a private enterprise economy.
   d. All of the above are true.
2. Which of the following statements is true regarding the law of demand?
   a. Consumers have unlimited resources to satisfy limited wants and needs.
   b. Consumers try to spend their money in a way that brings the highest satisfaction for the lowest cost.
   c. As the price of a product goes up, the demand for it increases.
   d. Both b and c are true.

THINK CRITICALLY

Answer the following questions as completely as possible. If necessary, use a separate sheet of paper.

3. **History** Use the Internet to locate information on how one of the major methods of distribution (air, boat/ship, truck, railroad, pipeline) has changed in the last century. Describe how those changes have affected the ways that businesses distribute products.

4. **Technology** The relationship between supply and demand is often shown as a set of intersecting lines on a graph. Use the Internet to find an example of a graph that illustrates supply and demand for a product. Print a copy of the graph. Write a description of the relationship between supply and demand as shown in the graph.

BUSINESS ORGANIZATION AND MANAGEMENT

LOGGING ON

Faster Internet connection speeds are affecting consumer purchasing. Broadband services through DSL (digital subscriber lines) and cable allow rapid connections and downloads. Businesses can now offer information instantly and in different formats, including graphics, movies, and live videophone conversations. An e-retailer, eBags, discovered that customers who view videos of products rather than just pictures are 19 percent more likely to place an order. Lands' End says new customers are 70 percent more likely to buy if they talk to a customer representative using online chat.

Work with a partner. Discuss why a faster Internet connection makes shopping more satisfying for consumers, resulting in higher product sales for businesses.

GOALS

Explain the changing role of management in e-commerce.

Describe new concepts of business organization.

MANAGING E-COMMERCE

Management is a part of every business. It is especially important for new and innovative businesses. While there are many different management jobs in a variety of companies, the basic work of managers is much the same. **Management** is the process of setting direction and accomplishing the goals of an organization through the effective use of people and other resources.

Successful managers are good leaders. **Leadership** is the ability to influence and motivate people to cooperatively achieve important goals. Not all leaders are managers. An employee can provide leadership in an organization without being a manager. Both effective managers and leaders are needed as business operations adapt to meet new challenges.

MANAGEMENT ACTIVITIES

All managers are responsible for four major activities—planning, organizing, implementing, and controlling.

- **Planning** involves analyzing information and making decisions about what needs to be done. E-commerce managers must be innovative in order to determine new ways of operating the business using technology.
- **Organizing** is concerned with determining how the business's work can be effectively accomplished. Managers need to organize the business to implement the e-commerce strategy. They may need to blend the e-commerce strategy with a traditional brick-and-mortar strategy.

With any type of business, unethical people will find ways to take advantage of consumers. The number one Internet-related complaint is auction fraud. A consumer pays for a winning bid but never receives the merchandise.

- **Implementing** means that managers help employees and others work effectively to carry out the plans of the business.
- **Controlling** involves gathering and analyzing information to determine if the business's plans are being accomplished. Based on the evaluation and changes that are occurring, new plans are made to move the company forward.

THE IMPORTANCE OF ORGANIZING

Businesses organize to accomplish their work by completing five major steps.

1. Identify the work that needs to be done.
2. Organize the work into jobs and departments.
3. Identify and obtain equipment and materials to complete the work.
4. Hire and train people to fill the jobs.
5. Develop policies and procedures to guide completion of the work.

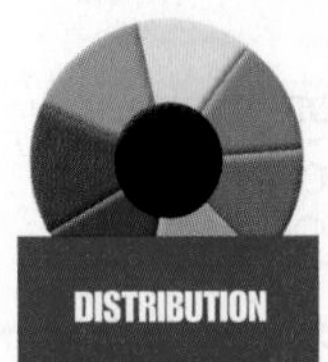

Jeff Bezos, who started and leads Amazon.com, is an example of an effective e-commerce manager. In the mid-1990s, Bezos recognized the Internet's potential to be a popular resource for consumer shopping. He developed plans to sell books on the Internet in a way that no brick-and-mortar store could. An Internet site could provide customers with access to any available book title. Bezos needed only a few large warehouses and efficient transportation to fill customer orders. Delivering customer orders would be important. Bezos decided to develop relationships with established shipping companies such as UPS rather than to create a company-owned delivery service.

Based on the plans for Amazon.com, Bezos and other managers determined the resources needed, including the technology and equipment. They hired personnel with the skills to develop and maintain the web site, process orders, manage huge amounts of data, and answer customer questions. Training programs for the jobs and the use of technology and equipment were prepared. Relationships were developed with book suppliers.

The business opened in 1995. Managers, employee teams, and suppliers worked together to build the rapidly growing business. From the beginning, detailed information was collected on the number of web site visits, the amount of time customers spent shopping, and whether orders were placed. Data also was gathered on the types of books that sold and did not sell, the time required to fill and deliver customer orders, and the cost of each business activity. Based on that information, problems were solved, improvements were made, and the business was expanded. Amazon.com started selling new types of products. It also began serving as an Internet sales site for the products of many other businesses, including Target, Old Navy, Lands' End, and Office Depot. Management efforts resulted in one of the most admired e-commerce businesses today.

THE NEW LEADERSHIP

What happens when employees believe that the company for which they work does not value them? They likely will not work as hard as they could and may not be as careful with their work. Further, they will not look for ways to make the business more successful. Leaders know that the culture of a business is important. A **business culture** is the shared purpose, values, and commitment of the people who work for a company. Leaders work hard to develop and maintain a positive business culture.

Successful leadership in an e-commerce organization keeps everyone focused on the company's mission and top priorities. Employees understand the mission and know how their work contributes to the business's success. Leaders encourage innovation and creativity. It is acceptable for new ideas to fail as long as lessons are learned from the failures. Leaders help employees build technology expertise and find ways to improve the use of technology.

©GETTY IMAGES/PHOTODISC

E-commerce leaders build flexible and adaptable organizations that allow for the free flow of information. Less attention is paid to someone's seniority or job title. More attention is paid to the person's knowledge and ability. Teams are formed to increase the knowledge available to solve problems. Employees believe they should contribute to problem solving and decision making. They are rewarded for their contributions to organizational success.

Working for an e-commerce company can be exciting. The organization is involved in a new way of doing business. Employees often have different jobs than in traditional businesses. They develop new skills and expertise. Leaders foster a team spirit where everyone is focused on the same purpose and goals. Each person takes responsibility, not only for his or her own work, but also for that of the team as a whole.

How do leadership skills and management skills differ?

Management is the process of setting direction and accomplish. leadership-is the ability to influence and motivate people

HOW BUSINESSES ARE ORGANIZED

In the past, organizational decisions about a business were made by a company's managers. A complex structure often resulted. The company had specialized divisions and departments as well as several layers of managers and employees. Communication was difficult. Managers and employees were isolated in their specialized areas. Individual workers had little interaction with other managers and employees inside the company. They also had little communication with other companies and customers. An example of a complex organizational structure is shown in the following chart.

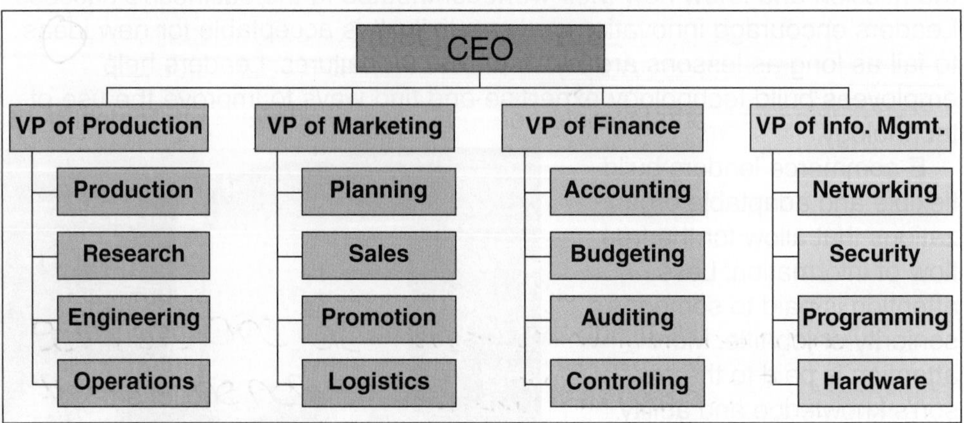

The old organizational structures required too much time for decision making. Information flowed slowly from the top executives down through other managers to the employees. Little input was received from those employees who were actually doing the work. Now, individual employees and work teams are *empowered* (given authority) to make decisions. People working in marketing need to communicate quickly and accurately with people in production or finance. The company must have effective partnerships with other businesses that supply products and resources or that help with the distribution, sales, or servicing of its products.

RESTRUCTURING BUSINESSES

Businesses involved in e-commerce are developing new organizational structures and operating procedures to gain advantages over their competitors. The new organization is *flatter*, meaning there are fewer layers of management and employees. There is *less specialization*. Each employee may have more job responsibilities, requiring a broader set of knowledge and skills. *Employee teams* are organized to complete the work. Often, employees from different parts of the organization are members of work teams designed to encourage new ideas and cooperation. Employees have *easy access to information* to improve the quality and speed of decisions and work. *Technology* is used to gather, organize, and distribute information and to encourage communication and teamwork. The organization often uses *distance workers* who are not required to work at the business's geographic location. Distance workers **telecommute**, or work from their homes using computers and Internet access to the business. Distance workers may be part of a virtual team. A **virtual team** meets and communicates using technology such as online video conferencing rather than face-to-face contact.

IMPROVING WORK PROCESSES

In addition to new organizational structures, successful e-commerce businesses have developed different ways of accomplishing work. Customers have high expectations when purchasing from an e-commerce business. They want to receive the products they purchase in the correct form and at the time and place they want. It should be easy for customers to place orders, make payments, or receive customer service.

Business processes are the activities that transform the resources of a business into products and services and deliver them in a way that meets customer expectations. Processes combine the work of many people and often more than one company. A business works with suppliers and distributors to develop and market its products and services. Those involved must work together effectively for the business processes to be successful.

Consider the activities and resources involved in serving an individual customer who makes an online purchase. The web site must be easy to use and provide the needed information. The customer should be able to confidently place an order and arrange payment. The business must process the order quickly and accurately. The product should be available in the quantity ordered and ready for shipment. The shipper must transport the product to the customer rapidly without damage. The customer needs the ability to have questions answered about the product and to conveniently return the product if necessary.

Within the business processes, there are many places where errors can occur. These mistakes often result in customer dissatisfaction and higher expenses for the business. There are also many opportunities for businesses to improve the business processes. Companies devote much time and many resources to studying and improving their business processes.

Many companies are reluctant to allow employees to telecommute even though their jobs don't require that they be in the businesses' facilities. Many managers believe that employees will not work as hard while alone and may make mistakes that cannot be easily corrected. There is also a concern that even with technology, communication will be less effective than with face-to-face interaction.

THINK CRITICALLY

1. **Do you believe that an employee will be more or less productive as a telecommuter? Justify your answer.**
2. **If you wanted to telecommute, how would you reassure your manager that you would still be an effective employee?**

What are the characteristics of new organizational structures?

They want to receive the products they purchase in the correct form and at the time and place they want

LOGGING OFF

UNDERSTAND MARKETING CONCEPTS

Circle the best answer for each of the following questions.

1. The four major management activities are
   a. planning, organizing, leading, and empowering.
   b. planning, organizing, implementing, and controlling.
   c. leading, innovating, directing, and controlling.
   d. managing, leading, training, and communicating.

2. A difference in employee roles in new organizational structures compared to traditional ones is
   a. there are more levels of management in new organizations.
   b. employees are more specialized and work more independently.
   c. individual employees and work teams are empowered to make decisions.
   d. all of the above

THINK CRITICALLY

Answer the following questions as completely as possible. If necessary, use a separate sheet of paper.

3. Describe the culture of your school. How do you believe it is different from the cultures of neighboring schools?

4. **Technology** Review the activities that Jeff Bezos completed to develop Amazon.com. Use a word-processing program to create a four-column table. Use the four major management activities as column headings. List each management activity that Bezos completed in the appropriate column. Compare your decisions with those of other students.

PRODUCTION AND OPERATIONS

LESSON 3.3

LOGGING ON

If you walk through a department store, you see counter after counter of women's beauty products. Literally thousands of choices of skin care, hair care, makeup, and fragrances are available. Finding the right products just for you can be difficult.

Reflect.com provides an online beauty consulting service. It promises that "each Reflect product is created one at a time, just for you." For each product ordered, the customer completes a detailed survey to identify individual traits and preferences. The survey results are used to develop a specific formulation of the product. The customer can even design a package and a personalized brand name. Reflect saves the formula so that it is easy to reorder. If the customer is not satisfied with a product, the company will develop a reformulation at no charge or refund the purchase price.

Work with a partner. Discuss why Reflect is willing to develop personalized products for women while most other companies are not. Will enabling a customer to personally design products provide enough incentive to overcome resistance to purchasing online? Explain your answer.

Describe product and service development, and explain the effects of e-commerce on products.

Discuss the importance of effective business operations.

PRODUCTION PROCESSES

Every exchange between a business and its customers begins with a product. Many businesses are responsible for developing their own products. Even companies that are not involved in production must be able to obtain the products their customers want from other businesses. If those products do not meet expectations, customers will be dissatisfied with the sellers as well as with the original producers. Identifying products that meet customer needs better than alternatives is an important business activity. Companies that make the products must have effective production processes so that customers' quality, quantity, and availability needs are met.

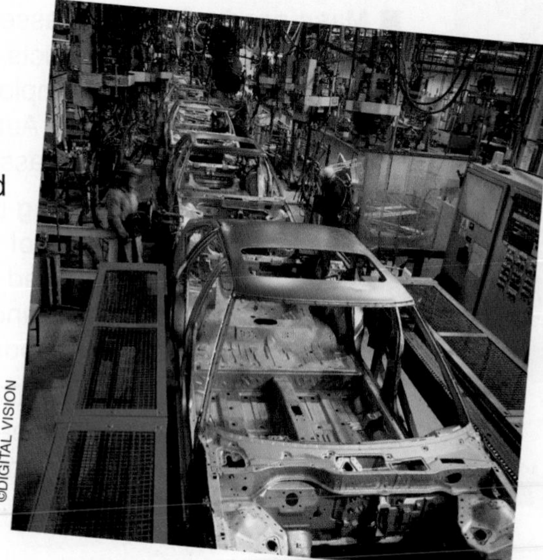

©GETTY IMAGES/PHOTODISC

PRODUCT AND SERVICE DEVELOPMENT

Production is all of the activities involved in creating products for sale. Products can be classified into three categories.

- **Consumer products** are purchased by individuals for final use and consumption. For example, consumers purchase groceries, CDs, gasoline, clothing, and personal computers.
- **Industrial products** are purchased by companies for business use, for integration into other products, or for resale. Examples of industrial products include steel used in automobile production, computers used in a business office, or swimwear resold to vacationers at a resort.
- **Services** are activities of value performed for the benefit of a consumer or a business. Consumers attend concerts and purchase insurance to protect the investment in their homes and cars. Businesses hire lawyers to prepare contracts, cleaning services to maintain buildings and equipment, and transportation companies to deliver their products.

Product Development Constructing an office building is much different than assembling a computer or preparing a meal in a restaurant. Yet each of those activities requires a multi-step production process. If a company believes in the marketing concept, the process begins with identifying customers that the company wants to serve and considering their needs. The product is then planned and designed. What will the office building look like? How will the computer be used? How many courses and what types of foods and beverages should be part of the meal?

Based on the design, the materials needed for production are acquired. The process, personnel, and equipment needed to construct, assemble, or prepare the product are organized. In some cases, an assembly area (for example, a factory, assembly line, or kitchen) is used. In other cases, personnel and equipment are taken to the production site and where construction occurs.

There are several production processes used to develop products.

©GETTY IMAGES/PHOTODISC

- **Mass production** is an assembly process whereby a large number of identical products are produced. Parts move on an assembly line as each employee performs a specific task until the product is completed. Automobiles, agricultural equipment, and large appliances are assembled using mass production.
- **Intermittent processing** uses short production runs to make limited quantities of various products. Different models of a car may be produced using intermittent processing. Various blends of juice and different designs of kitchen also use this type of production.
- **Custom production** allows for the design and assembly of a new product to meet the unique and specific needs of a customer. For example, custom production can result in a gourmet meal, a wedding video, a customized van, or a house.

Production schedules are developed to ensure that customer orders can be filled on time. Production is closely monitored. Products are tested to maintain quality control. When complete, products are delivered directly to the customer, shipped to another business for final sale, or stored for later sale.

Service Development Services are quite different from products, so development requires a different set of processes. Services differ from products in four ways.

1. Services are *intangible*. They are not a physical product. They cease to exist once they are provided to the consumer.
2. Services are *inseparable* from the provider. Lawn care cannot be completed without the personnel who are doing the mowing and fertilizing.
3. The quality of services is derived from the *expertise* and *commitment* of the provider. A legal service requires expert lawyers and support staff. A service performed poorly or with variable quality will not satisfy the customer.
4. Services are *time-specific*. When a concert begins, you cannot recapture the opening moments. If a plane departs with empty seats, those seats cannot be sold at a later time.

Service development requires an understanding of customer needs. A service business needs to know the type of service wanted and the expected quality. It also needs to know when and where the customer expects to purchase and receive the service. Suppose a person wants to watch a recent movie at home. A theater showing won't meet that need. The customer must be able to rent the movie or possibly select it for viewing through cable or satellite television service. Personnel must be well trained and highly motivated to provide consistent quality each time they deliver the service to the customer. Finally, the business must have the appropriate quantity to meet customer needs at the time the service is wanted. If adequate resources are not available to meet customer needs at a particular time, the sale cannot be recaptured and the unserved customer will be dissatisfied. If resources exceed demand for service, the business's costs will be higher than necessary.

Businesses are demanding that software producers improve product quality. Businesses currently spend an average of $5 on software installation and repair for every $1 spent on the actual software.

E-COMMERCE EFFECTS ON PRODUCTS

In some cases, e-commerce does not change a business's products at all. The same products are available to customers whether they are purchased in a brick-and-mortar store, from a catalog, or through a web site. The Internet acts as a means to access the business, gather information, and order products.

In other cases, the Internet can result in an entirely new form of product—the digital product. CDs and movies can be downloaded in digital format. Postage can be accessed and printed from a home or business computer. Paperless airline tickets, called *e-tickets*, allow travelers to present a confirmation number and a photo ID rather than a paper ticket when boarding an airplane. Airlines save as much as $50 per ticket when e-tickets are purchased. E-tickets are delivered instantly. The customer no longer needs to pick up the tickets from a travel agent or wait for delivery by mail.

One of the major changes in product development and production for e-commerce is known as mass customization. **Mass customization** is a process of large-volume production that offers specific design choices for customers. Mass customization combines the cost advantages of mass production with the customer satisfaction of custom production. Dell, Inc. provides one of the best examples of mass customization. Each customer can make specific choices of computer features on Dell's easy-to-use web site. The online order is used to assemble the computer in Dell's facilities. Some parts of the computer system, such as a specific monitor, are not stored in the assembly facility. Dell orders them from the manufacturer to be delivered to the shipper and combined with the customer's computer order just in time for delivery. E-commerce combined with effective order processing, production planning, and assembly systems allows Dell to move a customer order from receipt to completion in only eight hours.

In what ways are services different from products?

services are activites of value perfoimed for the benefit of a consumer or a business. products computer or prepaing meals

BUSINESS OPERATIONS

The major ongoing activities of a business are known as **operations**. Various types of operations are quite different, but all are critical to the success and profitability of the business. A manufacturing business is most concerned about *production operations*. Production operations include obtaining materials, maintaining production facilities and equipment, scheduling and completing product assembly, and preparing the products for delivery. A retailer is most concerned about *store operations*. Store operations include ordering products, receiving and displaying products for sale, providing customer service, providing security, and preparing employees' work schedules.

The common elements of operations management are

- Facilities and equipment
- Personnel
- Work organization, procedures, and policies
- Information requirements and systems
- Communication processes and systems
- Safety and security

©GETTY IMAGES/PHOTODISC

PLANNING AND MANAGING OPERATIONS

Each area of an organization has its own operations requirements. Production operations are unique from marketing. Finance and accounting operations are focused on planning, budgeting, and managing financial resources. Information technology operations are directed at the hardware, software, and systems used to collect, analyze, and use information.

Effective planning and organizing are important parts of operations management. Planning helps to coordinate the operations of one area of the organization with the operations of other related areas. For example, production plans should match the quantity of products needed to fill expected customer orders. Planning also helps managers and employees know how to effectively complete the work assigned to them.

IMPROVING OPERATIONS WITH TECHNOLOGY

Technology connects businesses to customers and other organizations. It provides rapid access to and collection of information. Technology can monitor business operations and identify when quality problems are occurring so they can be corrected. Technology also allows a business to extend its markets outside of its geographic area.

Classic Furniture has been in the retail furniture business for over 60 years. It purchases furniture from all over the world for resale. Furniture is stored in one of its two 300,000-square-foot distribution centers until a customer orders from one of Classic Furniture's 25 retail stores. In the past, the company often lost track of items. Distribution center workers had difficulty locating a specific piece to fill an order.

©GETTY IMAGES/PHOTODISC

The retailer now requires its suppliers to place a bar code on every piece of furniture that is shipped to its distribution centers. When loaded for shipment, the bar code is read and the data transmitted to Classic Furniture's computers. This process allows the order to be tracked. When the furniture arrives at one of the distribution centers, the storage location is entered into the computer. When an item is sold, the salesperson enters the bar code information. The data is transmitted to the billing department and the correct distribution center. The information allows the distribution center's employees to identify exactly where the furniture is located.

Technology has integrated information between suppliers and Classic Furniture as well as among all of the company's locations and departments. Inventory information is always up to date. Orders are filled accurately and more quickly. Time and space are saved in the distribution centers. Quality of work increases while costs are reduced.

How does technology contribute to improved business operations?

Tchnology also allows abusiness to extend its markets outside of its geograhic area.

LOGGING OFF

UNDERSTAND MARKETING CONCEPTS

Circle the best answer for each of the following questions.

1. An assembly process where a large number of identical products are produced is known as
   a. mass production.
   b. intermittent processing.
   c. customized production.
   d. mass customization.
2. Which of the following is *not* a common element of operations management?
   a. facilities and equipment
   b. personnel
   c. marketing
   d. communication processes and systems

THINK CRITICALLY

Answer the following questions as completely as possible. If necessary, use a separate sheet of paper.

3. **Technology** Use the Internet to find an example of a product that is now offered in a different form due to the Internet. Examples include airline tickets, postage, music, newspapers, magazines, and education. Provide a brief description of the original form of the product and the new form that is available on the Internet. Which form do you believe is more satisfying to consumers? Explain.

4. **Management** You are the manager of a retail department store. One of your duties is to develop a weekly work schedule for five full-time and three part-time employees. List the information you will need to prepare an effective work schedule.

FINANCE AND INFORMATION MANAGEMENT

LOGGING ON

Do you have scientific knowledge and research skills? If so, you might be able to use them to solve important problems facing Eli Lilly and Company. The medical drug company spends millions of dollars each year to solve difficult chemistry problems. The answers often result in new products for the company. Lilly has its own scientists but also relies on a worldwide network of experts to help solve its problems.

Eli Lilly created InnoCentive, an online research forum. Problems that Lilly is trying to solve are posted on the Web as "InnoCentive challenges." Individuals or teams of scientists can work on a challenge. If they discover a workable solution, Eli Lilly will pay them as much as $100,000. The company believes that InnoCentive will achieve more and better research results at a lower cost.

Work with a partner to discuss why investments in scientific knowledge and research are important to many companies. Why would a scientist be interested in solving one of Eli Lilly's problems without being an employee of the company?

Explain the importance of finance in business.

Discuss principles of information management.

BUSINESS FINANCE

Finance is one of the most important activities of a business. Business owners and stockholders (people who own "shares" of a public corporation) invest money in businesses to make a profit. A profit results when revenues exceed expenses. A business needs to determine whether a profit is made, the size of the profit, and what parts of the operations are most successful. To do so, careful records must be maintained on all investments, income, expenses, and other business costs.

Businesses face government regulations regarding financial record keeping. Companies that sell publicly traded stocks are required to regularly file financial reports. Business income is taxed, and businesses must maintain detailed records in order to file accurate tax forms. Businesses must provide payroll expense reports to each employee and to federal and state governments. They are required to withhold income taxes from employees' wages. They are also required to make regular payments for social security, employee retirement programs, and other employee benefits such as health insurance.

Many of the original e-commerce businesses failed in the 1990s. Those that survived as well as newer e-commerce companies are much more successful. Over 40 percent of U.S. e-commerce businesses showed a profit in 2002 despite a struggling economy.

One of the most important reasons for keeping financial records is to aid managers in decision making. Without financial records, managers will not know which products and customers are most profitable or where expenses are increasing and declining. Financial records are used to determine whether a business should hire more personnel or rely on other companies to supply some of its products and services. Financial records also influence price increases or decreases and other important operating decisions.

IMPORTANT FINANCIAL RECORDS

Financial records help to organize and provide information on a business's financial activities. Financial records are planned and maintained by people who are experts in accounting, finance, and financial laws and regulations. These individuals are responsible for maintaining accurate records and reporting the financial status of a business. They must follow specific rules and procedures so that everyone can trust and rely on the information provided. In recent years, some financial personnel and accounting firms were not honest and ethical in record keeping and reporting. Consequently, the companies they worked for and investors in those companies suffered huge financial losses.

There are several types of financial records maintained in businesses.

- **Asset records** list the resources owned by a business. Records include the original and current values as well as any amounts the business owes on the assets. Business assets include land, buildings, equipment, products, and materials.
- **Receipt and payment records** track everything a business buys and sells. Items may be sold and purchased with cash and various types of credit. Common receipt and payment records are *accounts payable* (the amount owed to others for purchases), *accounts receivable* (the amount customers owe for sales made to them), and *cash records* (the amount of cash payments and receipts).
- **Payroll records** track the wages and benefits paid to each full-time and part-time employee. The government requires detailed records of tax, social security, and Medicare withholdings from each employee's paycheck.
- **Budgets** are written financial plans for a specific time period. Almost all managers and many employees rely on budgets to help with planning and decision making. A budget is used to predict the amount of money that will be needed for specific business activities. Budgets help ensure that the costs of the activities do not exceed their contributions to the business's profitability. If costs are higher than the amount budgeted, changes must be made to prevent financial losses.

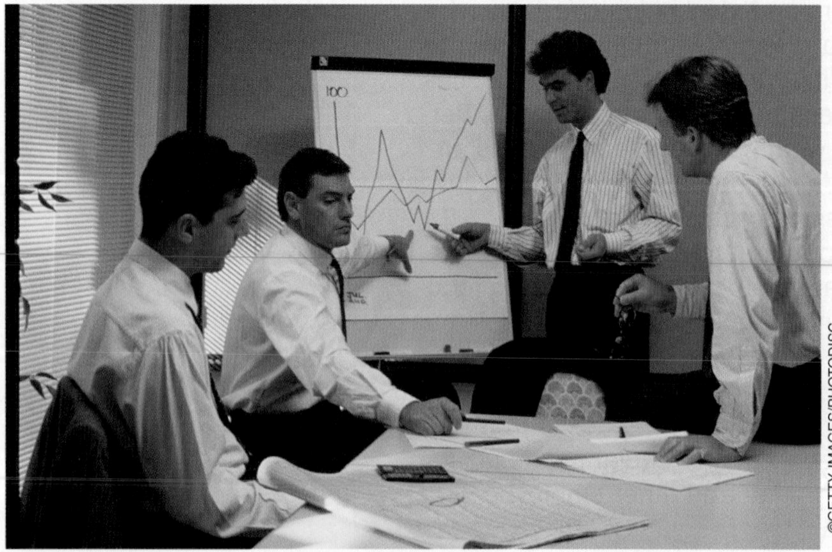

ISSUES IN E-COMMERCE FINANCE

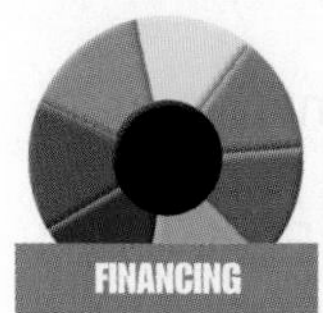

In the first few years of e-commerce, many of the dot-com pioneers were able to attract large amounts of money from investors and financial institutions. The investments were made with the expectation that e-commerce would grow rapidly. Costs would be much lower than with traditional businesses, and large profits would result. The promises did not materialize. Most of the early e-commerce businesses were forced to close before ever realizing a profit. Investors lost a great deal of money. The importance of careful financial planning is still evident as many e-commerce businesses and the e-commerce operations of brick-and-click businesses struggle to make a profit. E-commerce businesses must be able to demonstrate their financial strength to investors, banks, and suppliers who plan to extend credit to the business.

The procedures and technology used for customer payments affect the financial success of an e-commerce business. It is not possible for Internet customers to pay for their purchases with cash. Therefore, an easy-to-use and secure method of processing credit transactions or other forms of noncash payment must be available. As many as two-thirds of consumers who begin an online order terminate the process before they actually place the order. A primary reason for order incompletion is lack of customer confidence in the payment process. If businesses are losing more than half of their possible sales based on that factor, it is an important problem to solve. New forms of technology are offering customers alternative payment methods and increased security when submitting credit information online. Some businesses develop and maintain their own secure-payment systems. Others use online payment clearinghouses such as PayPal, VeriSign, or TeleCheck to provide a secure means for customers to submit payments. Some credit cards now guarantee secure transactions.

Another issue in developing a profitable e-commerce business is cost control. Consumers are able to easily compare prices of similar products from several companies using the Internet. Customers become more cost-conscious in their purchasing. Businesses whose products have significantly higher prices than competitors will likely lose sales. Many businesses have tried to attract customers by offering services such as free shipping. Often, the added expense to the business results in a sales loss. E-commerce businesses must have accurate information on all expenses in order to price products competitively yet profitably.

List three important reasons for maintaining accurate financial records and reports.

Asset records, payroll and budgets

MANAGING INFORMATION

Business in the twenty-first century will be defined by information management. **Knowledge workers** who successfully manage and use data and information in their work will be in high demand. Businesses that have the capability to instantly gather, analyze, and use information will have a competitive advantage over those who do not have effective information-management technology and procedures.

MARKETING INFORMATION MANAGEMENT

Information is becoming an increasingly important resource to businesses. Organizations are increasing the amount of technology used to generate, collect, store, analyze, and report information. Managing both the information and the technology is an important responsibility. The **chief information officer (CIO)** is the manager responsible for information systems and technology in a business. The CIO reports directly to the top business executive. The CIO helps other managers use information and related technology effectively.

BUSINESS INFORMATION NEEDS AND PRINCIPLES

Business operations are guided by information. To make effective decisions, business people need information about

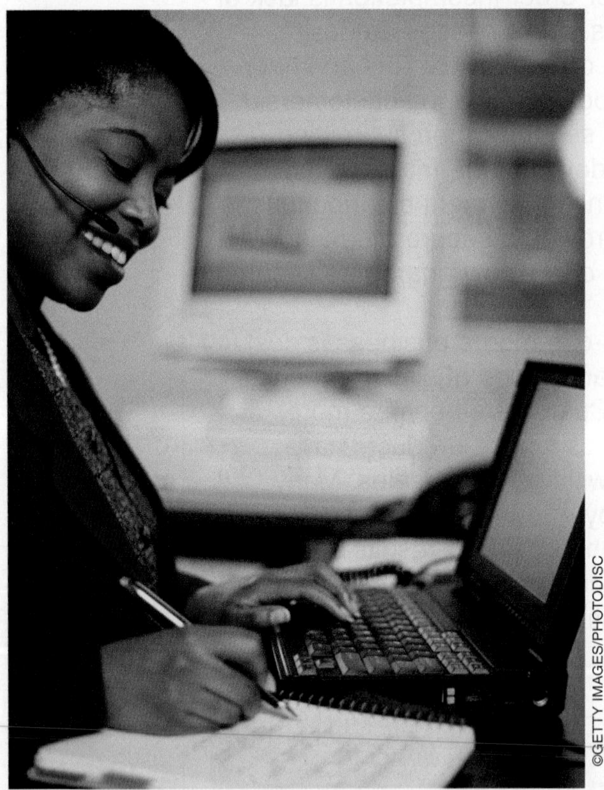

©GETTY IMAGES/PHOTODISC

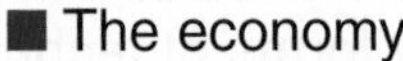

- The economy
- Competitors
- Customers
- Suppliers, distributors, and other contributing businesses
- Internal operations
- Company goals and performance

People who work in information management are responsible for ensuring that needed information is available to business decision makers. They develop and manage information technology and data following an important set of information-management principles.

- Adequate information is available to guide long-term business planning and day-to-day business operations.
- Data are collected in a way that is not disruptive to the business or its customers. Data collection does not add excessively to business costs.
- Information systems and data to be collected are planned cooperatively with those who need and use the information.
- Information-systems hardware and software are up to date, reliable, and user friendly.

- Information systems throughout the organization are compatible so that information can be exchanged and understood.
- Only the data needed for decision making are collected and maintained in the information-management system.
- Efforts are made to ensure that the data collection and analysis process is accurate and objective.
- Specific information is readily available to those who need it but restricted from all others.
- Security of information is a primary concern. Systems are tested regularly to confirm security.
- Privacy of personal information is protected. Privacy policies are communicated to those from whom data are collected and those who use the information.

VIRTUAL VIEWPOINTS

Less than 50 percent of Internet users speak English as their primary language. Yet, many businesses continue to use English as the only language for their web sites. Some B-to-B e-commerce businesses justify this policy by saying that most international executives speak and read some English. However, even people who are fluent in English as a second language often prefer to be addressed in their primary language. They believe this courtesy shows that the business values them as important customers.

THINK CRITICALLY

1. **Only a small amount of your company's sales comes from customers who do not speak English as their primary language. Should the company spend the time and money to translate its web site to other languages? Why or why not?**
2. **Why do fewer U.S. companies provide web site information in languages other than English than do businesses from other countries?**

IMPROVING INFORMATION MANAGEMENT

E-commerce increases the need for quick delivery of accurate information. It also provides a means to improve information availability and management. The Internet is an efficient resource for sharing information across a business or among business partners. With adequate security, salespeople can easily access information about the business's products, prices, and distribution. Marketing managers can access sales reports and communicate product information to the sales force. Production managers can gather information on inventory levels, scheduled deliveries, or costs of materials and supplies. They can instantly communicate with suppliers to discuss a product quality report. They can collaborate with company engineers to plan for the redesign of an older product. Employees can access their own personnel records to check a change in benefits. They can update personal information or register for an upcoming training session.

New Internet tools are improving business-information management. Electronic surveys gather market research information. A data-tracking system records an Internet user's interactions with the company's web site. Purchases are tracked to determine the most profitable products and customers. The information is used to develop personalized promotions for key customers. A shared database allows suppliers, distributors, and other business partners to analyze information. Shared analysis helps to cut production time and reduce costs. All business process costs are monitored to improve budget accuracy.

WORKING ONLINE

Data-mining software is used in marketing to provide detailed analysis of customer data. The analysis is used for many purposes. New target markets are identified. Marketing mixes are matched to the specific needs of customers. Customer satisfaction is improved while profitability is increased.

As a *marketing data miner*, Ricardo ensures the accuracy of data in company databases. He also organizes the databases for efficient analysis. He works with marketing personnel to determine the information they need for marketing plans and activities. Ricardo selects the data, completes the analysis, and prepares reports that provide the needed information to the marketers. If requested, he offers recommendations based on the data analysis.

Ricardo's most critical skills as a marketing data miner are mathematics and statistics. He also has expertise in the use of database and statistical software as well as data-mining software applications. Effective written communication skills are needed to prepare informative, user-friendly reports. Finally, an understanding of marketing is important in order to analyze and provide the appropriate information to marketing personnel. Ricardo's position as a marketing data miner requires a bachelor's degree. Some advanced data-mining positions require a master's degree or higher.

THINK CRITICALLY

1. **Marketing data miner is a relatively new position in businesses. What factors have resulted in the development of this new career area?**
2. **What types of computer software would be helpful to Ricardo when he prepares and presents reports?**

cyber check

List the six types of information that business managers need in order to make decisions.

____

____

LOGGING OFF

UNDERSTAND MARKETING CONCEPTS

Circle the best answer for each of the following questions.

1. Which type of financial records is used to predict the amount of money that will be needed for specific business activities?
   a. asset records
   b. receipt and payment records
   c. personnel records
   d. budgets
2. The executive responsible for information systems and technology in a business is known as a
   a. database manager.
   b. chief information officer.
   c. marketing information specialist.
   d. computer systems manager.

THINK CRITICALLY

Answer the following questions as completely as possible. If necessary, use a separate sheet of paper.

3. **Technology** Use the Internet to locate information on a computerized accounting software system. Identify the types of financial records that can be prepared using the software. If available, locate examples of these financial records.

4. **Research** Locate a recent story on a company that has experienced problems with data security involving its computer systems and the Internet. Prepare a two-page report on the type of security problem that occurred. Describe any damage that resulted and what the company did to solve the problem.

CHAPTER 3 REVIEW

REVIEW E-COMMERCE MARKETING CONCEPTS

Write the letter of the term that matches each definition. Some terms will not be used.

a. business culture
b. business processes
c. chief information officer (CIO)
d. knowledge workers
e. law of demand
f. law of supply
g. leadership
h. management
i. mass customization
j. operations
k. private enterprise economy
l. production
m. telecommute
n. virtual team

e 1. The relationship between price and purchase decisions

f 2. The relationship between price and production decisions

H 3. The process of setting direction and accomplishing the goals of an organization through the effective use of people and other resources

m 4. Work from home using computers and Internet access to the business

n 5. Employees who meet and communicate using technology rather than face-to-face contact

a 6. The shared purpose, values, and commitment of the people who work for a company

g 7. The ability to influence and motivate people to cooperatively achieve important goals

B 8. The activities that transform the resources of a business into products and services and deliver them in a way that meets customer expectations

I 9. A process of large-volume production that offers specific design choices for customers

K 10. Recognizes that both consumers and businesses should have the freedom to make individual and independent decisions about what is produced and what is purchased

C 11. The executive responsible for information systems and technology in a business

Circle the best answer.

12. The process of determining how a business's work can be effectively accomplished is
    a. e-commerce marketing.
    b. management.
    c. leadership.
    d. organizing.

13. Which is *not* a difference between services and products?
    a. Services are tangible.
    b. Services are time-specific.
    c. Services are inseparable from the provider.
    d. The quality of services is derived from the expertise and commitment of the provider.

THINK CRITICALLY

14. How does a private enterprise economy benefit both businesses and consumers?

15. Why are marketers more successful when they focus on satisfying customer satisfaction rather than on product promotion?

16. Do you believe that employee teams can be as effective in making decisions about company operations as an experienced manager? Why or why not?

17. Why have many companies moved to mass customization when producing products rather than using mass production or customized production?

MAKE CONNECTIONS

18. **MARKETING MATH** If 200,000 units of a product are available for sale, customers are willing to purchase them at $6.50 each. If producers can receive $6.50 per product, they are willing to produce 148,000 units. Calculate the total revenue that would result from the supply and demand situations described. Why is there a difference in the total revenue? What do you believe will happen to the product price and the amount sold in this situation?

19. **TECHNOLOGY** You are the team leader of a virtual team. All of your work must be done using the Internet rather than face-to-face interaction. Use the Internet to identify three types of computer hardware and three software programs that would improve your team's productivity. Briefly describe each item. Provide your reasons for each selection.

20. **COMMUNICATION** Research the history and business practices of an online payment clearinghouse such as PayPal, VeriSign, or Telecheck. Write a two-page report on the company. Describe the services that it offers.

21. **PRODUCTION** Locate the web site of a company other than Dell, Inc. that allows consumers to customize a product to fit their needs. Describe the design choices available. How easy or difficult does the process of customization appear to be? Do you believe the choices offered are adequate to meet consumer needs? What other alternatives would you recommend that the business make available?

22. **RESEARCH** Locate an Internet site that lists career opportunities in e-commerce. Find a job title and description for a position that would be considered a knowledge worker. Prepare a three-minute oral presentation describing the position. Include the types of data and information with which a person in that job would work. Also mention the education and experience required to obtain the job.

23. **COMMUNICATION** You are planning to use a survey to gather some information from customers of a business. Prepare a memo that you will send to the customers. In the memo, explain why the information is important to the business. Describe what the business will do to protect the privacy of the customers and the information they submit.

This part of the project will focus on production, operations, and financial decisions for your business.

Work with your team members to complete the following activities.

1. List and briefly describe the major products and services your business will offer.
2. For each product, determine the type of manufacturing process to be used. Choices include mass production, intermittent processing, custom production, or mass customization. If your company will not produce the product, identify at least two companies that your business might hire to supply the item.
3. For each service, identify the steps you will take to ensure that an appropriate quantity and quality of services will be available to meet customer needs.
4. Identify three major areas of operations that will be a part of your business. For each area, list up to five activities that will be completed by its employees.
5. Prepare a simple budget for your business. Identify the assets that the business will have. Assets include buildings, equipment, products, and so forth. List the business's major expenses. How much money will you need to start the business? Finally, identify where you can obtain the money needed to start the business. (Possible alternatives are your personal savings, loans or investments from family and friends, loans from banks or other financial institutions, and other sources.)

CASE STUDY

SMALL BUSINESSES WIN BIG ONLINE

Size once mattered in the world of commerce. The biggest players made the largest impact in marketing and pricing. E-commerce has become a great equalizer in the retail industry. Small businesses can now compete in the retail game. Many score "niche" victories by using the same strategies available to bigger businesses.

Skill over Size

E-commerce experts state that the key to small-business success is smarts, not riches. Retailers must ensure that their web sites are noticed. Gene Alvarez, senior program director for e-business strategies at Meta Group, explains that a small retailer's site must be registered properly so that it shows up in premier search engines. Even the best web sites will not reap benefits if they do not appear in search results.

It is important that the web site is well designed and functional or customers will not return. Many small retailers hire experts outside the company to design and maintain their sites for them.

The small business must establish uniqueness by focusing on a particular product or a small geographic area. For example, the web site of a Phoenix-based bookstore could emphasize same-day delivery to local customers. It could also boast that the business has a bigger selection of books relevant to Arizona than do larger competitors. Small businesses need a focused market that they can serve better than major companies.

Knowing a community well or effectively catering to a specific group not served by the big players can be rewarding. Made in Oregon is a regional e-commerce business that sells only products made in Oregon. PetsWelcome.com is a web site that promotes hotels and motels that accept pets. Sites that cater to specific groups benefit from word-of-mouth advertising shared by group members. Sites that cater to distinct groups also are more likely found by search engines.

Customers Come First

Small companies are no different from big businesses when it comes to customer service. Customers must have a positive experience with the company's web site. Small-business sites can use personalized customer service to their advantage. They must focus on the one or two areas where they perform better than anyone else does. Follow-up is critical. Small businesses must ensure that customers are satisfied. They also must resolve any issues that might prevent return visits to the site. Building a loyal customer base will result in repeat sales.

Small businesses should choose their online battles. Sometimes it is fruitless to enter a market served successfully by large, established businesses.

Think Critically

1. **How has e-commerce become the equalizer for large and small retailers?**
2. **What is a "niche" market? Why is it important for a small e-commerce business to focus on a niche market?**
3. **How can an e-commerce company build customer loyalty?**
4. **What types of businesses would be good candidates for e-commerce? Why?**

BUSINESS SERVICES MARKETING ROLE PLAY

You are the web designer for a professional sports team. The team's new web site will be an interactive fan club. Fans will find updates on the latest team developments. They also may purchase team-related merchandise online.

Fans have indicated that team players need to be more visible in the community and more willing to communicate with fans. The team's goals are to increase team merchandise sales, to increase community outreach, and to become "America's favorite."

Consider how the web site can help the team reach its goals. You have a meeting to discuss your ideas with the team's owner. You will have ten minutes to role play the situation.

Performance Indicators Evaluated

- Understand the challenges and opportunities faced by the professional sports team.
- Explain the specific features of the web site that will meet the needs of fans.
- Explain the interactive features of the web site.
- Describe how the web site will be effectively used to increase merchandise sales.
- Describe how customers will learn about the web site.
- Explain how the web site will be updated.
- Display strong listening skills.

Go to the DECA web site for more detailed information.

1. Why is a web site a good medium for a fan club?
2. What features might be necessary to display and sell merchandise online?
3. Why is timeliness of information so important for this type of web site?
4. What special promotions will attract repeat visitors to the site?
5. How can the web site help to increase players' visibility in the community?

www.deca.org/publications/HS_Guide/guidetoc.html

CHAPTER 4
INFORMATION TECHNOLOGY BASICS

4.1 Telecommunication Infrastructure
4.2 The Internet Backbone
4.3 Cybercrime
4.4 Technical Applications

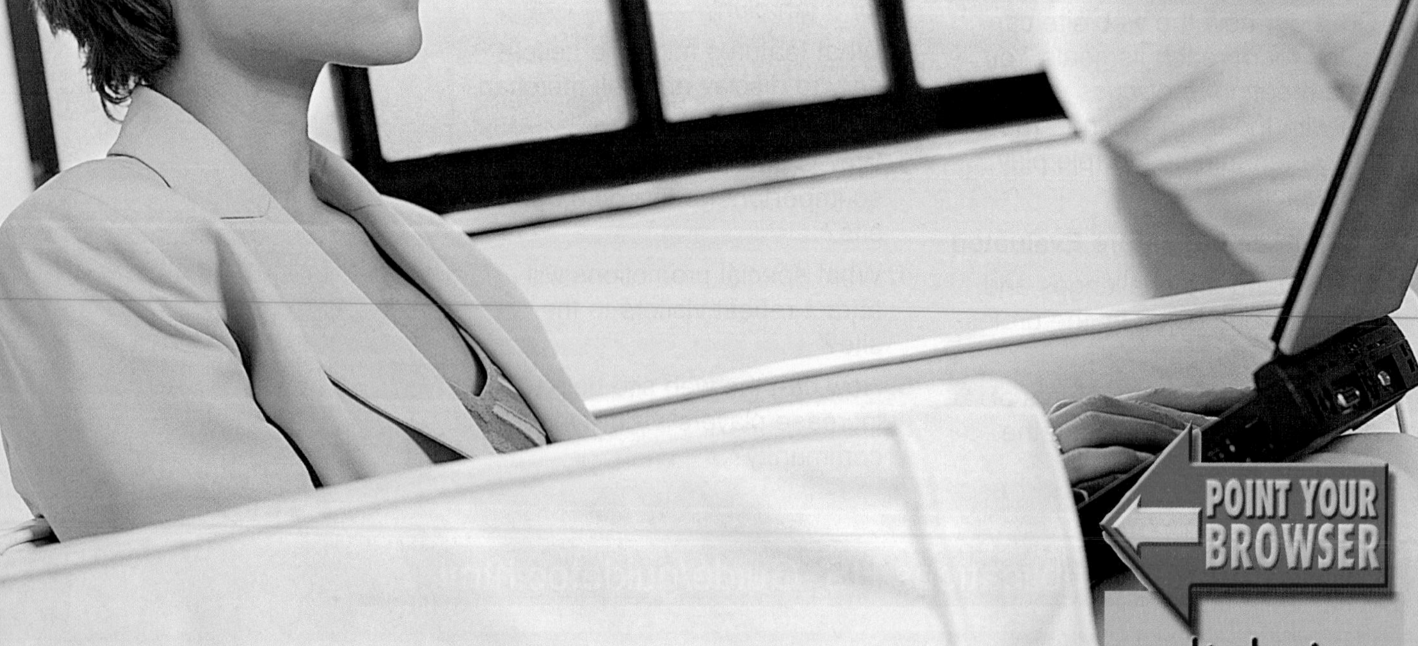

AOL EVERYWHERE

America Online (AOL) was founded in 1985. From 1993 to 2003, AOL grew from 500,000 members to 34 million members worldwide. AOL is the world's largest Internet service provider (ISP) with over 27 percent of U.S. Internet users as members.

AOL's mission is to connect people to information anywhere at anytime. Connection is primarily through the Internet, but AOL wants to bring its members information through wireless devices such as cellular phones and personal digital assistants (PDAs). AOL uses a number of communication platforms. Its web site allows access to online content. AOL also supports online chat, instant messaging, e-mail, and text messaging. Cellular phone services offer many of these features. AOL wants to be the point of contact when people go online to search for information, contact friends and family, and look for entertainment.

AOL's top managers believed that Internet users would want an abundance of online content. To supply this content, AOL and Time Warner joined in 2000 in a $110-billion merger. This partnership allows AOL to deliver Time Warner content such as HBO shows, Warner Brothers movies, music, and content from *Time* magazine. Customers need broadband connections to access the expanded content. The merger has not reached AOL's or Time Warner's goals. The Internet is highly popular as a means of communication for individuals. However, e-businesses have been less successful in persuading individuals to pay for information and entertainment. Consequently, AOL's stock price dropped from over $60 per share in 2000 to less than $15 per share by 2003.

THINK CRITICALLY

1. Explain how AOL plans to connect its members anywhere at anytime.
2. AOL/Time Warner wants to make money by selling content over the Internet. Would the company's plan work better if more people had broadband Internet access? Explain your answer.

LESSON 4.1

TELECOMMUNICATION INFRASTRUCTURE

Describe the history and importance of the telecommunication infrastructure.

Explain how the World Wide Web works.

LOGGING ON

The Internet requires a telecommunication *infrastructure* (underlying structure) to transfer information. The Internet's infrastructure includes telephone and television cables, broadcast systems, computer hardware, and software applications.

The Internet's infrastructure has evolved over time, allowing more information to be sent to a growing number of locations. Today, the Internet is connected not only to computers but also to televisions and wireless devices such as cell phones and personal digital assistants. The Internet's infrastructure is used to transfer e-mail, send web pages, transmit music, and view video files. The Internet continues to revolutionize how and where information is sent and received. Users are no longer bound to a stationary personal computer. They can carry the World Wide Web in their pockets!

Work with a partner. Analyze how life changes when you can access the Internet anywhere at anytime. Speculate on how this instant access can affect the way that businesses operate.

©GETTY IMAGES/PHOTODISC

INFRASTRUCTURE

The development of the telegraph in the early 1800s established the first electronic communication infrastructure. In the late 1800s, the telephone challenged the telegraph as both a business tool and a means of personal communication. Today, telephone infrastructure is changing around the world. Digital wireless cellular systems now cover more than 95 percent of the United States. In countries such as Finland, more than 75 percent of the population have cellular phones.

Over time, the global telecommunications industry has developed a complex infrastructure to send and receive information. When you make a telephone call, your voice travels from your phone to the local phone company to be transferred to a public telecommunications network. From there, it may travel through landlines (physical wires) or bounce around the world via satellites. The person receiving the call uses his or her local phone company's system to answer. The Internet initially relied on this basic infrastructure, but it did not stop there. It has taken advantage of newer telecommunication systems.

A number of companies have moved into the telecommunications business. Cable television companies provide not only television stations but also Internet access. Independent, wireless Internet-access companies are allowing individuals the opportunity to surf the Web at anytime and anyplace. Even electric utility companies are providing Internet access. The race is on to wire the world!

THE HISTORY OF THE INTERNET

The Internet began in 1969 as a U.S. government-funded project to develop methods of sharing information among computer networks. At first the Internet was used mainly by colleges, universities, researchers, and a few large companies that needed to send and share information. Most businesses and homes did not have Internet access. If they did, the access was through large mainframe computers.

The developers of the Internet needed to devise a way for it to operate across various computer systems. A critical piece of this development was the adoption of open standards. **Open standards** are basic sets of instructions that are not owned by a single company. The Internet can operate on any platform that adopts the open *Internet Protocol (IP) standards.* IP standards are used for Internet applications such as e-mail and the World Wide Web.

IP standards continue to evolve. Advancements in standards allow new devices to use the Internet and increase the Internet's functionality. New standards must be approved by the Internet's independent governing organizations. The approval process prevents any single company from controlling the Internet.

Today, the Internet "backbone" is a vast array of computers, telecommunication lines, and software standards that links businesses and individuals around the world. The infrastructure provides nearly everyone with the ability to connect and communicate.

List at least two reasons why open standards are important for the Internet.

___

___

The United States accounts for 29 percent of the world's Internet access. It has the highest rate of market entry with close to 75 percent of the population using the Internet. The United States is followed by Europe with 23 percent, Asia-Pacific with 13 percent, and Latin America with 2 percent of the world's Internet usage.

THE WORLD WIDE WEB

The **World Wide Web** is a set of open standards built on Internet standards that use the public telecommunication infrastructure to transfer information. The World Wide Web has so dominated the Internet that most people use the terms *Web* and *Internet* interchangeably.

Tim Berners-Lee developed the World Wide Web (or simply, the Web) in 1990. He envisioned the Web as a means of allowing hyperlinks to instantly connect to new information. A **hyperlink** is a reference from some point in a document to some point in another document or to another place in the same document. When clicked on, a web hyperlink sends a user to a new location. The Web was designed to work the same way as the human mind, allowing linkages between ideas and information. Berners-Lee developed the first web browser and a series of web standards including

- **URL** Universal Resource Locator—the web address
- **HTTP** HyperText Transfer Protocols—the instructions that allow hyperlinks to work
- **HTML** HyperText Markup Language—the set of design codes that are used to construct web pages

Berners-Lee gave away all of these ideas for free, allowing them to become open standards for use over the Internet.

©GETTY IMAGES/PHOTODISC

THE BROWSER

The **browser** is the key to the Internet's growth. A browser provides a graphical view of the Web. The first graphical browser to display pictures and formatted text was developed at the National Supercomputer Center and was offered to the public for free. A number of companies adapted and licensed the browser technology and attempted to sell their own versions. Netscape allowed users to download its browser for free. It then sold server software to Internet service providers that allowed users to access the Web via the Netscape browser. Today, Microsoft's Internet Explorer is the dominant browser for personal computers (PCs). Specialized browsers are used for Internet cellular phones, web-based television, and other non-PC access devices.

Web pages are usually created with web page editor software that automatically writes the HTML code. A user's web browser reads and translates the HTML code and graphically displays the pages. Browsers also allow *hypertext* to pull content from other locations.

INTERNET SERVICE PROVIDERS

An **Internet service provider (ISP)** allows an Internet user to "log on" or connect to the Internet. The ISP plays the same role for the Internet as the local telephone company plays for telephone service. An ISP uses specialized computers called *servers* to host, or store, web content and allow individuals to access the Internet.

When an individual goes online, he or she logs on to an Internet server. The server connects to the Internet backbone. The browser then acts like a telephone, calling up web content. When requested, an ISP sends copies of web pages to the user's browser.

Some ISPs specialize in providing consumers with Internet access. Others specialize in developing and hosting web pages for businesses and individuals. Some businesses use their own servers to host their web sites.

DOMAIN NAMES

Each web site has a unique name, known as its **domain name**. Amazon.com is an example of a well-known domain name. A domain name has an associated numerical IP address that acts as a telephone number to provide access to the site. The three letters to the right of a domain name's dot represent the *top-level domain.* The top-level domain distinguishes the type of web site. The most popular top-level domains are

- .com—for commercial enterprises
- .edu—for educational institutions
- .gov—for government agencies
- .org—for nonprofit organizations

Every country has a *national domain.* Canada has .ca, Mexico has .mx, and Germany has .de. Can you guess which country has .us?

The Internet began as a government-funded project. The Internet2 project is a new partnership between universities, industries, and the U.S. government to develop and organize an advanced Internet. The prototype (original model) of Internet2 sent digital information from Geneva, Switzerland to Chicago, Illinois 3,500 times faster than the typical home broadband connection. This speed would allow the transfer of a DVD-quality movie every 36 seconds.

THINK CRITICALLY

1. **Evaluate how you currently use the Internet. Determine how the increased speed of Internet2 would change your online activities.**
2. **Make a list of ways that Internet2 could affect how online business is conducted.**

Describe the role of browsers and ISPs in making the World Wide Web function.

Uses specializd computers called servers to host, or store, web content and allow inividuals to access the Internet.

LOGGING OFF

UNDERSTAND MARKETING CONCEPTS

Circle the best answer for each of the following questions.

1. The Internet is
   a. another name for browser.
   b. a worldwide network of interconnected computer networks.
   c. owned and run by the U.S. government.
   d. none of the above
2. Three standards used for the World Wide Web include
   a. URL, HTTP, and HTML.
   b. www, w3, and the Web.
   c. INTP, Cobol, and C+.
   d. .com, .edu, and .org.

THINK CRITICALLY

Answer the following questions as completely as possible. If necessary, use a separate sheet of paper.

3. The Internet and the World Wide Web are based on open standards. What might happen to the Internet if it was owned and controlled by one company? How would this change the marketing of the Internet?

____

____

____

____

____

4. **Technology** Assume you are Tim Berners-Lee. Describe to your manager the plan you have for developing the World Wide Web. Explain all of the technology that you will need to develop in order for the Web to work.

____

____

____

____

____

LESSON 4.2

THE INTERNET BACKBONE

LOGGING ON

The world is a noisy place crisscrossed with billions of miles of communication lines. Satellites receive and send information. Television and radio stations broadcast information. Cellular systems allow telephone calls to originate in New York and end in California. The amounts and types of information that communication systems are sending are rapidly increasing. For example, cellular phones are now able to send and receive video and download games and movies. All of this information does not necessarily travel into everyone's home quickly. The speed of receipt depends upon the type of connection that runs from the Internet backbone to the individual user.

Work with a partner. Determine how your school or your home is connected to the Internet. Recommend ways to increase the speed of your Internet connection. Explain the benefits and drawbacks of your recommendations. Choose one recommendation, and explain why you think it is the best choice.

Describe the various methods of digital delivery.

Explain the options available for last-mile connections.

DIGITAL DELIVERY

Information moves through the telecommunication infrastructure via analog and digital signals. **Analog signals** are waves of energy. Radio and television broadcasts and landline telephones mainly use analog signals.

MARKETING INFORMATION MANAGEMENT

The Internet uses digital signals. **Digital signals** are a series of ons (zeros) and offs (ones). Each on or off is called a *bit*. The more bits that can be sent per second over a communication system, the faster a computer file can be transferred.

You may have noticed that some Internet connections are faster than others. Internet-access speed is primarily dependent upon the bandwidth of the connection. The **bandwidth** is the number of digital signals that can travel per second. Many PCs use a telephone modem to connect to the Internet. A modem carries an analog signal from a telephone and translates it into a digital signal. The highest bandwidth for most PC modems is 56 kbps, or 56 kilobits (56,000 bits) per second. Many Internet users around the world are upgrading to **broadband** connections, where bandwidth is increased through direct digital signals. Information can travel much faster over digital connections. Currently, the Internet backbone can send information at 13 gbps (13 gigabits, or billion bits, per second). Experimental Internet backbones are so fast that they can send the entire U.S. Library of Congress in 71 seconds!

Canada has outpaced the United States in broadband usage. Almost 54 percent of Canadian home Internet users have broadband connections, compared to only 37 percent of U.S. home Internet users.

INTERNATIONAL ACCESS

The U.S. government sponsored and funded early versions of the Internet. Once the Internet had grown to a sustainable level, the government turned it over to the private sector (the part of the economy not controlled by the government). Governments around the world are following this same plan. Many countries are freeing their telecommunications industries of government regulation, allowing the private sector to provide Internet access.

Many governments have found that they need to improve their telecommunication infrastructures in order to provide Internet access. Improvement is no longer solely accomplished through landlines. Countries are developing wireless connections because they are often cheaper than laying land-based systems. France has set a goal to make broadband Internet access available to 95 percent of its population by 2005. Part of France's strategy is to provide wireless access to individuals' homes. Landlines are considered too expensive.

CYBERCAFÉS

Cybercafés are privately owned businesses that provide Internet access for a fee. Cybercafés are popular in countries that have a small percentage of home Internet access. The Himalayan kingdom of Bhutan received television broadcasts for the first time in 1999. By 2000, there were two cybercafés in the capital city. In 2001, China had an estimated 75,000 cybercafés.

Describe the difference between analog signals and digital signals.

Analog are waves of energy

Digital are a series of ons (zeros) and (ones)

THE LAST MILE

Regardless of how quickly information flows across the information superhighway, it can only travel as fast as the slowest connection to your home. The last connection between the Internet and your home or business is called the **last mile**. Last miles include landlines and wireless systems.

Early Internet access was supported by existing telecommunication infrastructures, such as the telephone. Technologies are now being developed that allow the Internet to expand into new areas.

LANDLINES

Landlines are physical wires that connect an Internet user to the Internet backbone. Landlines include telephone wires (called twisted pair lines), cable television (coaxial lines), and fiber-optic lines. Twisted pair lines and coaxial lines can deliver both analog and digital signals. Telephone analog signals require a modem and deliver 56 kbps. DSL (digital subscriber lines) allow telephone lines to deliver digital signals up to 1.5 mbps (1.5 million bits per second). Digital cable can deliver signals at speeds up to 3 mbps.

Fiber-optic lines use light to deliver digital signals. These lines are used throughout the Internet backbone and in many business computer networks. Fiber-optic lines are now being installed in homes around the world and can offer speeds up to 10 mbps.

WIRELESS SYSTEMS

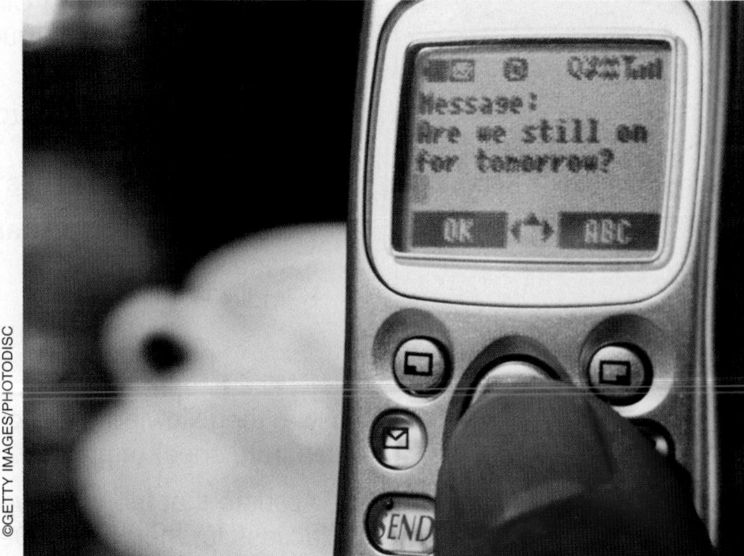

©GETTY IMAGES/PHOTODISC

Wireless Internet access sends signals without wires. Wireless access is provided through satellite broadcast, radio, and cellular telephone systems. Low power radio signals are used to support local wireless networks, or *hot spots*. Internet devices can link into the wireless fidelity (Wi-Fi) network of these hot spots. Some McDonald's restaurants have developed Wi-Fi technology to support hot spots so that customers can surf the 'Net while they eat. Home users can also take advantage of Wi-Fi technology, allowing them to access the Internet without wires.

Many cellular telephones can access the Internet. Services include sending short text messages as well as surfing full web pages. Web pages designed for cellular surfing are created for a much smaller screen. Many cellular phones can send and receive photos. Internet users around the world can use broadband cellular phones to download and play music, receive e-mail, and send and receive video.

THE FUTURE

The future of the Internet will be centered on high bandwidth. Many people question how this high bandwidth will be delivered. In the United States, broadband connections through digital cable television are growing faster than through DSL lines. In Europe, it is just the opposite—broadband connections through DSL are growing faster than through digital cable.

In the United States, the three largest regional phone companies have agreed to develop standards for fiber-optic connections to home users. Fiber-optic connections will allow the phone companies to deliver voice, data, TV broadcasts, and videoconferencing to home and business users.

List the two categories of last-mile connections and give two examples of each.

Landlines-house phone

Wirless Systems-cellphones

LOGGING OFF

UNDERSTAND MARKETING CONCEPTS

Circle the best answer for each of the following questions.

1. Which of the following provides the fastest Internet connection?
   a. telephone modems
   b. digital subscriber lines (DSL)
   c. digital cable
   d. fiber-optic lines
2. Which of the following can be used for wireless Internet access?
   a. satellite broadcast
   b. radio
   c. cellular telephone systems
   d. all of the above

THINK CRITICALLY

Answer the following questions as completely as possible. If necessary, use a separate sheet of paper.

3. Assume that friends have asked you for advice on obtaining Internet access for their home. Describe various last-mile options that you would recommend and the advantages and disadvantages of each.

4. Hold one end of a piece of thick string and have a partner hold the other end. Move your arm up and down to create waves in the string. Then pull the string tight. Next, use a series of short pulls to send a signal to your partner. Which of these actions represents an analog signal and which represents a digital signal? Explain your answer.

LESSON 4.3

CYBERCRIME

LOGGING ON

Is writing a computer virus or hacking a computer system really a victimless crime? Many people ask this question. The fact is, these crimes can generate extremely high costs, including lost productivity and lost information. Additionally, there is the time required to develop tools to block the viruses and hacking, as well as the cost to clean up the damage. One estimate indicates that costs due to viruses and hacking in 2000 reached as high as $1.5 trillion worldwide.

Work with a group. Discuss the computer viruses of which you are aware. How many of those viruses affected you or people you know? What kinds of damage did they do? What was done to prevent future infections?

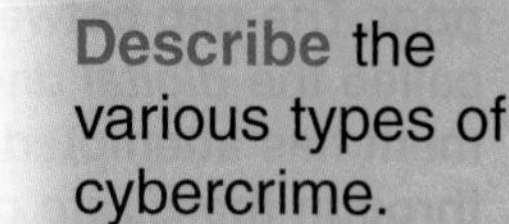

Describe the various types of cybercrime.

Describe security measures that can be used against cybercrime.

TYPES OF CYBERCRIME

In order for e-commerce to develop and succeed, businesses and customers must feel secure when they use the Internet. The Internet crosses international borders, tempting some unlawful people to believe that they can't be tracked online. This temptation can lead to **cybercrime**, or criminal activity on the Internet. Cybercrime includes hacking (economic espionage or infrastructure attacks) and viruses.

HACKING

One form of cybercrime is **hacking**, which involves the attempt by individuals to break through online security for fun or profit. They "hack" their way into computer networks. There are two types of hacking—economic espionage and infrastructure attacks. Hackers who hack just for fun do it for bragging rights. However, their actions can be just as damaging as those of hackers who plan economic espionage or infrastructure attacks.

©GETTY IMAGES/PHOTODISC

VIRTUAL VIEWPOINTS

People with low incomes are less likely to own PCs and have Internet access. This results in groups that are information rich and groups that are information poor. The gap between these groups is called the *digital divide*. The U.S. government has attempted to close this divide through the *E-rate program*. This program taxes long-distance telephone services in order to provide funding for Internet access in public schools and libraries.

The United States is not the only country concerned about the digital divide. Many poor countries cannot afford to develop the telecommunication infrastructure required to wire individual homes.

THINK CRITICALLY

1. **Do you think the government should play a role in providing Internet access to schools and libraries? Why or why not?**
2. **Why would a country be concerned about providing Internet access to its citizens? How could businesses in these countries benefit from a population that uses the Internet?**

Economic espionage takes place when individuals steal *intellectual property*, or information owned by another person or business. The most likely sources of economic espionage are employees who are disgruntled, who want to start their own businesses, who are about to be laid off, or who were recently fired. For-profit hackers often attack computer systems. They may be looking for credit card information or other valuable knowledge that would allow them to commit identity or data theft.

Companies hire *ethical hackers* to check network security. These individuals attempt to break through security measures and access a business's computer systems. Ethical hackers test for security weaknesses and report findings to the company.

Infrastructure attacks occur when individuals interfere with a computer system's operations. An infrastructure attack could involve something as prankish as changing the CIA's home page or something as serious as restricting access to bona fide users. *Distributed denial-of-service (DDoS)* attacks have been launched against Amazon.com, Buy.com, CNN.com, eBay, and other well-known businesses. A DDoS attack floods a business's web site with so much traffic that legitimate users cannot access the site.

Routers are used to direct Internet traffic. Cisco brand Internet routers are the most widely used in the world. In the summer of 2003, hackers learned of a vulnerability in the Cisco routers and coordinated attacks on them. The Internet's worldwide availability was hindered until the problem was resolved. Cisco Systems, Inc. issued software patches to protect the routers' operating systems.

VIRUSES

Computer viruses are software programs that copy and replicate (reproduce) themselves. The uncontrolled replication can consume system resources, slowing or halting tasks. Before the widespread use of the Internet, viruses were usually transmitted through the sharing of floppy disks. Today, e-mail allows for the sharing of computer files as well as the sharing of viruses attached to them. Once an e-mail virus is opened, it can take control of a computer and send itself to the e-mail addresses listed in the infected computer's address book.

The Melissa virus was the first virus to spread through e-mail. This virus used Microsoft's Outlook software to send itself to others in the victim's e-mail address book. In 2003, the SoBig virus became the fastest-spreading computer virus in history, causing an estimated $29.7 billion in damage worldwide. SoBig was designed to turn computers into spam (online junk mail)-sending machines. At its peak, SoBig increased total e-mail traffic by up to 25 percent.

List and briefly define two types of cybercrime.

Viruses-computer viruses are software programs that copy and replicate. Hacking which inveles the attemnt by individuals

SECURITY

Computer security is important to Internet users at work and at home. Businesses are often more aware of security issues because they have data and computer systems that are susceptible to hacking and viruses. Home users may have protection systems against viruses, but they are also becoming the targets of hackers. When home users engage in e-commerce, they sometimes leave information on their computers such as credit card numbers, bank account information, and other personal data that can be stolen.

By 2000, there were over 50,000 known computer viruses. Only about 180 of these were actively spreading. The rest were too poorly written or were variations of other viruses.

FIREWALLS

Companies defend themselves against hackers by using firewalls. **Firewalls** are software programs that block unauthorized computer usage. Firewalls check for authorized access to computer networks. Firewalls do not protect against improper computer usage by employees who have network access. Thus, in addition to firewalls, some businesses actively monitor employees' computer usage.

Firewall software for the home is designed to prevent hacking of a personal computer while it is connected to the Internet. Home users also typically use *virus-checker software*, which screens incoming files for viruses and other destructive programs.

ENCRYPTION

Encryption scrambles data to ensure that information is secure. The data travel in scrambled form over the Internet backbone. When the data are received, a decoding key is required to unscramble the information.

Wi-Fi networks can leak radio signals, which can be intercepted by unauthorized users. Wi-Fi encryption standards must be adopted before most individuals will feel secure engaging in e-commerce over wireless networks.

List strategies that can be used to improve online security.

Firewalls and Encryption

LOGGING OFF

UNDERSTAND MARKETING CONCEPTS

Circle the best answer for each of the following questions.

1. Which of the following is *not* a cybercrime?
   a. hacking
   b. an infrastructure attack
   c. a virus
   d. encryption

2. Which of the following is used to prevent hacking?
   a. computer virus
   b. firewall
   c. virus-checker software
   d. hacker-checker software

THINK CRITICALLY

Answer the following questions as completely as possible. If necessary, use a separate sheet of paper.

3. Your manager has asked you to explain if there is any danger in connecting her computer to the Internet. Describe possible problems she may encounter.

4. Recommend ways to prevent the problems you described to your manager in Activity 3 above.

LESSON 4.4

TECHNICAL APPLICATIONS

LOGGING ON

Developing an e-commerce web site may seem like a simple activity. All you need to do is create a few web pages and link them to the Internet. In reality, it is not that simple. Much expertise is needed.

Web sites require an Internet service provider (ISP). An ISP must be operational 24 hours a day. Many web sites require links to databases or other computer networks. These links may require complex programming. Web sites must meet customer expectations. Today, customers may want sound or high levels of interactivity. Tomorrow, they may want broadband applications such as two-way video.

Work with a partner. Create a list of skills necessary to develop a functioning web site. Determine the new skills that will be necessary as more people gain broadband Internet access.

Describe programming languages used for the Web.

List the considerations involved in choosing an ISP.

INTERNET PROGRAMMING LANGUAGES

Web pages use HTML tags, or codes, to tell the browser how to display text, where pictures should be located, and how a page should be formatted. A web page designer must be familiar with HTML code. However, most web page designers use web page editor software that writes the underlying code for them as the web page is created.

To set up a hyperlink, an HTML locator code must be included that directs the browser to access information from the desired site. For example, the code to link to South-Western's high school web site is

```
<a href="http://school.cengage.com">South-Western</a>
```

To turn this hyperlink red, the following code would be used.

```
<a href="school.cengage.com"><font
color="#FF0000">South-Western</font></a>
```

The tag within the brackets <> turns on a code and the tag preceded by a slash within the brackets </> turns the code off.

Other programming languages are also used in web page design. DHTML (Dynamic HTML) allows movement and layering. XML (eXtensible Markup Language) identifies various types of content and allows for programming that pulls customized information into an HTML document from a database.

Many web page editors work like word-processing software. They allow web page designers to apply tags and codes without keying in the coding details. For example, you can highlight a portion of text and click on the *Italic* button, and the program will apply the tags for italic formatting for you. The applied HTML codes can be read by any browser. Greater levels of technical skill are required in order to apply the advanced features for secure online purchasing, pulling database information into the page, or playing media files.

PLUG-INS

Web sites often do more than just display text and pictures. Many sites play sound and video and allow users to play games. These features are possible through plug-ins. A **plug-in** is a program that can be integrated into a browser to play media files. Some common plug-ins include

- Apple Computer's QuickTime—plays video
- RealNetworks' RealPlayer—plays video and audio
- Macromedia's Shockwave and Flash—allow for the streaming of multimedia and interactive games

Streaming allows a large file to be broken into small sections that are fed to the user's browser. The browser can begin playing the file as it streams in, instead of waiting until the entire file is downloaded. Companies use streaming for radio and video broadcasts.

Multimedia programs are used to create interactive content. These programs combine illustrations, animation, video, sound, and programming. The technical skills required to master these programs are more advanced than those needed for web page creation.

E-MARKETING MYTHS

The Internet everywhere? Microsoft's British Internet unit came up with the idea of putting Internet access inside of portable toilets to promote online services. The service was to be called the "iLoo." (The British word for toilet is "loo.") The iLoo idea was ridiculed in the press. Although the concept fit with Microsoft's slogan "Where do you want to go today?," the iLoo idea was dropped. Microsoft claimed it was an April Fool's joke, even though the iLoo press release was dated May 2.

THINK CRITICALLY

1. **How important is it that people have Internet access everywhere they go? Explain your answer.**
2. **Do you think Microsoft should have proceeded with the iLoo concept? Why or why not?**

What is the purpose of web page editor software?

ENABLING E-COMMERCE

The commerce process is complex. In order for a business to fully engage in e-commerce, it must provide customer access to product descriptions, product availability information, pricing that includes taxes and shipping, online ordering and payment, and a number of other applications. Access to these features requires links between commerce software, databases, online payment verification systems, and web servers.

E-commerce requires the networking, or linking together, of many computers and computer systems. Today, many companies use the Internet to connect their computer systems around the world.

The largest ISP providing access for home Internet users in the United States is AOL. It has over 27 percent of the market. Its closest competitor is Microsoft Network (MSN) with a little over 9 percent. The top five ISPs have 50 percent of the market. The other 50 percent is served by ISPs with less than 2 percent of market share each.

CHOOSING AN ISP

It can be extremely expensive for a business to host its own e-commerce web site. Costs can include hardware, software, personnel, programming, and content creation. A business must decide if it is going to host its own site or use an ISP. In most cases, a business finds that it makes sense to outsource (hire another company to manage) some or all of its web development and hosting needs.

When choosing an ISP, a business must consider a number of important issues.

- **Network Reliability** What percentage of time is the network up and running?
- **Value for Price** What services are offered for the price charged?
- **Customer Service Responsiveness** Does the ISP provide quick attention to problems and timely answers to questions?
- **Technical Support** How responsive and knowledgeable is the ISP's technical support staff?
- **Disk Space** How much disk space is the business allowed, and what is the cost?
- **Programming Support** What capabilities does the ISP have to provide database access, programming help, or special design skills?
- **E-commerce Support** Does the ISP allow for shopping carts, online transactions, and individualized marketing programs?
- **E-mail Services** How many accounts can be provided, and how can they be accessed?
- **Security** Does the ISP ensure security for data transfer and for transactions conducted online?

©GETTY IMAGES/PHOTODISC

Most companies do not want to allocate resources to activities that are not part of their core business. This decision has led most businesses to outsource their web hosting. Over 60 percent of large companies and more than 90 percent of small companies outsource their web sites. Businesses outsource their web sites for many reasons.

- The business does not have the in-house technology, and it does not want to pay for software and hardware upgrades.
- The business does not have the ability to maintain high levels of security.
- The business's technology requires rapid change.
- The business does not have the personnel to operate and maintain the web site.
- The business does not want to pay for around-the-clock technical support staff.

LeTisha graduated with two college degrees, one in marketing and the other in management. While in college, she learned how to create web pages. Upon graduating from college, LeTisha worked as a marketing director for a small business, developing advertisements and promotional pieces. She also gained graphic design experience by helping to develop online publications. LeTisha's experience led her to a job as a webmaster with a large manufacturer.

A *webmaster* is the person in charge of a web site. Webmasters design web pages, coordinate graphics, write HTML coding, and maintain servers. They also answer users' questions, aid in online strategic planning, compile statistics, and make purchasing decisions. Webmasters are often cross-functional experts who are able to understand the marketing and media aspects of a company as well as the technological requirements of developing and maintaining web sites.

LeTisha loves the challenges she faces every day. She has learned new skills to help her in her work. She works with web page editors, databases, graphical design packages, and multimedia software.

THINK CRITICALLY

1. **Evaluate LeTisha's job. Identify the skills that you would need to develop in order to succeed as a webmaster.**
2. **Outline a plan to obtain the needed skills.**

What should a business consider when choosing an ISP?

Network Reliability, Value for Price, Customer Service, Technical Support, Disk space, Programming Support, E-Commerce Support, Email Service, and Security

LOGGING OFF

UNDERSTAND MARKETING CONCEPTS

Circle the best answer for each of the following questions.

1. Which of the following is used to create and enhance web pages?
   a. HTML coding
   b. web page editors
   c. plug-ins
   d. all of the above

2. Which of the following is *not* a consideration when choosing an ISP?
   a. technical support
   b. security
   c. programming support
   d. location

THINK CRITICALLY

Answer the following questions as completely as possible. If necessary, use a separate sheet of paper.

3. **Technology** Use the Internet to find information on three types of web page editor software. Using spreadsheet software, create a table comparing the features and cost of each web page editor.

4. You work for a small retail business that wants to expand to the Internet. Your manager has asked you if the business should invest in a server and host its own web site or hire an ISP. Make a recommendation and justify it.

REVIEW E-COMMERCE MARKETING CONCEPTS

Write the letter of the term that matches each definition. Some terms will not be used.

a. analog signals
b. bandwidth
c. broadband
d. browser
e. computer viruses
f. cybercrime
g. digital signals
h. domain name
i. encryption
j. firewalls
k. hacking
l. hyperlink
m. Internet service provider
n. last mile
o. open standards
p. plug-in
q. World Wide Web

J ____ 1. Software programs that block unauthorized computer usage

A ____ 2. Basic sets of instructions that are not owned by a single company

L ____ 3. A reference from some point in a document to some point in another document or to another place in the same document

q ____ 4. A set of open standards built on Internet standards that use the public telecommunication infrastructure to transfer information

O ____ 5. Provides a graphical view of the Web

m ____ 6. Allows an Internet user to "log on" or connect to the Internet

B ____ 7. The number of digital signals that can travel per second

C ____ 8. Connections where bandwidth is increased through direct digital signals

f ____ 9. Criminal activity on the Internet

K ____ 10. Attempts by individuals to break through online security for fun or profit

n ____ 11. The last connection between the Internet and your home or business

P ____ 12. A program that can be integrated into a browser to play media files

g ____ 13. A series of ons (zeros) and offs (ones)

Circle the best answer.

14. Which of the following makes up part of the telecommunication infrastructure?
    a. telephone and television cables
    b. computer hardware
    c. software
    (d.) all of the above

15. Which of the following was developed first?
    (a.) the Internet
    b. the World Wide Web
    c. HTML
    d. the browser

THINK CRITICALLY

16. Assume that you are investing in the telecommunication infrastructure. Spend five minutes discussing with another student the type of last-mile technology in which you should invest. Justify your decision and share your thoughts with the class.

17. You have been hired to speak to high school students about the damages caused by hacking computer systems and developing computer viruses. Outline the main points of your talk that will persuade students not to commit cybercrime.

18. You have decided that you would like to be a professional web page designer. How will you go about determining the skills you need and the ways to obtain them?

MAKE CONNECTIONS

19. **MARKETING MATH** In the past, you have used a 56-kbps modem to download Internet pages on your home computer. You have just upgraded to DSL with a 1.5-mbps connection. How much faster will the new connection be?

20. **HISTORY** Write a two-page report that outlines the history of the Internet. Point out the most important technologies that have allowed the Internet to grow to a worldwide medium. Speculate on the Internet's future.

21. **TECHNOLOGY** Use a browser to call up a web page. View the web page source code (right-click on the page and choose "View Source"). Scroll through the HTML code. Do you think this code was written by a person or by web page editor software? Explain your answer.

22. **COMMUNICATION** Your manager believes that wireless cellular phone Internet communication will not grow because the browser screen is too small. Develop an argument that supports the idea of cellular Internet growth.

23. **COMMUNICATION** You are developing an advertisement for an ISP. Write the ad copy for the ISP's main selling points. Include information on why a business should use this ISP to host its web site.

This part of the project will focus on how your business plans to deliver web content to its market.

Work with your team members to complete the following activities.

1. Identify the type of web access that your market will use. Will this access be through a PC, digital cable, wireless systems, or some other connection? Determine the type of last-mile connection speed that the majority of your market will likely have. Indicate whether you expect the market to have access to broadband connections.
2. Determine if your team will host its own web site or outsource the hosting to an ISP. Develop a list of criteria for choosing an ISP.
3. Develop a strategy to keep your web site secure. How will you communicate assurance of online security to your customers?
4. Within your team, decide who will create the web pages. Identify the skills that these team members will need.

E-COMMERCE—THE CONVENIENCE FACTOR

More consumers are opting to shop online from the comfort of their homes. Online shopping allows consumers to find the exact items they are looking for without having to dress up and go out.

Convenience is one of the primary advantages of digital shopping. Shoppers are becoming less intrigued with traditional retail stores, where they have to sort through racks and shelves to locate the merchandise they want. Consumers want to find items quickly and easily when they have a need for a specific product. Online shopping also allows consumers to bypass salespeople who are not skilled in providing customer service.

Guidelines for Customer Satisfaction

Businesses must follow several guidelines in order to satisfy customers and maintain a successful e-commerce web site.

- Provide pictures and accurate descriptions of all products available for purchase.
- Accept a variety of payment options, including credit cards. Few sales will be generated by a site that requires payment by money order or check sent through the mail.
- Maintain an adequate supply of merchandise to fill orders in a timely fashion. Customers will quickly become frustrated if they have to wait long to receive their orders.
- Confirm customer orders with e-mail responses. Customers should not be inconvenienced by having to print the order page for their records.
- Don't overwhelm the customer with unnecessary market research questions during the time of the order. Ask only for basic data such as customer name, address, and payment information. Market research questions are more appropriate once a positive customer relationship has been established.
- Offer the customer a variety of shipping options, including overnight express. Last-minute shoppers often are willing to pay the extra price to receive merchandise on time rather than risking late delivery through standard shipping methods.
- Ensure that the site is searchable by keywords or phrases. Customers appreciate finding an item quickly and checking out of the web site without a hassle.
- Make all company contact information highly visible, including a toll-free number and an e-mail address for the customer service department. Customers occasionally need the answer to a question before finalizing a purchase.
- Confirm that the web site (text, graphics, and interactive elements) loads quickly. Frustration builds as customers wait for pages that load slowly or don't load at all.

Businesses will gain loyal, repeat customers by providing a shopping experience that is quick, convenient and painless.

Think Critically

1. Why are more people opting to shop online?
2. Why are convenience and ease of use so important for a retail web site?
3. What should mall stores do to improve customer service?
4. List three ways that an online retailer can build a solid customer base.

MARKETING MANAGEMENT ROLE PLAY

Sports Past is a small e-commerce business that sells popular retro jerseys of professional sports teams. You have been hired to improve the business's customer service.

The popularity of retro jerseys has increased dramatically. Orders of the jerseys have tripled in the past year. Sports Past attributes much of its success to the absence of excess inventory and related storage expenses.

Jerseys are manufactured in China to reduce labor costs. Customers have complained about the length of time that it takes to receive their orders. All orders are sent by the U.S. Postal Service. Most orders take eight weeks to process.

You have been asked to advise management on ways to streamline the customer ordering/receiving process. Sports Past is also counting on your expertise to improve its inventory strategy. The business's goal is to keep just enough inventory on hand to avoid any out-of-stock situations. You must offer realistic suggestions to improve both areas of concern.

You will have up to ten minutes to role play the situation with the store's owner.

Performance Indicators Evaluated

- Understand why customers are unhappy with the service provided by Sports Past.
- Explain the need to improve delivery of retro jerseys.
- Discuss reasons that the business should offer more shipping options through alliances with delivery service providers such as FedEx.
- Describe how the business needs to improve its inventory strategy in order to provide quicker delivery.
- Explain how the Sports Past web site can help to determine production quantities of the various retro jerseys.

Go to the DECA web site for more detailed information.

1. Why is good customer service so important for an e-commerce business?
2. What role does delivery of merchandise play in customer satisfaction?
3. Should Sports Past continue to outsource its jersey production to China? Why or why not?
4. Why does Sports Past need to reconsider its inventory strategy?

www.deca.org/publications/HS_Guide/guidetoc.html

CHAPTER 5
EFFECTIVE INTERNET COMMUNICATIONS

MSN: PORTAL IN PROCESS

Microsoft Network (MSN) is designed to be a portal, or window, to the Internet. MSN's web site provides access to informational content, advertising, searches, e-commerce, and e-mail. MSN also delivers broadband content such as music and video. Users of MSN can instantly send messages to others online through its instant messaging services. MSN attempts to retain its users by offering high-value information. MSN Money offers online personal financial services, tools, and content. Links to MSNBC and ESPN are provided, so visitors can find interesting, up-to-date information.

In order to reach its communication goals, MSN's site must appeal to over 84 million people worldwide. The MSN site is designed with easily identifiable areas of content, allowing visitors to move quickly to desired information. MSN attracts a larger number of visitors than AOL. On average, however, America Online users spend four times longer at the AOL portal than Microsoft Network users spend at the MSN portal.

In addition to adding valuable content and resources to its site, Microsoft spent millions of dollars to revise its MSN Internet-browsing software to appeal to new users. Part of Microsoft's strategy was to design the new MSN site to utilize features for high-speed broadband access. MSN wants to be more than just a portal to the Internet.

THINK CRITICALLY

1. Visit the MSN web site. List at least three reasons that a visitor would want to return to the site.
2. Explain why it might be difficult for MSN to build a web site that appeals to millions of people around the world.

LESSON 5.1

INTERNET COMMUNICATION

GOALS

Explain the e-commerce communication model.

Describe the various e-commerce communication platforms.

LOGGING ON

The Internet is an information superhighway allowing you to communicate with others in a number of different ways at any time and any place. This ability is changing how people interact.

A survey from AOL found that the Internet is the primary communication tool used by teenagers in the United States. Among older teens (ages 18 and 19), 56 percent prefer the Internet to the telephone. Of this age group, 91 percent use e-mail and 83 percent use instant messaging (IM). For teenagers between the ages of 12 and 17, up to 81 percent e-mail their friends and relatives and 70 percent use instant messaging. Over 61 percent of teens use the Internet for schoolwork and other types of online information. While younger teens play online games, older teens listen to and download music.

Work with a partner. Analyze how you communicate with others. Compare and contrast the advantages of telephone communication with online communication.

COMMUNICATION BASICS

©GETTY IMAGES/PHOTODISC

The process of transferring a *message* from a *sender* to a *receiver* is called **communication**. The sender must *encode*, or design, the message in a way that it can be understood by the receiver. The receiver must *decode*, or interpret, the message. *Feedback* from the receiver to the sender is important to ensure that the message is understood. Businesses communicate with a number of receivers, including customers, employees, and other businesses. Many types of media are used to carry the messages. These media include broadcast (television and radio), print (books, magazines, and newspapers), telephone, and the Internet. The Internet is playing an increasingly important role in supporting the communication process as part of a multi-platform strategy. Figure 5.1 illustrates the e-commerce communication model.

Figure 5.1 E-Commerce Communication Model

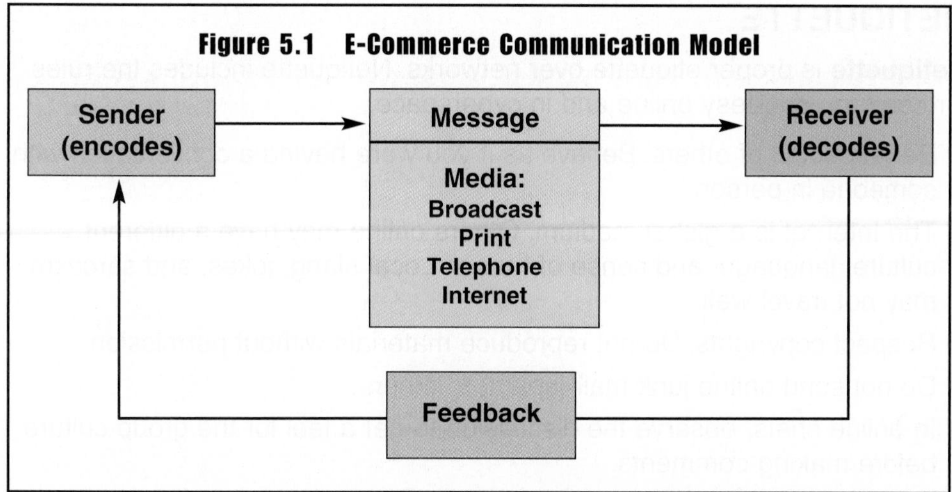

Broadcast and print media do not allow for immediate feedback from the receiver. Surveys are used most often to determine if broadcast or print media are seen and understood. Telephone calls allow for person-to-person communication with immediate feedback. This instant communication allows the sender to offer new information based on the feedback of the receiver. The Internet allows for the receiver to obtain new information by using a hyperlink.

©GETTY IMAGES/PHOTODISC

The Internet is one form of hypermedia. **Hypermedia** use hyperlinks. While the Internet is dominant, it is not the only example of hypermedia. Interactive television, cellular phones, DVDs, and other electronic media allow for the linking of content.

Individuals use a variety of media to communicate with each other and with businesses. For young people around the world, the Internet is overtaking television as the most popular entertainment platform. It is also overtaking the telephone as the most heavily used communication platform. In business settings, e-mail is now used more often than telephones.

THE MANY-TO-MANY COMMUNICATION MODEL

The **many-to-many communication model** places hypermedia in the center of the communication process. The model can be thought of as a meeting place where anyone can communicate with anyone else. For example, a business (B) can design a web site that allows consumers (C) to post comments. Employees (E) of the business can respond to the consumers' comments. The many-to-many communication model allows hypermedia to foster a number of interactions.

- consumer-to-consumer (C-to-C)
- business-to-consumer (B-to-C)
- consumer-to-business (C-to-B)
- employee-to-business (E-to-B)
- business-to-employee (B-to-E)
- employee-to-employee (E-to-E)
- business-to-business (B-to-B)
- employee-to-consumer (E-to-C)

The youth market is a large audience. Pre-teens ages 8 to 12 spend $19.1 billion annually ($946 per person) on products and services. Teens between the ages of 13 and 19 spend $94.7 billion annually ($3,309 per person).

NETIQUETTE

Netiquette is proper etiquette over networks. Netiquette includes the rules for common courtesy online and in cyberspace.

- Be respectful of others. Behave as if you were having a conversation with someone in person.
- The Internet is a global medium. Others online may have a different culture, language, and sense of humor. Local slang, jokes, and sarcasm may not travel well.
- Respect copyrights. Do not reproduce materials without permission.
- Do not send online junk mail (spam) to others.
- In online chats, observe the discussion to get a feel for the group culture before making comments.
- Use mixed case when sending messages. UPPER CASE LOOKS AS IF YOU ARE SHOUTING.

Explain the e-commerce communication model.

place hypermedia in the center of the communication process.

E-COMMERCE COMMUNICATION PLATFORMS

The Internet supports a number of communication platforms including web pages, e-mail, chat, instant messaging (IM), discussion forums, and rich media. Text-based e-mail is the most common communication platform used over the Internet. Web pages allow for more complicated messages to be communicated.

The most common content on web pages includes text, graphics (images), and hyperlinks. Web pages can also support other communication platforms. For example, a web site can host e-mail, chat rooms, or discussion forums.

Chat, IM, and discussion forums allow for two-way communication, such as C-to-C. With chat and IM, each person types a real-time message that is seen immediately, allowing for instant feedback. Discussion forums allow a message to be posted to which viewers may respond at a later time. Chat and IM can be used to provide instant information and feedback between employees and the company's customers. *Rich media*, such as multimedia, 3-D virtual environments, streaming videos, and other digital technologies, allow web sites to play audio and video as a means of conveying information to site visitors. Companies that use rich media must consider bandwidth restrictions, the access devices used by their target markets, and the markets' ability to view and interact with online content.

INTRANETS AND EXTRANETS

Internet protocols are used to develop communication systems within and between businesses. Because business employees are generally familiar with web-based interfaces, these systems have been adopted as major business communication tools.

Businesses often set up internal web sites, called **intranets**, to communicate with their employees. The sites are generally not open to outsiders and are protected by firewalls. Intranets allow employees to share information and knowledge, work together on projects, learn new skills, and obtain company news. Intranets use the same communication platforms as the Internet.

Extranets securely connect companies with suppliers and partners using Internet protocols. They allow companies to transact business-to-business activities quickly. Extranets facilitate order processing by linking suppliers to a company's inventory data. Contractors can share design information and immediately see when design changes are made. Suppliers can submit proposals and bids, provide documents, and receive payments in real time.

To develop extranets, a company must work with its suppliers and partners outside of the organization. Extranets require more security and technical consideration because private information must be sent securely over public networks.

Young people worldwide are changing the way they communicate. People between the ages of 18 and 24 are increasingly using cellular phones, e-mail, and instant messaging. The Internet is dominating this age group's media time, causing decreased rates in the amount of time spent watching television, reading magazines and newspapers, and listening to the radio.

THINK CRITICALLY

1. **Track your own media time for 24 hours. Determine how much time you spend with the Internet, television, magazines and newspapers, and radio. Speculate on which of these media are growing and which are declining.**
2. **How will these trends affect a business's strategy to communicate with its customers?**

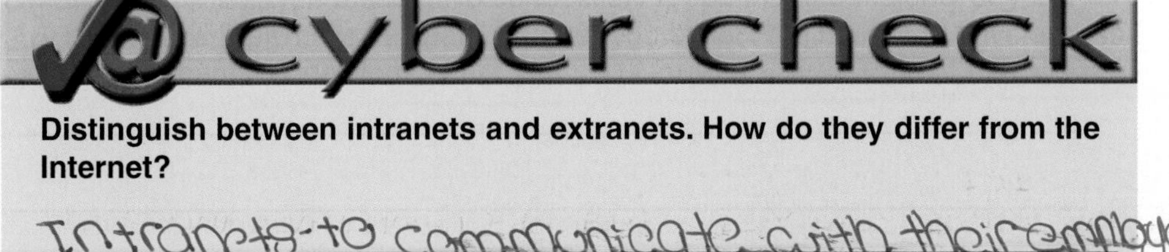

Distinguish between intranets and extranets. How do they differ from the Internet?

Intranets-to communicate with their employees
Extranets-securely connect companies with
Summiers and partners using Internet protocols

LOGGING OFF

UNDERSTAND MARKETING CONCEPTS

Circle the best answer for each of the following questions.

1. The components of the communication process include
   a. sender and messenger.
   b. broadcast, print, telephone, and the Internet.
   c. sender, message, receiver, and feedback.
   d. sender, broadcast, and receiver.
2. Which of the following statements about e-commerce communication platforms is false?
   a. The most common content on web pages includes text, graphics (images), and hyperlinks.
   b. Chat, IM, and discussion forums allow for two-way communication.
   c. Text-based e-mail is the most common communication platform used over the Internet.
   d. Businesses do not generally use chat or IM.

THINK CRITICALLY

Answer the following questions as completely as possible. If necessary, use a separate sheet of paper.

3. **Communication** Choose a well-known company. Describe the various media that this company uses to communicate with its customers.

   ____

   ____

   ____

   ____

   ____

4. **Communication** Describe communication platforms you would recommend for a large home construction business. Justify your answers.

   ____

   ____

   ____

   ____

   ____

DIGITAL COMMUNICATION STRATEGIES

LOGGING ON

Businesses develop communication strategies and goals before they decide what and how to communicate to their audiences. Every message that a business sends costs money and must have some advantage to the business.

If you were in charge of the communication strategy for a business, you would need to consider the most cost-effective way to deliver a message to the audience. This becomes more complicated when you have multiple audiences and media from which to choose. The Internet offers a variety of new, cost-effective means of communicating.

Work with a partner. Brainstorm a variety of communication goals that a company could set. Pick one goal, and describe a communication strategy that includes the use of hypermedia to meet that goal.

Describe the various types of hypermedia communication goals.

Explain the role of e-mail marketing in a communication strategy.

Define the tools that are used for time-dependent communication.

HYPERMEDIA COMMUNICATION GOALS

Web sites have moved beyond acting as simple electronic brochures. Today, web sites are the public face of companies. A business's web site is often the first place that an individual will look to find information about the company and its products, services, and employment opportunities. Visitors differ in the amount of information they want to receive. A single web site must be designed to meet all visitors' needs and to grab the attention of those merely surfing.

A business's communication goals should always be set based on the information needs of the market being served. These goals should direct the development and design of the web site. Some examples of communication goals that businesses set include supporting the sales process, informing customers of products, reinforcing brand images, and recruiting employees. Often, a web site will be designed to reach all of these goals, allowing different audiences to find different information. A single site can act as a brochure and be designed to develop and maintain relationships. Brochure sites, relationship sites, e-commerce sites, and web portals are each designed to reach specific communication goals.

©GETTY IMAGES/PHOTODISC

VIRTUAL VIEWPOINTS

The Internet allows for a variety of communication platforms. But perhaps the greatest social benefit of the Internet is its ability to act as a free speech venue. At one time, it was expensive to communicate ideas around the world. Today, individuals develop web sites and engage in discussion forums, chats, and other many-to-many communication systems to discuss ideas, companies, products, and various topics.

Sometimes rogue sites are designed to allow individuals to express their feelings about companies, products, or organizations. Some companies attempt to find out what is said about them online. They look through discussion forums and chat rooms for defamatory comments. In some cases, companies may sue individuals for *cybersmearing*, or defaming online.

Free speech is not always welcomed around the world. Some countries snoop the Internet to find individuals who express ideas that go against the beliefs of the government.

THINK CRITICALLY

1. **Why is the Internet an important tool in fostering free speech? Why would the Internet be better for the individual than other communication outlets?**
2. **Do you think that companies should snoop to find out what you say about them online? Should the government be allowed to do the same thing? Discuss your opinion.**

BROCHURE SITES

A business develops printed brochures to communicate its products, services, and image to customers. **Brochure sites** are designed to reach these same goals. These sites may not support relationship building or online selling.

A business may decide to develop a brochure site because it is the simplest and least expensive type of web site to design. For some businesses, a brochure site may provide all the content that customers require. The site's content must be updated often to keep its audience returning.

RELATIONSHIP SITES

Customers must have a compelling reason to return to a web site. If a company has only a brochure site, customers may view it once or twice and never return. To develop relationships with customers, a site must support communication that interests its customers.

Relationship sites are designed to bring customers back over and over again. These sites may provide games, chat groups, or other interactive components to foster relationships with customers.

E-COMMERCE SITES

E-commerce sites have specific goals geared toward having customers make purchases. E-commerce and brick-and-click businesses must provide enough information on products, prices, and shipping options to make customers feel comfortable purchasing online. However, many customers use web sites only to find out about products, and then they go to brick-and-mortar stores to make purchases. Many e-commerce sites combine brochure information, relationship-developing content, and online selling.

WEB PORTALS

A *web portal* is a site designed to act as an access point to content on the Internet. AOL, MSN, Yahoo!, and other portals attempt to draw web users to their sites as an initial point of contact. AOL and MSN achieve this because they are large ISPs. Yahoo! allows individuals to access the Internet through its search engine.

A *corporate portal* is an internal web site that provides company information to employees. It also provides access to selected web sites such as those of benefit providers and suppliers.

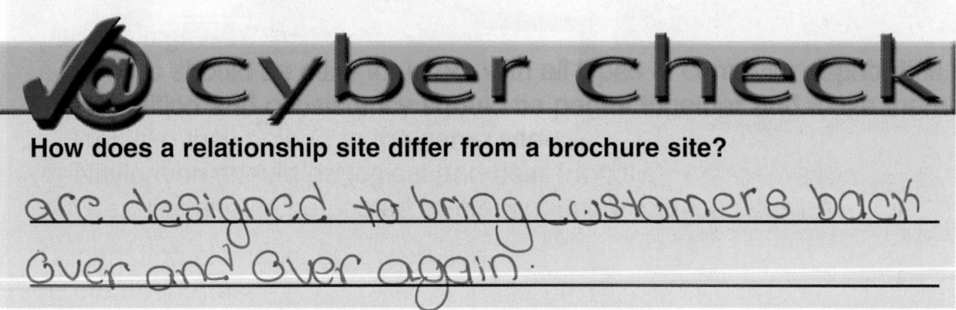

@ cyber check
How does a relationship site differ from a brochure site?
are designed to bring customers back
over and over again.

E-MAIL MARKETING

The most commonly used e-business communication platform is e-mail. **E-mail marketing** works like direct mail (often called junk mail), targeting messages to the individuals most likely to purchase the company's product or service.

PERMISSION-BASED MARKETING

E-mail marketing is most effective when it is targeted to individuals who give their permission, or *opt-in*, to receive information from the company. **Permission-based marketing** allows businesses to target only customers who have expressed an interest. Often, the individual registers on the company's web site to receive e-mail. Registration allows for the personalization of the e-mail. Studies have shown that adding the recipient's name to e-mail can double the response rates over non-personalized e-mail.

Targeted e-mail marketing is one of the most effective hypermedia platforms for reaching communication goals. E-commerce marketers set goals such as having customers click-through to a web site or purchase from an e-mail offer. A study found that 69 percent of U.S. e-mail users made online purchases after receiving permission-based e-mail marketing. E-mail responses are much faster than through direct mail. Customers often respond within 48 hours, while postal responses can take as long as six weeks.

©GETTY IMAGES/PHOTODISC

©GETTY IMAGES/PHOTODISC

In 2002, approximately 31 billion e-mails were sent around the world each day. By 2005, this number could reach as high as 60 billion!

HTML E-MAIL

E-mail is delivered in both text and HTML formats. **HTML e-mail** can include graphics with text and looks similar to a web page. The most-used form of permission-based e-mail marketing in the United States is HTML e-mail. HTML e-mail is effective in reaching communication goals. Click-throughs to web sites can be up to four times higher for HTML e-mail than for text-only e-mail.

SPAM

The effectiveness of e-mail marketing has been hampered by **spam**, or unwanted e-mail, sent to a large number of receivers. Spam accounted for over 50 percent of all e-mail sent in 2003. Businesses spend close to $50 per employee to protect workers' mailboxes from spam.

Why do people spam? Spammers believe that the more e-mail they send, the better their chances of a response. E-mail spammers do not need to purchase postage for every message sent and, therefore, can greatly increase the number of people they can reach. Spam is also difficult to block. Some spammers set up temporary ISP accounts and then broadcast their spam before they are caught. Then they move to a new account.

Name two things an e-mail marketer can do to increase the effectiveness of messages.

is targeted to indivduals who give their permission or opt-in to recive information

TIME-DEPENDENT COMMUNICATION

Most e-commerce communication platforms are not *time-dependent*, meaning that they do not require the sender and the communicator to interact at the same time. Time-dependent platforms allow for real-time communication in which multiple individuals interact.

DISCUSSION GROUPS AND MAILING LISTS

Discussion groups (also called newsgroups or forums) apply protocols to place user-submitted messages on a server. An online discussion may go something like this.

- A person places a message on a discussion board. The initial message may be a question or a description of a situation for which the originator is seeking advice. A company may post a request for opinions regarding a new service or product.
- Visitors read and may respond, placing messages after the comment to which they are responding.
- People can visit the discussion board whenever they want to read the string of messages.

Mailing lists allow e-mail to be sent to all members of a group at once. Mailing lists can send articles of interest, or they can simply collect and send comments from members.

Mailing lists and discussion forums can be moderated or unmoderated. In *moderated* communication, a moderator checks and approves the messages before they are sent or posted. *Unmoderated* communication is automatically posted or redistributed to the names on the mailing list.

INSTANT MESSAGING AND CHAT

Individuals do not need to wait until they check their e-mail to receive messages from others. Internet protocols allow for time-dependent, instant connections between users. Such connections allow multiple individuals to meet in a chat room or send messages back and forth through instant messaging (IM).

Instant messaging is being used more frequently in business communication. Employees use IM to rapidly communicate with each other and with customers. Some firms use IM as a means of delivering service information to customers. The service representative can communicate with more than one customer at a time through IM technologies.

Name reasons a company may utilize a discussion group on its web site.

• A person places a message on a discussion board
• Visitors read and may respond placing message after the comment to which they are responding
• People can visit the discussion board whenever they want to read the string of messages

LOGGING OFF

UNDERSTAND MARKETING CONCEPTS

Circle the best answer for each of the following questions.

1. Which of the following would be designed to communicate only the image and products of a company?
   a. a brochure site
   b. a relationship site
   c. an e-commerce site
   d. none of the above
2. Each of the following statements about e-mail marketing is true *except*
   a. e-mail marketing is one of the most effective hypermedia communication platforms.
   b. e-mail marketing works best without user permission.
   c. e-mail can have an HTML format.
   d. spam is hurting e-mail marketing as a communication tool.

THINK CRITICALLY

Answer the following questions as completely as possible. If necessary, use a separate sheet of paper.

3. **Technology** Visit a web site. Determine if it is designed as a brochure site, a relationship site, or an e-commerce site. Identify its communication goals and how it is reaching them.

4. **Communication** Assume a toy store has consulted you regarding how it can best use e-mail in a communication strategy to reach its current customers. Recommend a plan for this business.

WEB DESIGN BASICS

LOGGING ON

The Internet was not originally created for personal computers, even though they have become its main delivery system. Wireless devices, such as cellular phones and personal digital assistants (PDAs), also provide access to the Internet but do not allow for rich, complex content. Current cellular technology limits both the size of the viewing screen and the bandwidth available to carry data.

Web page developers must be concerned with design and content and how they display in a variety of platforms. Text and graphics currently dominate the Internet. Some sites include enhanced communication with motion, sound, and video. As the Web moves toward broadband, new formats of content will be developed. Future cellular systems are expected to allow rich media, including motion and video, to be downloaded over wireless networks.

Work with a partner. Describe three designs for a business web site—one for PC users, one for wireless device users, and one for a broadband audience. Compare and contrast your designs for each platform.

List principles of good web design.

Explain the considerations when planning a web site.

PRINCIPLES OF DESIGN

Good web page design for an e-commerce business must satisfy a number of criteria. Foremost, it must reach the communication goals of the business. A design should be logical and consistent and, at the same time, must enhance the image of the company. The design must also allow the visitor to easily navigate the site. The design process starts with the **home page**. The home page is the initial page that a viewer sees. There are a number of design considerations in developing good web pages.

- **Accessibility** Access should be easy for Internet users with all types of computer capabilities. Sometimes simple is best when appealing to a mass audience. If your site has flashy components that require sophisticated *plug-ins* (tools that allow the components to run), you should have an alternative link for users whose systems are not advanced so that they may view the same information in a simpler format. There should also be links to sites where users can download the needed plug-ins.
- **Advertising** Do not clutter the web site pages with excessive advertising. The type and number of ads on a page should fit the market's needs and should not overpower the main content for which the viewer is visiting.

Site design is important. Sixty-five percent of surveyed U.S. Internet users stated that they won't patronize a poorly designed site. Thirty percent stated that web site design is more important than a great product.

E-MARKETING MYTHS

In 1994, a news report attributed to the Knight-Ridder news service stated that Microsoft Corporation was going to purchase the Vatican. While untrue, this was one of the first Internet hoaxes.

E-mail is a great medium for spreading hoaxes and rumors, including everything from false virus warnings to safety warnings for nonexistent threats. This misuse leads Internet users to question the reliability of online information. Internet users must become *net literate*, or learn to evaluate online information.

THINK CRITICALLY

1. **List reasons why an online hoax could be dangerous.**
2. **Develop a strategy to determine if information you receive online is a hoax.**
3. **Visit the Hoaxbusters web site. Describe its recommendations for checking out hoaxes.**

- **Alignment** Choose a style of alignment and stick with it. Vertically, do not have some elements left-aligned, some centered, and others right-aligned. Varying alignments will make your page look messy.
- **Consistency and Repetition** Throughout your site, repeat certain elements such as your navigation buttons and company logo. These repeated elements will tie everything else together. Navigation buttons should be the same color, size, order, and position on every page. Treat main headings the same throughout the site. Basic text should be the same font, size, and color on every page.
- **Content** The organization and type of information on the site should be based on the needs of the target market. Care should be taken to ensure that the content is clearly written and free of grammar, punctuation, and spelling errors.
- **Contrast** Contrasting elements draw the viewer's eye into the page, create interest, and show hierarchy. If two elements are not the same or are of unequal importance, treat them differently. For example, main heads should be bigger and bolder than subheads. Contrast creates a focal point, emphasizing what is most important. Text should stand out clearly from any background colors or graphics.
- **Customization** Delivering personalized content is best.
- **Feedback** Contact information should be visible. Responses to any queries or feedback should be timely.
- **Links** Links to other content should be appropriate, topical, and of interest to the target market. If the linked content is on another web site, open it in a new window. Do not pull it into a frame of your own web page as if the content were your own. Respect others' creations.
- **Navigation** Navigation should be logical and user friendly. Navigation buttons should have the same treatment and position on the web pages throughout the site.
- **Ordering** Purchasing should be simple, convenient, and secure.
- **Privacy** There should be an effective privacy policy that is easy to find on the site.

- **Searches** Search tools should be accurate and easy to use.
- **Speed** Fast-loading graphics and text are important. If a page loads slowly, users will get bored and move on. Graphics originally created for high-quality print do not need the same resolution for good viewing on the Web. Save them down to a smaller resolution that will load quickly on the page. Do not let pages run so long that the user must wait for them to load and then scroll to see all the content. Instead, make smaller pages that load quickly and link to each other in a logical fashion.
- **Updates** The site's content and format should be updated frequently. Links to other sites should be checked frequently and updated as necessary. Freshen the look of the site regularly but not drastically enough to confuse the regular visitor.

List at least five elements of good web design.

•Alignment •Consistency and Repetition

•Content •Contrast •Customization

PLANNING THE SITE

©GETTY IMAGES/PHOTODISC

Today, most people who use the Internet have experience navigating web sites. They have expectations based on sites they have used in the past. When you start the web design process, it is useful to evaluate competitors' sites and determine how your site can be more appealing. At the same time, you don't want to confuse your audience by creating navigation systems that are too different from what they are currently using.

The first step in designing a web site is to outline the main topics and subtopics of the information that you want customers to find. Initial navigation ideas can be presented in a *thumbnail* format, a rough sketch of the site design showing each page and how the pages will link together. The thumbnail can be used to evaluate the design before actual page construction begins. Figure 5.2 shows the structure of a bed and breakfast's site presented in thumbnail format at the early planning stage.

Why is it important to sketch a web site in thumbnail format *before* building the pages?

shows the structure of a bed and break

fasts sits presented in thumbnail format

the early planning stage.

Figure 5.2 Thumbnail of Navigation

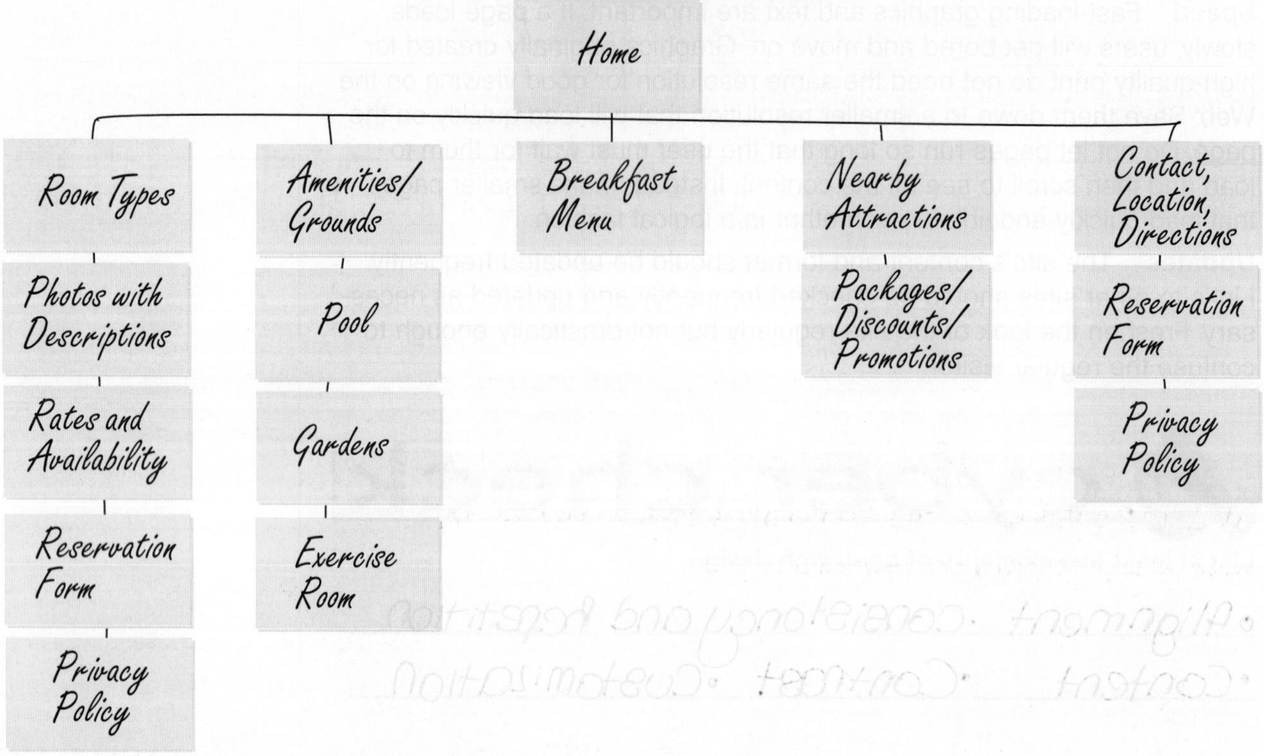

WORKING ONLINE

Matt graduated from college with a degree in marketing. In college, he was interested in web page design and e-commerce strategy. Upon graduation, he took a job with a large pharmaceutical firm. Soon, he moved into a position as a *communication team leader* in web page development.

Matt leads a team of seven people in developing and executing communication strategies. His responsibilities include developing the company's web site for external communication and developing the intranet for communication within the company. His team manages over 2,000 pages of content. Matt must ensure that content is collected, proper design tools are used, and information is structured properly on web pages. He also must ensure that the site design is user friendly.

Matt communicates with graphic designers, programmers, managers, and customers. He turns the company's communication goals into strategies and then delivers the final web site. Matt's skills have put him on the fast track to a leadership position.

THINK CRITICALLY

1. **Evaluate Matt's job. Identify the skills that you would need to develop in order to succeed as a communication team leader.**
2. **Explain why someone with a background in marketing would be effective in this position.**

LOGGING OFF

UNDERSTAND MARKETING CONCEPTS

Circle the best answer for each of the following questions.

1. Which of the following would *not* be considered a principle of good web page design?
   a. Access should be easy for users with all types of computer capabilities.
   b. Repetition and consistency should tie pages together and make them look like they belong to the same site.
   c. Navigation should be logical and user friendly.
   d. Graphics should be posted at the highest resolution possible.
2. Contrasting elements on a web site
   a. create interest.
   b. show hierarchy.
   c. draw the viewer's eye into the page.
   d. all of the above

THINK CRITICALLY

Answer the following questions as completely as possible. If necessary, use a separate sheet of paper.

3. **Technology** Visit a web site. Rate how well you feel the site uses the principles of web design. Indicate what could be done to improve the site's design.

____

____

____

____

____

4. **Technology** Assume a retail clothing business has asked you to design a web site with rich media for broadband users. Develop a thumbnail of the site structure that includes how you would utilize rich media to deliver content. Justify your design.

____

____

____

____

CHAPTER 5 REVIEW

REVIEW E-COMMERCE MARKETING CONCEPTS

Write the letter of the term that matches each definition. Some terms will not be used.

a. brochure site
b. communication
c. e-commerce sites
d. e-mail marketing
e. extranets
f. home page
g. HTML e-mail
h. hypermedia
i. intranets
j. mailing lists
k. many-to-many communication model
l. netiquette
m. permission-based marketing
n. relationship sites
o. spam

__E__ 1. Securely connect companies with suppliers and partners using Internet protocols

__L__ 2. Proper etiquette over networks

__b__ 3. The process of transferring a message from a sender to a receiver

__K__ 4. Places hypermedia in the center of the communication process

__H__ 5. A media that uses hyperlinks

__M__ 6. Allows businesses to target only customers who have expressed an interest

__J__ 7. Allow e-mail to be sent to all members of a group at once

__I__ 8. Internal web sites used to communicate with employees

__O__ 9. Unwanted e-mail sent to a large number of receivers

Circle the best answer.

10. The first page that a visitor sees on a web site is
    a. the front page.
    b. the opening page.
    c. the home page.
    d. none of the above

11. Cellular phones, interactive television, and DVDs are examples of
    a. rich media.
    b. hypermedia.
    c. spam.
    d. none of the above

12. A discussion group
    a. allows individuals to place a message for others to see.
    b. allows individuals to respond to placed messages.
    c. may be moderated or unmoderated.
    d. all of the above

13. A site designed to communicate a company's products, services, and image to customers is
    a. an e-commerce site.
    b. a brochure site.
    c. a relationship site.
    d. none of the above

THINK CRITICALLY

14. Your employee has been sending e-mail that violates the rules of netiquette. Explain the basic rules of netiquette and why your employee should follow these rules.

15. You are attempting to develop a communication strategy to reach a youth market. Choose the e-commerce communication platforms that you think would best reach this market. Justify your choices.

16. You have been hired to develop the web site for a new e-commerce business that sells home decor. Outline the goals that should be set for this web site in order to be successful with its communication strategy.

MAKE CONNECTIONS

17. **COMMUNICATION** Use the many-to-many communication model to evaluate the communication flows within a business of your choice. Indicate the kinds of information that would flow in each of the following types of interaction (C-to-C, B-to-C, C-to-B, B-to-E, E-to-E, and B-to-B).

18. **COMMUNICATION** Web-based interfaces for the Internet, intranets, and extranets provide a consistent design. Explain how the interfaces can improve the communication in a business.

19. **HISTORY** Assume that you are running a business at the end of the 1800s. A new technology called the telephone is being adopted by businesses and individuals. Write a paragraph indicating how the telephone will change communication patterns among businesses, employees, and customers. Write another paragraph explaining how these new patterns parallel communication over the Internet today.

20. **TECHNOLOGY** Instant messaging, chat, and discussion boards offer new means of communication among people. Write a paragraph indicating how these online communication platforms are likely to be used over wireless systems such as cellular phones.

21. **COMMUNICATION** Pick a business. Assume that this business has hired you to develop a relationship web site. Develop a thumbnail indicating what you will include to help ensure that customers return to the site. Compare your site to competitors' sites, and explain why your design is best.

This part of the project will focus on your business's communication strategy, including its communication goals, target audience, and design strategy.

Work with your team members to complete the following activities.

1. You have developed an e-commerce strategy. It is now time to design your web site. Develop a list of the communication goals you are setting for your business. The goals should include the company's image, product information, and anything else you feel needs to be communicated to your target audience. List the hypermedia communication platforms you plan to use.
2. Visit competitors' web sites. Evaluate these sites based on the design principles outlined in the chapter. Develop a thumbnail of your site. Justify your design based on the principles of web design.
3. Develop an e-mail marketing strategy. Recommend how you will use e-mail to reach your communication goals.
4. Specify how you will use rich media and wireless technology to communicate to your audience. Explain how these components will fit with your company's communication strategy.

CASE STUDY

CAN CATALOG RETAILERS SAVE MONEY BY DOING BUSINESS ONLINE?

Catalogs containing hundreds of glossy pages of merchandise are expensive to produce and mail to potential customers. Catalog customers who make minimal purchases must be identified and removed from retailers' mailing lists in order to reduce costs.

Catalog retailers are increasing sales and lowering start-up costs by selling merchandise online. In some instances, online sales can reduce catalog mailings and trim order-taking costs. However, printed catalogs are still a major contributor to online businesses' success.

Catalogs Stimulate Online Sales

Mailings of catalogs to customers stimulate Internet sales. A recent survey indicates that three of the top five consumer activities at a catalog retailer's web site relate directly to their printed catalogs. Catalogs have a strong influence on customers who visit retail web sites. Surveys indicate that 71 percent of consumers who visit a catalog retailer's web site research or buy a product they first saw in the company's printed catalog.

Although catalogs are still popular, they do not reduce a catalog retailer's need for a web site. Nearly 45 percent of consumers indicate that they order online instead of by mail because they prefer the convenience of the Web. Many customers even order their catalogs online.

The best e-commerce web sites allow customers to determine how complex products can fit their needs. For example, automobile enthusiasts can visit the Crutchfield.com web site and click on "what fits my car" to determine what audio components will best fit their vehicles.

Customer-ordering preferences are as varied as learning styles. Online sales do not eliminate the need for printed catalogs. The Internet and catalogs complement each other. The key to success is determining the amount to invest in catalogs and the amount to invest in the online ordering system.

Think Critically

1. **Why do some customers prefer catalogs to the Internet?**
2. **What advantage does the Internet have over catalogs?**
3. **How could a business encourage catalog customers to make more use of the Internet?**
4. **Have you ordered merchandise over the Internet? Why or why not?**

APPAREL AND ACCESSORIES MARKETING ROLE PLAY

The Post and Nickel is a highly successful, upscale clothing store located in a large city with a major university. The Post and Nickel sells the latest clothes for college students as well as suits for young business professionals. The Post and Nickel has maintained success with an award-winning catalog that is sent to current college students, college graduates, and young business professionals throughout the state. The catalog is extremely expensive to produce and mail. Last year, the store decided to initiate a web site to reach more current and potential customers.

Old habits are hard to break. The majority of traditional customers are not ordering online. The Post and Nickel has hired you as a consultant. Your challenge is to develop ideas to encourage traditional customers to make online purchases from The Post and Nickel web site. The Post and Nickel also wants your advice on how to retain both the catalog and the web site without increasing the store's advertising budget.

You have ten minutes to review this information and determine how you will handle the role-play situation. You will have up to ten minutes to present your ideas to the class. The class will have five minutes to ask questions.

Performance Indicators Evaluated

- Understand the challenges and opportunities facing The Post and Nickel.
- Explain The Post and Nickel's need to expand its business to the Web.
- Describe how more customers will learn about The Post and Nickel's web page.
- Explain how the web site can make customers feel more comfortable about ordering merchandise online.
- Identify a strategy that will encourage dedicated customers to use The Post and Nickel's web site.
- Explain how the web site will allow The Post and Nickel to expand sales.
- Discuss the importance of using both the Web and the catalog to maximize sales of The Post and Nickel's merchandise.
- Demonstrate an understanding of meeting budget constraints.

Go to the DECA web site for more detailed information.

1. Why is it important for The Post and Nickel to maintain its catalog?
2. How will presence on the Web attract a larger market and increase sales?
3. Why would dedicated customers be hesitant to order merchandise over the Internet?
4. What advantages does the Internet have over The Post and Nickel's traditional catalog?

www.deca.org/publications/HS_Guide/guidetoc.html

CHAPTER 6
MARKETING-INFORMATION MANAGEMENT

6.1 Marketing-Information Systems
6.2 Marketing Research
6.3 Data Mining and Customer-Relationship Management

BANKING ON E-COMMERCE

Banks are service businesses. So why are some banks charging customers to use live tellers? These banks have used marketing information to determine the customers who were most profitable and the services that were losing money. Marketing information has also helped to predict how customers would react to changes in service strategies. Such changes include charging for traditionally free services.

The banking industry uses marketing information to increase overall profits. At the heart of marketing-information systems are databases. The databases are used to develop customer profiles. These databases identify customers who are likely to accept new products. They can also identify customers who are likely to default on loans and customers who are most profitable. Marketing-information systems forecast customers' reactions to changes in interest rates and the profitability of households. The databases can even project the lifetime value of customers.

Banks do not necessarily drop low-value customers. One bank's data showed that 30 percent of its low-value customers were college students. Many of these students will later become high-value customers if the bank can maintain their loyalty.

Research has shown that customers want the same banking services across all delivery channels. A combination of the Internet and in-person channels is often the best way to meet customer needs. Banks are also deploying customer-relationship strategies. Satisfied consumers are 50 percent more likely to recommend their bank's web site. Happy customers are 19 percent more likely to purchase additional services.

THINK CRITICALLY

1. Explain the types of customer information that banks are collecting.
2. Speculate how banks collect this information.

MARKETING-INFORMATION SYSTEMS

LOGGING ON

Marketers must make decisions in a constantly changing environment. Customer needs change. Competitors change. Technology changes, along with many other factors. Marketers must have a systematic way of collecting information. Data collection helps make sound strategic decisions in a changing environment.

Marketers collect information in a number of ways. They collect information from news sources such as trade magazines. They also collect information directly from customers. E-commerce has introduced a new set of tools for collecting and analyzing information. At one time, marketers had to reach out to collect information. Marketers are now automating information collection to assist with managerial decisions.

Work with a partner. Determine what types of information a business needs to collect in order to make strategic decisions. Make a list of where and how a business could collect this information.

Describe the goals of a marketing-information system.

Describe the sources of consumer data.

SYSTEMS GOALS

Information is the lifeblood of decision making. The better information a marketer has, the higher the quality of the decision. Marketers face a unique problem today in that there can be too much data. One study estimates that more data will be collected between the years 2002 and 2005 than has been collected since the dawn of civilization. Companies have problems organizing these data into useful information for decision making.

©GETTY IMAGES/PHOTODISC

Marketers must make sense of the vast amount of data available. A formal **marketing-information system (MkIS)** is designed to collect data and provide meaningful information. There are three major categories of data that marketers collect. Categories include data on current and prospective customers, data on the environment, and data related to marketing-mix elements. (Marketing-mix elements include factors that affect product, price, promotion, and distribution decisions.) The goal of a marketing-information system is to turn raw data into information that is useful for managerial decision making.

SCANNING THE ENVIRONMENT

A marketing-information system should provide a systematic way of capturing data. Consumer data can be collected from customer actions or through a marketing-research process. **Environmental scanning** is a process in which managers regularly review information about competitors and environmental trends. These trends include changes in the economy, new technology, and new competitors entering the market. The data can come from government sources or industry sources. It can also come from careful observations of media articles and competitive behavior.

The most common tool used for environmental scanning is the Internet. However, it should not be the sole source. While the Internet is low-cost, it may not provide timely, accurate, and relevant information. Companies should also collect data from customers, suppliers, trade publications, and employees. Industry experts, industry conferences, and commercial databases also supply data that are useful for understanding competitive environments.

Businesses collect large amounts of information on their marketing-mix elements. The collection process includes capturing data on product sales, sales fluctuations with price or promotion changes, and sales by location geographically or within a store. The large amount of captured data is analyzed and used as a basis for managerial decisions.

While the areas of data collection may be clear, implementing a strong marketing-information system can be complicated. An MkIS requires that data be obtained from both internal and external sources. Computer databases are used to both store and analyze data in many businesses. A database becomes the hub of a business operation. It provides valuable information to managers who control and coordinate business operations.

Merchants were asked to indicate what they considered important in their e-commerce sites. They stated cross-selling (50 percent), personalization (50 percent), improved search (35 percent), and live customer service (25 percent). Customer service in the form of online response to visitor feedback was used at 100 percent of the sites.

THINK CRITICALLY

1. **Rank the four web site features mentioned above in terms of importance to you as a customer. Explain your rankings.**
2. **Have you ever contacted a customer service representative online? What was your experience?**

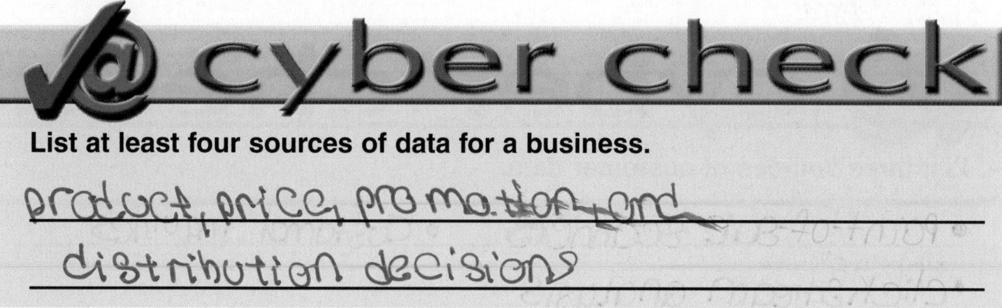

List at least four sources of data for a business.

product, price, promotion and distribution decisions

Over one-third of Internet users in the United States have done their banking online. Customers are most interested in checking the status of their accounts. Banks are most interested in persuading customers to pay bills online. Banks charge for online bill-paying services. Online bill payers are also less likely to switch banks.

CUSTOMER DATA

Marketers collect data to maintain relationships with current customers and to find new customers. Customer data is collected in three ways.

POINT-OF-SALE SCANNERS

The first data collection approach is to capture data on actual customer behavior. The most common method for this collection is the use of *point-of-sale scanners*. Every time a sales associate scans a product bar code, it records the sale along with associated data such as other products sold. A customer is linked to a purchase when he or she uses a debit or credit card, check, or store card. The transaction data is collected and placed into the business's database.

There are many advantages to the collection of scanner data. The data help businesses determine shopper profiles and personalized marketing strategies. Businesses can target *heavy users*, or those individuals who are the highest-spending customers. Businesses can also develop product mix strategies. A marketer can apply scanner data to determine the effects of an advertised "featured" product or shopper discounts. Marketers can also use the information to plan sales for specific time periods.

CLICKSTREAM ANALYSIS

E-businesses also collect data related to online behavior by using **clickstream analysis** to monitor individual web site use. Clickstream analysis systems track the sites from which visitors link, surfing paths within the sites, and time spent at the sites. This information is more valuable if the data can be matched to individuals who have registered at the sites. E-businesses also track and maintain order information of online customers in their databases.

CUSTOMER INQUIRIES

A third method businesses use to understand customer needs is to track customer complaints and questions. Customer inquiries can be used to spot product or service problems. Lands' End, a large catalog clothing business, tracks customer complaints and questions by keying them into a computer database. The data are then analyzed to produce information on problem trends that can be addressed. Otis Elevator receives over 600,000 calls per year from around the world requesting unscheduled repair service. This information is used to develop repair histories of elevators. It is also used to identify possible design problems.

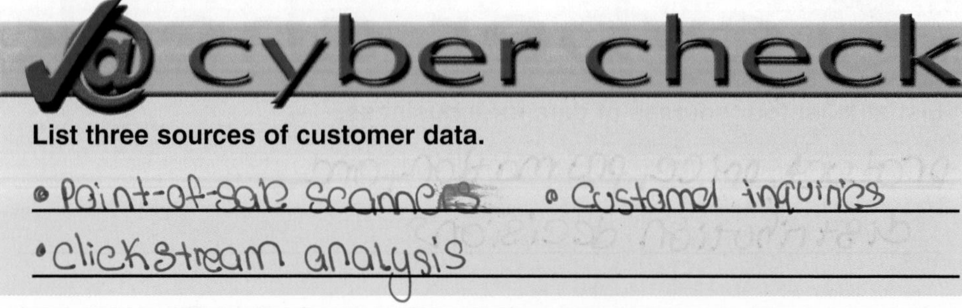

List three sources of customer data.

• Point-of-sale scanners • Customer inquiries
•Clickstream analysis

LOGGING OFF

UNDERSTAND MARKETING CONCEPTS

Circle the best answer for each of the following questions.

1. A marketing-information system is likely to collect information from
   a. current and prospective customers.
   b. data on the environment.
   c. data related to the business's marketing-mix elements.
   d. all of the above
2. Marketers collect data on customers by
   a. capturing actual customer behavior.
   b. using clickstream analysis.
   c. tracking customer inquiries.
   d. all of the above

THINK CRITICALLY

Answer the following questions as completely as possible. If necessary, use a separate sheet of paper.

3. **Research** Collect a number of business-oriented print magazines. Conduct some environmental scanning by reviewing articles in these magazines. Specify how information you find could impact strategies developed by businesses.

4. **Technology** Use the Internet to find three trade support sites. (Using a search engine, key in "*industry name* trade industry.") Review each site. Identify the type of information it supplies to the industry. Discuss the kinds of business decisions that would be aided by the information found on the site.

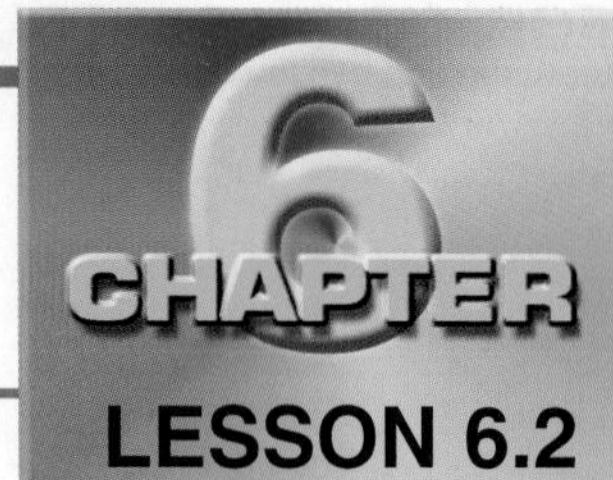

LESSON 6.2

MARKETING RESEARCH

LOGGING ON

Not all data a business needs can be obtained by tracking customer behavior or through environmental scanning. Often, a business has specific questions that need to be answered. To answer these questions, a business will conduct marketing research. This process begins with identifying a marketing problem. Background information is collected. Then, a marketing research plan is structured. Data are collected and analyzed. Finally, reports are generated.

Work with a partner. Brainstorm questions that marketers might ask that would require research to answer. Explain how you would collect data to answer those questions.

GOALS

List the steps in the marketing research process.

Explain how the marketing research process is implemented.

Discuss guidelines for online privacy policies.

MARKETING RESEARCH PROCESS

The systematic and objective process of generating data for marketing decisions is called marketing research. The **marketing research** process follows a number of steps.

1. **Problem Definition** Identify the problem and develop research objectives.
2. **Research Design** Specify how the data will be collected.
3. **Sample Selection** Identify from whom the data will be collected.
4. **Data Collection and Analysis** Collect raw data and organize them into useful information for managerial decisions.
5. **Report Preparation** Formally present the information developed from data analysis.

©DIGITAL VISION

Online marketing research has many advantages over traditional research methods. Data can be collected in a much shorter time and at a lower cost. Studies have found that the Internet can cut research time in half. It can cut costs by as much as 80 percent. There are also drawbacks with online data collection. Internet users may not necessarily reflect the attitudes and opinions of the overall population. Thus, online survey results might be skewed.

List the steps in the marketing research process.

• Problem Definition • Sample Selection

• Research Design • Data Collection and analysis

• Report Preparation

IMPLEMENTATION

There are many techniques that marketing researchers use to collect and analyze data. The Internet offers newer, faster, and more efficient means of collecting information. Online marketing research will become more common in the years ahead.

PROBLEM DEFINITION

Managers want to reduce the risk in decision making by obtaining information related to specific problems. These problems can be as varied as determining the best price at which to sell a product, which advertisement to use, or what factors will increase the chances of selling a product.

RESEARCH DESIGN

Marketing research will take one of two forms. **Qualitative research** involves collecting data in an open-ended form. Questions asked are similar to those found on an essay test. **Quantitative research** controls possible answers and allows for statistical analysis of data. Think of an objective test with multiple-choice and true-false questions. Web-based research can collect both qualitative and quantitative data.

SAMPLE SELECTION

A researcher needs to collect information from only a **sample**, or subgroup of a larger population. Currently, a major limitation to online data collection is that Internet users do not represent the overall population. Not everyone has access to the Internet or chooses to use it regularly. If a research problem specifies individuals who match the profile of typical Internet users, then the Internet can be a useful research tool. Internet users are an attractive target market to some researchers because they represent the higher-income, heavy users of some product categories. Increasingly, the profile of Internet users is beginning to match that of the general population. The growing similarity is making online research a stronger option for data collection.

Researchers often use online panels. A **panel** is a collection of individuals who have volunteered to participate in surveys. Panels give the researcher control over who answers survey questions. Researchers may use a database to identify a pool of individuals with specific characteristics. From that pool, individuals are asked to become panel members. Panel members are typically compensated with reward points or entered into a drawing for prizes.

DATA COLLECTION AND ANALYSIS

Qualitative research is typically conducted through focus groups, observation, or other techniques that require the researcher to use judgment to interpret the results. **Focus groups** are led by a moderator who collects qualitative data from eight to fifteen individuals who respond to open-ended questions. The moderator uses two-way communication to gain a deep understanding of consumers' thoughts and decision-making processes. Focus groups can be conducted in an online environment. Online focus groups use discussion forums or chat rooms to discuss a research topic.

Researchers also collect qualitative data by "mining" online forums and chat rooms related to products or businesses. Mining allows researchers to see what individuals are saying without interfering in the communication process.

Researchers collect quantitative data through surveys and experiments. Surveys are typically conducted by telephone or mail or through personal interviews. Those surveyed must generally choose from a given set of possible answers. The responses can be loaded into a computer database and the answers readily compared. For example, the computer can quickly calculate the percentage of respondents who chose answer A over answer B. The Internet allows researchers to post online surveys. These online systems can collect and analyze data automatically.

Online surveys have a number of advantages over traditional data collection methods. Online surveys can include pictures, links to other web sites, multimedia files containing audio or video, and interactivity. Survey software can limit common research errors such as nonsensical answers, incorrect data entry, or unanswered questions. For example, suppose you were a survey participant and had failed to answer a question. When you hit the submit button, a pop-up message would prompt you to go back and answer the overlooked question. Survey software can also analyze data and automatically create charts and tables.

VIRTUAL VIEWPOINTS

When gathering competitive intelligence, it is important to maintain both ethical and legal boundaries. Recommendations for maintaining *ethical snooping*, or fairness in the collection of data, include the following.

- **Observe all legal restrictions. Do not steal trade secrets, offer bribes, or hack other sites.**
- **Avoid misrepresentations. Do not disguise your or the company's identity. Clearly state the reason for the data collection.**
- **Do not try to thwart competitors by releasing false information. Dishonesty can backfire and erode the image of your firm.**
- **Never ask for or exchange price information with competitors. The exchange could violate antitrust laws.**

THINK CRITICALLY

1. **Review the recommendations for ethical snooping. Why do you think these rules are suggested?**
2. **What could happen to the quality of information if these rules were broken?**

Secondary Research The data collection process is often aided by third-party specialists who conduct secondary research. **Secondary research** is data that already exists. Parties outside the company have collected the data for other purposes. Secondary data can come from publications. Previously collected data can be purchased. Many companies specialize in collecting data. The data are purchased by many businesses. The information is used to help target customers and develop promotional campaigns.

The Internet provides easy access to trade information, articles from magazines and journals, and other secondary sources. Good secondary research can help solve a managerial problem without the collection of *primary data*, or data collected by the business itself.

Catalina Marketing collects data from more than 184 million shoppers and 15,600 supermarkets in the United States as well as 2,700 supermarkets worldwide.

REPORT PREPARATION

Online survey systems can help with report preparation. Many online survey software packages and web sites automatically create summary reports of data. As new data are collected online, charts and reports are automatically updated. Many of these survey software packages and web sites can perform statistical analysis as well.

Explain how the Internet can be used to collect data.

by using surveys to collect data

PRIVACY

The right to privacy is a major concern for both marketers and customers. E-commerce businesses benefit from using customer data. At the same time, customers want control over their personal information. Research has shown that consumers would use the Web more if they could be sure their privacy was protected.

When customers engage in a transaction with a U.S.-based business, that business is free to use the personal information, sell it, or pass it on to others. This is not true in all countries. In the European Union, customer data belongs to the individual. Customers must give their permission for the data to be used.

PRIVACY POLICIES

The Federal Trade Commission (FTC) requires businesses that ask for personal data to post a privacy policy outlining how the information will be used. The Online Privacy Alliance has developed the following guidelines related to the privacy of personal data.

- **Adoption and Implementation** A business should take steps to develop an effective online privacy policy.
- **Notice and Disclosure** A business's privacy policy must be easy to find, read, and understand. It should clearly state what information is being collected and how it will be used.
- **Choice/Consent** Individuals should be able to choose if and how their information will be used. They should also be given the choice to opt out.
- **Data Security** Businesses that collect personal information should take steps to protect that data from loss, misuse, or alteration.
- **Data Quality and Access** Businesses must ensure that personal data are accurate, complete, and timely for their intended purposes.

EMPLOYEE PRIVACY

Employees have limited privacy rights on the job. The Electronic Communications Privacy Act gives U.S. employers the right to monitor and control how employees use private property such as computers and telephones. Employees' web surfing and e-mail can be monitored by their employers. Businesses that engage in this practice should post their privacy policies to ensure that employees are aware of them. Posting may also help to avoid possible liability for employees' misuse of company property.

Monitoring and filtering software can be used to track and block employees' web usage. A business should use this type of software cautiously. Some employees may be *cyberloitering*, or surfing the Web without a specific business purpose. Others may be gathering information on competitors, site designs, or other topics of practical use to the company.

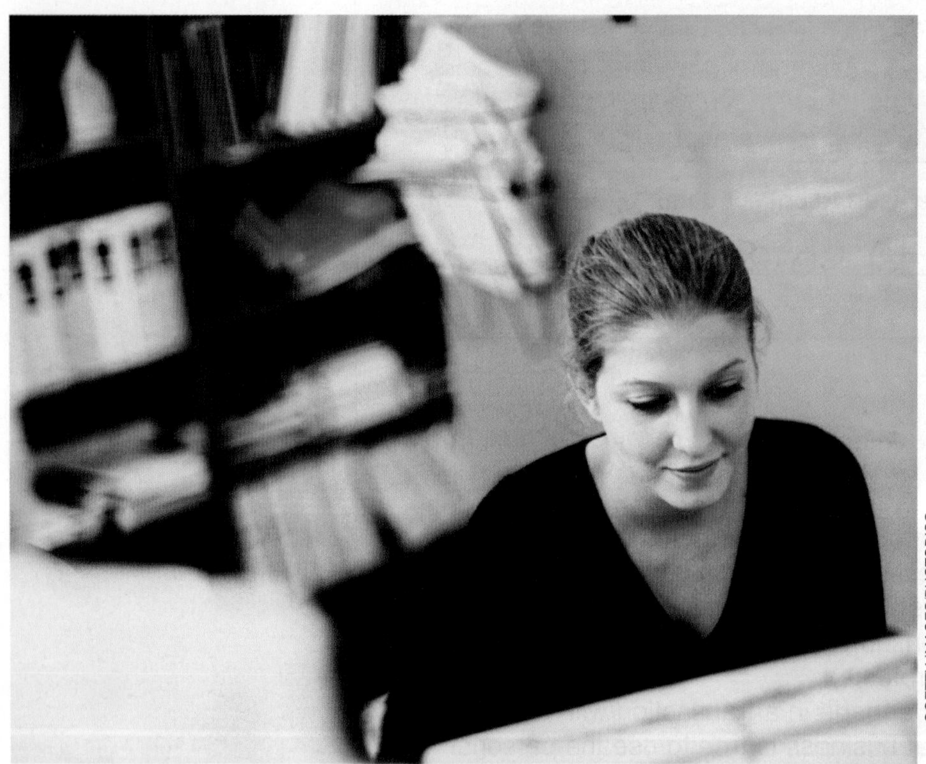

List guidelines for the privacy of personal data.

• Adoption and Implementation • Data Security
• Notice and Disclosure • Data Quality and Access
• Choice/Consent

LOGGING OFF

UNDERSTAND MARKETING CONCEPTS

Circle the best answer for each of the following questions.

1. Which of the following is *not* a step in the marketing research process?
   - a. problem definition
   - b. sample selection
   - c. data collection and analysis
   - d. economic analysis
2. Which of the following research methods can be conducted online?
   - a. mining
   - b. surveys
   - c. focus groups
   - d. all of the above

THINK CRITICALLY

Answer the following questions as completely as possible. If necessary, use a separate sheet of paper.

3. **Communication** Your manager has asked if it is possible for your company to conduct marketing research online. Write a brief report indicating the advantages and disadvantages of online marketing research.

4. **Communication** Develop a privacy policy for your school. Indicate how you would implement this policy.

DATA MINING AND CUSTOMER-RELATIONSHIP MANAGEMENT

Describe how database marketing is used in a business.

Explain how a customer's value is determined.

Describe the role of databases in business systems control.

LOGGING ON

Databases are the heart of many organizations' knowledge strategies. Electronic databases are used to store, manipulate, and analyze data. These databases can be small enough to operate on laptop and desktop computers. They can also be large enough to require supercomputers to store and analyze the data.

Despite their power, databases cannot make a single managerial decision. It is up to marketing managers to determine if the information provided by the databases is useful.

Work with a group. Discuss what types of data a company would want to collect and place into a database. What makes this data useful? Create a list of the decisions a manager would be able to make if the database could provide the pertinent information.

DATABASE MARKETING

Databases are used to store data that are collected and analyzed by a business. The data may come from customers, sales tracking, inventory records, suppliers and other business partners. Data may also come from trade magazines and third-party researchers. The data are collected, sorted, organized, and analyzed. Databases are used for many purposes.

- **Market Segmentation** Databases help identify common characteristics of customers who are likely to react to similar marketing strategies. Databases allow for personalized marketing strategies and identification of customer profitability.
- **Customer Churn** Databases help predict which customers are likely to switch to a competitor.
- **Fraud Detection** Databases can rate the likelihood that a transaction is fraudulent.
- **Customer Service** Databases allow businesses to provide customer service based on the customers' past experience. Databases can also detect patterns of customer problems.
- **Direct Marketing** Databases identify the prospects most likely to respond to direct marketing efforts.

- **Interactive Marketing** Databases can predict what a web site visitor is most interested in seeing. Databases can then customize the site's content accordingly.
- **Market-Basket Analysis** Databases group products or services that are most likely to be purchased together.
- **Trend Analysis** Databases identify differences and trends among groups of customers over a given period of time. This analysis aids in short-, medium-, and long-term decision making.

Database marketing is designed to strengthen relationships with customers. Database marketing limits wasted promotional efforts, such as junk mail, by targeting only interested customers.

DATABASE DEVELOPMENT

Data are collected from a variety of sources. When customers send in warranty cards, sweepstakes applications, or coupons, data from these sources can be entered and combined with data purchased from third-party researchers. A credit card company stores virtually every customer transaction in a database. This process allows the company to look at patterns and flag behavior that falls outside of an individual's normal purchasing habits. The credit card company can then contact the individual or the store to verify abnormal purchases.

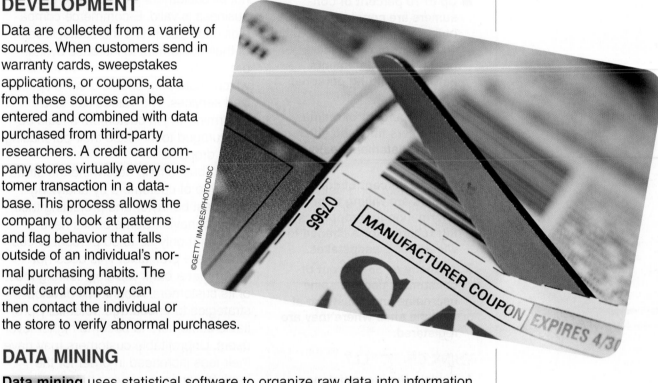

©GETTY IMAGES/PHOTODISC

DATA MINING

Data mining uses statistical software to organize raw data into information that is useful for managerial decisions. One telecommunications company used supercomputers to develop 22 profiles of customers. The company analyzed 140 million households on up to 10,000 customer attributes such as income, lifestyle, and past calling habits. The analysis reduced the cost of attracting new customers from 65 cents to 4.5 cents per customer.

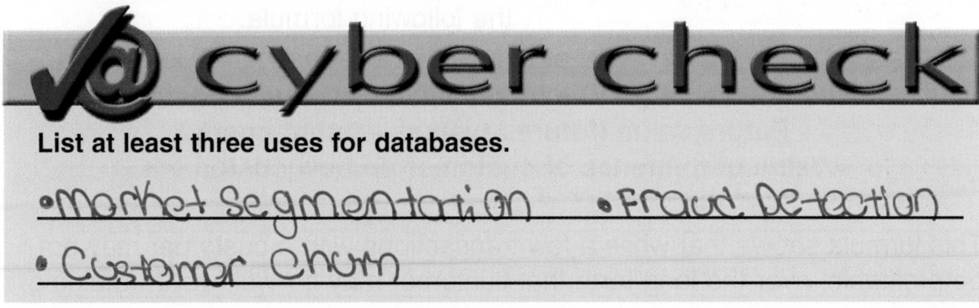

List at least three uses for databases.

•Market Segmentation •Fraud Detection
• Customer Churn

STRATEGIC VALUE OF CUSTOMERS

Privacy is a major concern in e-commerce. However, research has shown inconsistencies between privacy concerns and consumer behavior.

- **Up to 70 percent of consumers are concerned about online privacy. However, only 40 percent of consumers read privacy statements before submitting personal information.**
- **Only 30 percent of online consumers find web site privacy statements easy to understand.**
- **Over 80 percent of consumers are willing to provide information to shopping sites in exchange for a chance to win a $100 sweepstakes.**
- **As many as 53 percent of consumers use the same username and password at multiple sites where they are registered.**

THINK CRITICALLY

1. **Explain the inconsistency between privacy concerns and consumer behavior.**
2. **What would happen to online sales if privacy could be guaranteed? Explain your answer.**

All customers are not equal. Some customers are more profitable than others. Some can even cost a company money. The *80–20 rule-of-thumb* dictates that 80 percent of profits come from 20 percent of a business's customers, known as heavy users. Although the percentages may not be exact, the idea that not all customers are profitable to a business is valid. E-commerce companies often determine the strategic value of their customers to increase overall profits. The assigned values determine which customers should receive specialized services. The values can also determine which customers should be encouraged to increase their purchasing or be dropped.

Databases help determine the strategic value of customers by analyzing their past behavior and projecting their future behavior. Some banks have found that only 20 to 30 percent of customers are profitable. This does not mean that a bank will stop serving most of its customers. A bank will develop strategies to encourage potentially profitable customers to become higher-level users. Unprofitable customers may have their fees increased in order for the bank to continue serving them.

LIFETIME VALUE

Companies have a number of ways to measure the value of their customers. One measure determines the **lifetime value (LTV)** of a customer by using the following formula.

Lifetime value (LTV) = Initial value (revenue – costs)
+ Future value (future revenue – future costs)
+ Value of influence of customer on new customers

This formula shows that while a few transactions with a customer may not be profitable, over the long term that customer may be well worth retaining.

RFM MEASURES

Another technique used to determine the strategic value of customers includes **recency, frequency, and monetary (RFM) measures**. Customers are seen as more valuable if they have made a large number of purchases in the recent past for a high-dollar value. Once marketers have determined an RFM profile, strategies may be implemented to increase purchase frequency and the total amount spent.

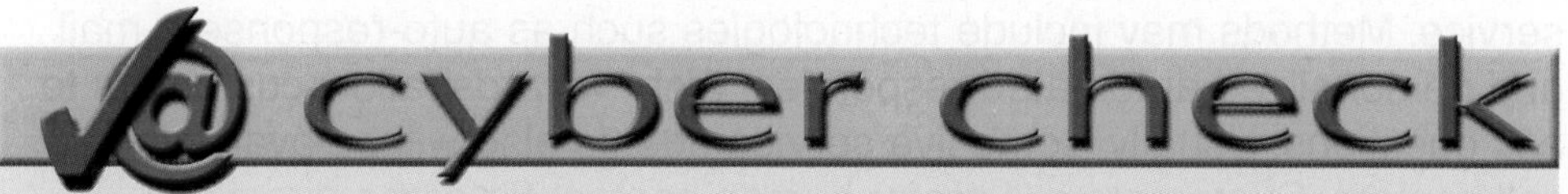

Describe two methods used to determine the value of a customer.

• LTV -of a customer by using the folloing formula
R.FM measures another technique used to determine
the strategic value of customers

BUSINESS SYSTEMS CONTROL

Databases are used to control business systems and the business processes needed to complete a transaction. Databases provide information for customer support, aid salespeople, and provide links to inventory. For example, if you order a product online from an e-commerce business, your order goes into a database. The database automatically provides information to the sales, manufacturing, inventory, accounting, and shipping departments. If you call to inquire about your order, a customer service representative can look at the status by using the database. It is possible for some companies' customers to check order status online without ever communicating with a customer service representative.

©GETTY IMAGES/PHOTODISC

Spending for customer-relationship management systems is expected to reach $148 billion worldwide by 2005. The major uses of these systems will be in developing reports and mining data to determine market segments.

CUSTOMER-RELATIONSHIP MANAGEMENT SYSTEMS

Customer-relationship management (CRM) systems combine software and management practices to serve the customer from order to delivery and to provide after-sale support. Businesses have adopted the Internet as a cost-effective means of providing customer service. A typical service transaction with a live representative costs $5. A voice-response system costs 50 cents per transaction. A transaction through a web-based system costs only pennies.

Most businesses use a combination of methods to provide customer service. Methods may include technologies such as auto-response e-mail and personalized automated responses. Web "wizards" allow customers to ask questions. Usually, some live service agents also will be available at call centers. Customers still prefer human contact for some questions.

List the advantages of using the Internet for customer service.

____

____

WORKING ONLINE

An-Li is graduating from college with a degree in marketing. She is pursuing a career as an *online marketing researcher*. She has found openings at a number of marketing research firms. Job responsibilities include developing and working with consumer panels, developing online surveys, and working with online focus groups. Duties also include administering customer tracking systems and conducting customer satisfaction surveys.

The job requires a bachelor's degree in marketing. An understanding of consumer behavior is essential. The ability to conduct surveys, interviews, and focus groups is necessary. Job candidates must also be able to compile reports and communicate study results. An-Li knows that she will need to be a team player. She must have the interpersonal skills to develop relationships with business partners. She must be willing to learn new research methods. She will need strong verbal and written communication skills. Project-management and analytical skills will be crucial. The ability to work in a multi-tasking, fast-paced environment is critical.

An-Li is excited about her opportunities. At the same time, she is nervous about the new duties she will be taking on.

THINK CRITICALLY

1. **Evaluate An-Li's career choice. Identify the skills that she will need in order to succeed as an online marketing researcher.**
2. **Assume you would like to follow in An-Li's footsteps. Outline a plan to obtain the skills you will need.**

LOGGING OFF

UNDERSTAND MARKETING CONCEPTS

Circle the best answer for each of the following questions.

1. Which of the following is *not* a purpose of a business's databases?
   a. market segmentation
   b. fraud detection
   c. career tracking
   d. customer service

2. Measures used to determine the strategic value of a customer include
   a. recency measures.
   b. frequency measures.
   c. monetary measures.
   d. all of the above

THINK CRITICALLY

Answer the following questions as completely as possible. If necessary, use a separate sheet of paper.

3. **Communication** You work for a pet supply company. Your manager has asked you to investigate a database-marketing strategy for the business. Prepare a brief report for your manager. Explain the types of data needed, the methods of data collection, and the purposes for which the data will be used.

4. **Communication** Your manager at the pet supply company has also asked you to recommend a way to implement a strong customer-relationship management system. Prepare a memo outlining your suggestions.

6 CHAPTER REVIEW

REVIEW E-COMMERCE MARKETING CONCEPTS

Write the letter of the term that matches each definition. Some terms will not be used.

- a. clickstream analysis
- b. customer-relationship management (CRM)
- c. data mining
- d. environmental scanning
- e. focus groups
- f. lifetime value (LTV)
- g. marketing-information system (MkIS)
- h. marketing research
- i. panel
- j. qualitative research
- k. quantitative research
- l. recency, frequency, and monetary (RFM) measures
- m. sample
- n. secondary research

A 1. Data that already exists, having been collected by parties outside the company for other purposes

H 2. The systematic and objective process of generating data for marketing decisions

J 3. Involves collecting data in an open-ended form

G 4. A formal system designed to collect data and provide meaningful information

E 5. Led by a moderator who collects qualitative data from eight to fifteen individuals who respond to open-ended questions

C 6. Uses statistical software to organize raw data into information that is useful for managerial decisions

f 7. Initial value + future value + value of influence of customer on new customers

b 8. Combine software and management practices to serve the customer from order to delivery and to provide after-sale support

D 9. A process in which managers regularly review information about competitors and environmental trends

I 10. A collection of individuals who have volunteered to participate in surveys

Circle the best answer.

11. Secondary research includes all of the following *except*
    - a. surveys conducted by the company.
    - b. information found in trade publications.
    - c. focus groups.
    - d. all of the above

12. Which of the following marketing research methods would collect data for statistical analysis?
    - a. qualitative research
    - b. quantitative research
    - c. focus groups
    - d. none of the above

THINK CRITICALLY

13. Identify a business in which you are interested. List the types of data that are collected by this business. Tell how this business collects and uses the information.

14. You work at the national headquarters of a restaurant chain. Your manager wants to use the Internet to collect data for managerial decisions. Write a paragraph outlining an Internet strategy for collecting information for the business.

15. Keep track of your interactions with various businesses for two weeks. Determine the types of information these businesses collect from you. Note if any information can be traced to you as an individual.

MAKE CONNECTIONS

16. **MARKETING MATH** Determine the lifetime value of a customer using the following information.

    current revenue = \$500, current costs = \$550, future revenue = \$1,200, future costs = \$700, value of influence = \$150

17. **HISTORY** Assume you are a shopper living 100 years ago. Most of the businesses from which you buy are small enough to know you and your family on a personal level. Write a paragraph describing your feelings about the storeowners knowing you as a shopper. Contrast this with another paragraph indicating your feelings about current businesses keeping your personal data in their databases.

18. **TECHNOLOGY** Indicate how the various e-commerce communication platforms could be used effectively for marketing research. Speculate how effective the Internet will be for marketing research purposes.

19. **COMMUNICATION** One of the main barriers to data collection is the lack of understanding individuals have about the use of their private information. Write a paragraph explaining to customers the benefits of allowing businesses to collect personal data.

20. **COMMUNICATION** Choose a business. Devise a plan that would allow customers to obtain online service from this business. Indicate if you believe that a "live" service representative is also needed.

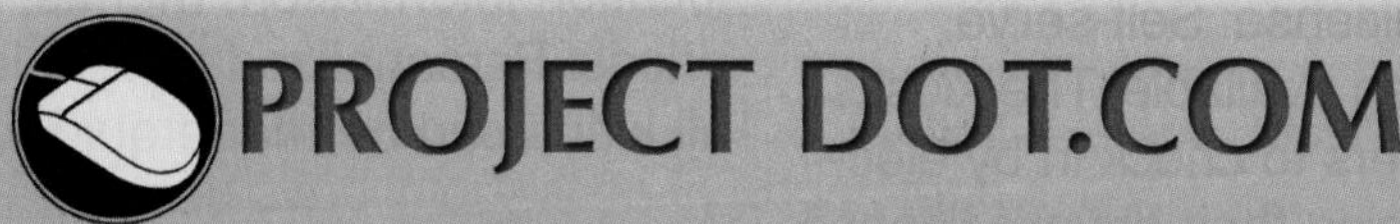

This part of the project will focus on how your business plans to develop a marketing research system.

Work with your team members to complete the following activities.

1. Make a list of the types of information that will be helpful in aiding your strategic decisions.
2. Develop a systematic way of scanning the environment. Explain how you will use the information collected.
3. Develop a systematic way of collecting data on customers. Explain how you will use the information collected.
4. Identify a specific marketing research question that you feel needs to be answered for your business. Outline a marketing research process to answer the question. Indicate how you will collect the necessary data in an online environment.
5. Assume that all collected data will be placed into a database. Specify the types of data you will collect. Explain how you will use the information.

DECA PREP

An Association of Marketing Students

SHOPPING ONLINE FOR ALL OF YOUR TRAVEL NEEDS

"Please remain on the line. An operator will assist you in approximately eight minutes." Nothing is more frustrating than being put on hold when trying to make an airline or hotel reservation by telephone.

Financially strapped airlines have almost totally replaced paper tickets sent through the mail with paperless e-tickets confirmed online. Airlines are now encouraging customers to purchase tickets online in order to receive the best rates and reduce costs for the airline industry. Travelers who purchase tickets online are often awarded bonus frequent-flyer miles.

Easy Check-In

Travelers with e-tickets can quickly check in at curbside by presenting their driver's license. Self-serve kiosks are also available. The kiosks allow customers to check in by electronically swiping their driver's license or credit card. Customers key in their final destination and the number of pieces of luggage they will check for the flight. The boarding pass is printed for the customers to take to the departure gate. Airlines now even make check-ins for domestic flights accessible online. Boarding passes can be printed at home before going to the airport.

Airline web sites include timetables of all flights. Up-to-date departure and arrival times and delay information can be found online as well.

Accommodations and Transportation

Airlines and hotels use pop-up advertisements to announce great travel prices. Most airlines offer special packages that include airfare, hotel, and car rental. Hotels also offer specials for customers who book online. Reservations can be made directly by using individual hotel web sites or discount travel sites like Travelocity, Priceline.com, and Hotels.com. Cost-conscious consumers can use the Web to find prices that meet their budget needs.

AAA members traveling by car can map the best route using the Internet. The Internet is a great source of information about entertainment at the traveler's final destination. Restaurant web sites provide location information, menus, and prices. Personalized travel plans of all kinds can be made quickly online.

Think Critically

1. **Why are e-tickets becoming increasingly popular?**
2. **Why do airlines and hotels offer special rates to customers who make online purchases?**
3. **Will tighter security at airports have any impact on the purchase of e-tickets? Explain.**
4. **How can e-tickets reduce the number of employees required by an airline?**

FOOD MARKETING ROLE PLAY

The supermarket industry has become extremely competitive. Smaller grocery stores have gone by the wayside. Bigger and better venues continue to enter the market. Grocery store customers are usually price conscious. Their loyalty can be fickle.

Ideal is an independent neighborhood grocery store. Ideal is noted for fresh meats, vegetables, and fruits. Customer service is a top priority that has kept the local grocer in business. Ideal takes great pride in carefully bagging groceries and carrying them to the customers' cars. Ideal also excels at fulfilling and delivering telephone orders. Employees know customers by first name.

Some major supermarkets have unsuccessfully tried to operate web sites where customers can order groceries. Ideal believes that the uniqueness of its store could make a web site a successful promotional tool.

You have been asked to design a web site for Ideal. The site will inform customers about weekly specials. It will emphasize the store's unique services and offer specials to online customers. The site will also provide a weekly newsletter that includes recipes for healthy living.

Ideal also wants your ideas on collecting e-mail addresses of loyal customers. The store believes its web site would provide a valuable means for customers to place delivery orders.

You will have ten minutes to review this information and determine how you will handle the role-play situation. You then will have up to ten minutes to present your ideas to the store's manager. The manager will have five minutes to ask questions.

Performance Indicators Evaluated

- Understand the opportunities and challenges facing Ideal.
- Explain the value of a web site for the grocery store.
- Describe the features and information to be included on the web site.
- Explain how the web site will set Ideal apart from the supermarket giants.
- Describe how customers will learn about the web site.
- Explain how the store will maintain/update the web site.

Go to the DECA web site for more detailed information.

1. Why should Ideal consider a web site when the Internet has been unsuccessful for other supermarkets?
2. How can a web site make Ideal's operation more efficient?
3. What type of campaign should be implemented to advertise the new web site?
4. Should Ideal also keep non-web promotional strategies in place? Why or why not?

www.deca.org/publications/HS_Guide/guidetoc.html

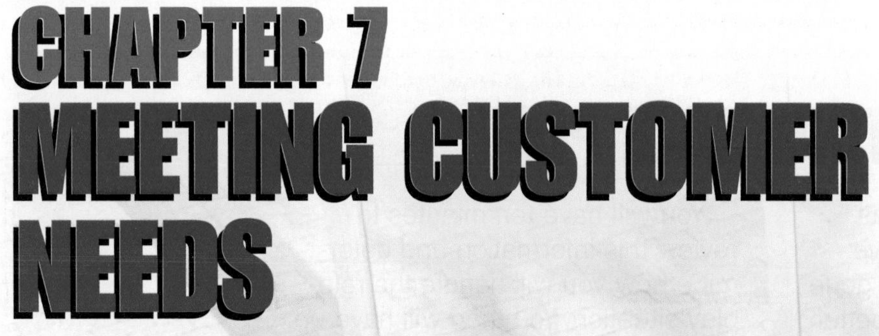

CHAPTER 7 MEETING CUSTOMER NEEDS

7.1 Identifying E-Business Customers
7.2 Principles of Consumer Behavior
7.3 Building Virtual Customer Relationships

POINT YOUR BROWSER
ecommkt.swlearning.com

CARS, VIRTUALLY ANYWHERE

People enjoy a new car shopping experience—sitting in the vehicle, inhaling the odor of new leather, listening to the stereo, and sensing the handling of the vehicle during a test drive. Yet, many customers dread the sales negotiations, the complex financial discussions, and the pressure to make a decision.

Will automobile shoppers give up the visit to dealerships and shift their purchasing online? The answer may dictate the future of local dealerships and the jobs of many salespeople. It may also indicate the power of the Internet to change longtime buying habits of consumers. Almost all automobile manufacturers worldwide have web sites that allow a customer to order a new vehicle online. Statistics show that the Internet is changing the way people shop for automobiles. However, the Internet does not currently meet all of the purchasing requirements of most consumers.

According to a recent survey, 83 percent of Internet users in the United Kingdom who purchased an automobile used the Web extensively to help them make their purchase decisions. Four of the top eight sites visited by car shoppers were the web sites of automobile manufacturers. In a similar survey of U.S. consumers, 82 percent who were currently considering a new car purchase were using the Internet to help them gather information. Contrasted with web sites visited by U.K. car shoppers, the top ten web sites visited by U.S. consumers were information or buying assistance services rather than manufacturers' sites.

THINK CRITICALLY

1. Explain possible reasons for the differences in the types of web sites visited by U.K. and U.S. automobile shoppers.
2. Do you believe that most automobile shoppers eventually will make their purchases completely online? Why or why not?

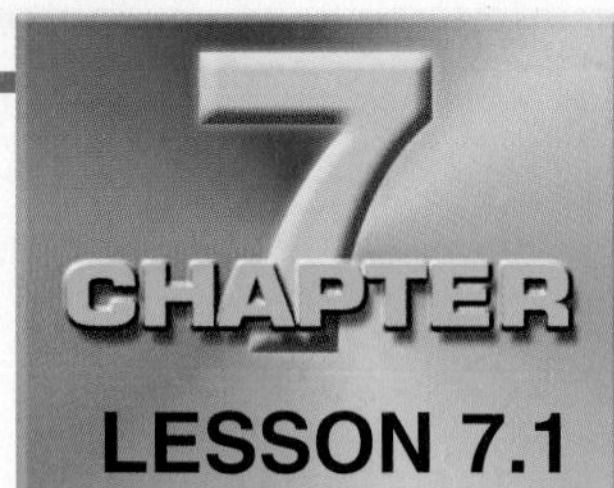

IDENTIFYING E-BUSINESS CUSTOMERS

Recognize the value of market segments.

Identify the categories of customers for e-businesses.

LOGGING ON

Consumer surveys are an important part of marketing research. Companies use the gathered information to develop and improve products. The information also helps to ensure that customers are satisfied with the marketing mix. Surveys are expensive and time consuming. Most companies send surveys to consumers by mail. They often provide a small cash incentive or gift to encourage responses. Even so, because surveys require time and effort to complete and return, the response rate is often quite low. Sometimes only five to ten percent of the mailed surveys are returned.

Online surveys are a new way for companies to gather information. They save money and result in a higher response rate. *Consumer Reports* is shifting its annual survey of products and services online. In 2002, it mailed four million surveys to its magazine subscribers at a cost of $700,000. About 14 percent were returned. In 2003, 900,000 subscribers received their surveys online while the rest received their surveys by mail. The total cost was about half that of 2002, and the response rate increased to over 25 percent.

Work with a partner. Discuss why response rates to online surveys are usually much higher than to mailed surveys. Are there instances when the Internet should not be used for consumer surveys?

THE IMPORTANCE OF CUSTOMERS

Customers are the lifeblood of a business. They decide whether to purchase a company's products or the products of a competitor. They may be persuaded to try a product once. If satisfied, they are more likely to purchase from the company again. They may encourage friends and family to buy as well. Companies with satisfied customers are likely to be successful. Those that are unable to satisfy customers will soon fail.

One of the most important tasks of marketing is to identify prospective customers for a company. The activities needed to attract customers include marketing research and promotion that gets the attention and interest of new prospects. Also important are some type of incentive to encourage customers to make their first purchase and follow-up activities that ensure customer satisfaction. Any concerns the customer has about the product must be identified and resolved. Companies that have clearly identified their potential customers can concentrate their marketing resources on those prospects.

Many new Internet-based businesses believe that obtaining customers will be easier online than through traditional routes. However, the Internet presents several challenges. First, a large percentage of prospective customers do not yet have reliable Internet access or are not comfortable shopping online. Second, when a business goes online, it becomes one of thousands with a web site. It is not likely that a prospective customer who is unaware of a business will locate its web site and choose it as a purchasing source. If the prospective customer does locate a business's web site, a successful sale requires that the site be well designed and easy to use. It must offer the best product choices from among all of those available online as well as through traditional channels.

CUSTOMER CHARACTERISTICS

When consumers want to make a purchase, they usually have thousands of products and services from which to choose. Some consumers will find that the products of a specific business meet their needs. They will return to that same business to purchase those products again and again. Other consumers will not be interested in that company's products. Trying to turn a consumer who is not interested in a company or its products into a regular, satisfied customer is both difficult and expensive. If a company is able to identify the people who are satisfied with its products and services, it will be much easier and less expensive to retain them as customers.

Every business has access to thousands and sometimes hundreds of thousands of consumers. The Internet provides an even greater number of prospective customers. While many potential customers do not have Internet access, most of those who do are using that connection to gather product information and to search for businesses that offer products. However, only a small percentage of the people who use the Internet to gather information actually make their purchases online. A business needs to develop an effective method of identifying those consumers who are most likely to purchase. It should concentrate its marketing efforts on attracting and satisfying those customers.

The process of identifying high-potential customers is known as *market segmentation*. A **market segment** is a group of individuals within a larger market who share one or more important characteristics resulting in similar purchasing needs and behaviors.

Markets are segmented by a number of characteristics that can be used to identify prospective customers. Factors often used to segment markets are demographics, psychographics, product usage, and specific needs and benefits.

Demographics are the descriptive characteristics of consumers. Common demographic characteristics are age, income, education level, gender, race, ethnicity, marital status, family size, geographic location, and occupation.

Psychographics refer to people's interests, activities, lifestyles, and values. People make choices based on their interests. Someone who is interested in health and nutrition may be attracted to certain types of products and choices. Another person who is involved in investing and financial planning will have other product and service interests.

Product usage identifies the frequency and quantity of use of a category of products. Segmenting a market of people who rent movies might identify

Even young children are using the Internet. Fourteen million 2- to 12-year-olds are online in the United States today. However, that is only 32 percent of all children in this age group. Internet use by pre-teens is expected to expand to 62 percent by 2008.

those who rent more than twice a week, those who rent one to two times a month, and those who rent less than five times a year. Segmenting may also identify those who typically rent more than three movies at the same time and those who rent only one at a time.

Needs and benefits segmentation divides a market based on the primary reasons that customers make a purchase or the value they receive from the use of the product. People need to rent automobiles for business travel, family vacations, or emergencies when their own cars have been damaged or are being serviced. Benefits derived from selecting a particular bank may be convenience, personal attention, a high level of service, or financial gain.

IDENTIFYING MARKET SEGMENTS

Companies gather and analyze consumer data in order to segment a market. When a business has identified all of the segments that exist in a market, it can make decisions about which segments to serve. It can also decide the marketing mixes that will be needed to satisfy those segments. The segments of a business's market selected for attention are its target market. To be effective as a target market, the segments must meet four criteria.

1. The people in the segments must have common, important needs.
2. The people in the segments should respond in a similar way to marketing activities designed to address those needs.
3. The people in the segments must be identifiable.
4. Adequate information about the segments should be available so that effective marketing mixes can be developed.

A number of web sites provide information on personal health and healthcare. WebMD has been successful by focusing on business customers. One of its primary services is to process insurance claims for businesses online.

THINK CRITICALLY

Personal health is an important concern of many people. Use the Internet to locate several businesses that serve healthcare needs. Why do you think many companies that provide online health information have found it difficult to succeed?

Each of us belongs to several market segments based upon our personal characteristics and needs. You are an important member of a market segment for some businesses. Other businesses are not interested in you at all. For some businesses, demographics are the most important factor in segmenting a market. For others, it might be needs, previous purchase experiences, or interests. Consider a company that produces and sells uniforms. If the company manufactures school uniforms, an important market segment would be school-age children and their parents. If the company manufactures military uniforms, then government agencies would be an important segment. If the company sells work uniforms, the market might be segmented by occupation or industry.

Need segmentation is an important way to study a market. For example, people who have a need for entertainment and socialization have a variety of demographic characteristics. There may be a wide range in age, income, and education levels. Yet, people who are in your age group are likely to have different entertainment and socialization needs than their parents, grandparents, or younger siblings. People in high-income brackets may make different entertainment choices than those with limited resources.

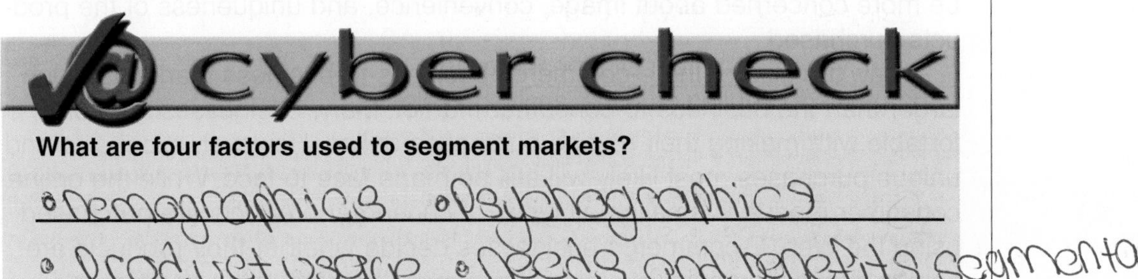

cyber check
• Demographics • Psychographics
• Product usage • Needs and benefits segmentation

What are four factors used to segment markets?

CHOOSING CUSTOMERS FOR E-COMMERCE

Many years ago, businesses believed that if they offered good products and services, customers would find them and their companies would succeed. We know today that it takes more than a good product to be successful. As consumers choose among all of the available products and services, they will select those that best meet their needs. A business must be able to offer a valuable marketing mix. The mix must exceed what customers can obtain from other businesses offering the same product. In order to do that, businesses must gather information about potential customers and use the information to understand the customers as well as possible. Then, they must target groups of customers that the business can serve effectively. Finally, they must develop products and services that are superior to those offered by competitors.

©GETTY IMAGES/PHOTODISC

BUSINESS CUSTOMERS OR FINAL CONSUMERS

Businesses and final consumers may purchase the same products but for different reasons and uses. A business chooses an automobile that is efficient and comfortable for its salespeople. A family chooses an automobile with available space to transport children and their friends to school, soccer games, and dance lessons. A retailer orders hundreds of computers from a manufacturer to sell in its stores. A college student orders a laptop from the same manufacturer's web site, but it will be used for schoolwork, personal entertainment, and communication. The products may be the same, but the quantities ordered and the uses of the products will be quite different.

Final consumers make purchases primarily for their own personal consumption. **Business consumers** purchase products for use in their business operations or for resale. Business purchasers use a rational basis for their decisions. **Rational decisions** are based on facts and logic. Final consumers are likely to be more emotional when making purchase decisions. **Emotional decisions** are based on feelings, beliefs, and attitudes. A business may be concerned about price, consistent quality, and the ability of the seller to quickly deliver the quantity ordered. An individual consumer may be more concerned about image, convenience, and uniqueness of the products purchased.

Today, the size of the e-commerce business-to-business market is much larger than the business-to-consumer market. Many businesses are comfortable with making their routine purchases online. However, expensive and unique purchases most likely will still be made face to face. While the online consumer market is smaller, all types of consumer products are purchased using the Web. E-commerce businesses decide whether their products are sold to final consumers, business consumers, or both. If the decision is made to serve both, a different marketing mix will be required for each group. Often, a separate web site and purchasing process will be developed for each type of customer.

MARKETING TO INNOVATORS

Online sales to U.S. consumers currently total about $100 billion. That is only five percent of total retail sales. Business-to-business sales are over $1 trillion. That accounts for less than ten percent of total business purchases. These facts suggest that there is much room for growth in e-commerce. The statistics also suggest that most businesses and individual consumers are not attracted to the Internet as a purchasing destination.

Who should e-commerce businesses target? There are certain types of consumers who are likely to be Internet customers. They are people who are comfortable with technology and innovation. An **innovation** is a new and unique product, process, or idea. Most people are reluctant to try something that is totally new. However, a small percentage of the population (about two percent) is considered to be *innovators*. Innovators want to be the first to try new products. When the public could access the Internet in the early 1990s, innovators were the first to try it. When businesses began selling products online, innovators were their first customers.

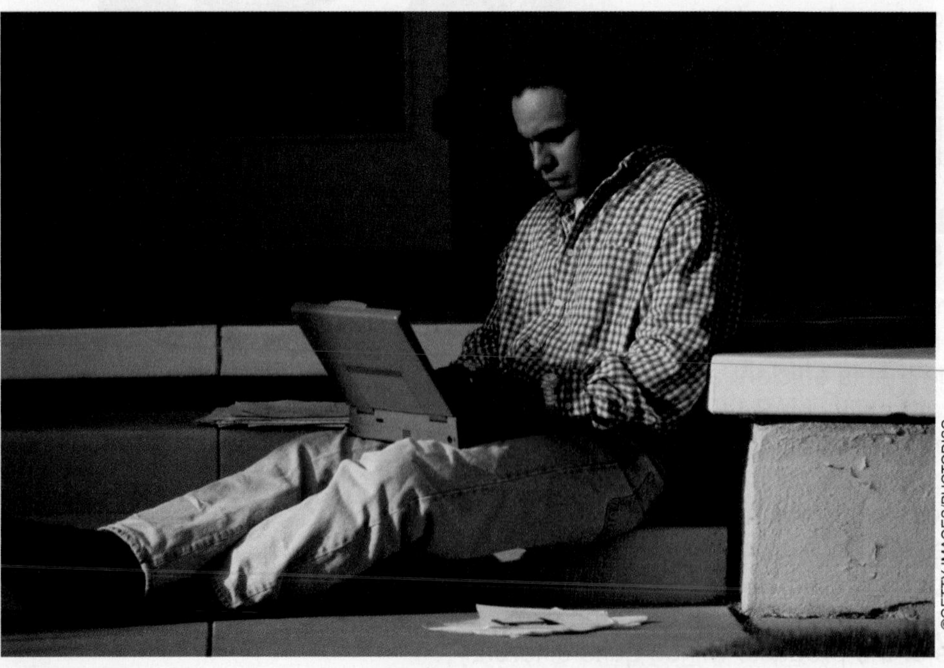
©GETTY IMAGES/PHOTODISC

Innovators have characteristics that differentiate them from other consumers. These traits make it possible for businesses to identify them. Innovators are generally younger and more educated and have a higher income level than others. They are also considered social leaders and enjoy taking risks.

The adoption sequence shown in Figure 7.1 illustrates how consumers accept innovations. Innovators are first, followed in sequence by early adopters, early majority, late majority, laggards, and non-adopters. Currently, about 24 percent of consumers in the United States do not use the Internet. Today's average Internet user is somewhat older, is less educated, and has a lower income level than in the past decade. The adoption sequence for Internet use has progressed from innovators and early adopters to early majority and late majority adopters. However, innovators and early adopters are the consumers who view the Internet as a source to purchase products and services.

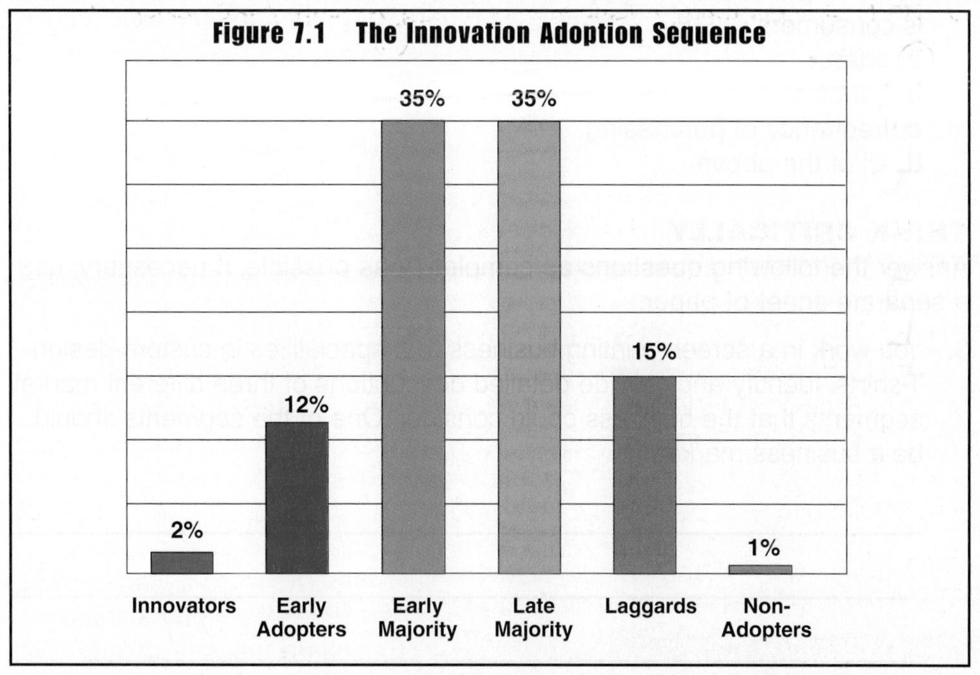

Figure 7.1 The Innovation Adoption Sequence

If a business uses the Internet to attract consumer interest and to provide information to aid decision making, its target market can include all Internet users. However, if the business expects consumers to use the Internet to purchase its products, marketing efforts should be directed toward innovators and early adopters.

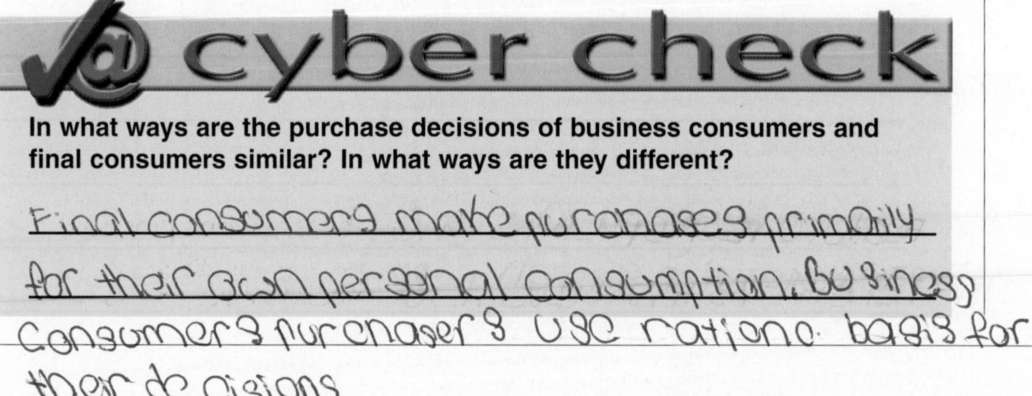

In what ways are the purchase decisions of business consumers and final consumers similar? In what ways are they different?

Final consumers make purchases primarily for their own personal consumption. Business consumers purchasers use rational basis for their decisions

LOGGING OFF

UNDERSTAND MARKETING CONCEPTS

Circle the best answer for each of the following questions.

1. Businesses have difficulty attracting customers on the Internet because
   a. it is illegal to advertise on the Internet.
   b. only a small percentage of consumers have reliable Internet access.
   c. there are not enough product choices on the Internet.
   d. product prices are usually higher on the Internet.
2. An example of a demographic characteristic used to segment a market is consumers'
   a. ages.
   b. hobbies.
   c. frequency of purchasing.
   d. all of the above

THINK CRITICALLY

Answer the following questions as completely as possible. If necessary, use a separate sheet of paper.

3. You work in a screen-printing business that specializes in custom-design T-shirts. Identify and provide detailed descriptions of three different market segments that the business could consider. One of the segments should be a business market.

4. **Research** Use the Internet to gather information on a widely used product or service that was considered innovative many years ago. Describe how the product changed as more and more people accepted it. Provide a time line for the development and acceptance of the innovation.

PRINCIPLES OF CONSUMER BEHAVIOR

LOGGING ON

Wal-Mart is the world's largest retailer. It is also a huge customer. Manufacturers work hard to sell their products to Wal-Mart. These businesses know that a sale to the giant retailer can have a dramatic effect on their success. Because of its size, Wal-Mart can often dictate how other businesses operate.

A new wireless technology known as radio frequency identification (RFID) is used to identify products. The RFID consists of a small computer chip and antenna placed on a product when it is manufactured. It replaces the traditional bar code. The RFID transmits a signal so the product can be located and identified at any time. It can be used by businesses to track a product's location, inventory level, and sales. It can even be used to deter shoplifting, since it is almost impossible for the consumer to locate and remove.

Many manufacturers don't want to use RFIDs because they are more expensive than bar codes. However, Wal-Mart is requiring its top suppliers to begin using them by 2005.

Work with a partner. Discuss why companies might choose to replace bar codes with RFIDs even though they are more expensive. Why might the technology be especially important to Wal-Mart?

Recognize the importance of understanding consumer behavior.

Identify the steps in the consumer decision-making process.

NEEDS, WANTS, AND BENEFITS

Why do you purchase a certain product? When is a brand name important? What causes you to return a product? Do you frequently try new products or buy from companies with which you are not familiar? The answers to these questions describe your behavior as a consumer.

Consumer behavior is the study of how people make decisions about the purchase and use of products and services. Businesses study consumer behavior in order to understand what they must do to satisfy customer needs. With careful study, businesses can make better decisions about the target markets they plan to serve and the marketing mixes they will use to satisfy their customers. Effective marketing results in satisfying exchanges. Understanding consumer behavior helps businesses improve customer satisfaction.

E-commerce presents new challenges for businesses. Many of the principles of consumer behavior that have worked in traditional businesses will apply to e-commerce. However, purchasing on the Internet is different in some ways.

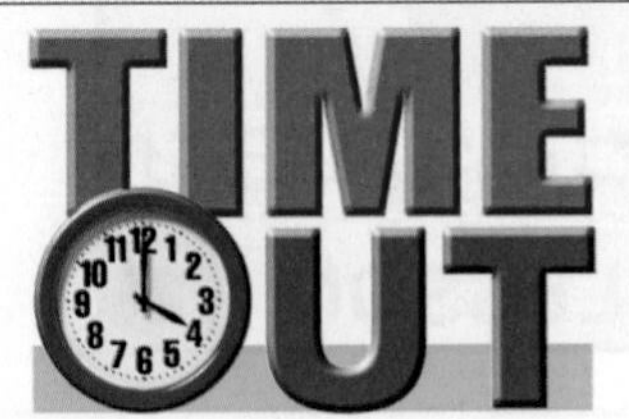

Seventeen percent of the population is considered to be "'Net dropouts." These people once used the Internet but no longer do. Reasons include their frustration with technical problems and Internet connections. Some simply lost interest in the Web.

UNDERSTANDING CONSUMER NEEDS

Consumers use resources (money) to purchase products and services that satisfy their needs and wants. Most people do not have enough money to purchase everything they want. They must gather information and decide if a purchase will provide enough satisfaction to be worth the price.

Needs are those things that are required for you to live. **Wants** are unfulfilled desires. Examples of needs are food that prevents you from starving and shelter that provides you with a safe and comfortable place to live. Many consumers have adequate resources to meet basic needs. Therefore, they don't devote a great deal of time and effort in making decisions about need satisfaction. Instead, they must decide which of their wants are most important and the products and services that will best satisfy these wants. A number of factors influence a consumer's choices.

Consumers usually want to make rational decisions. They will consider several alternatives to determine which is the greatest value. The "greatest value" does not always mean the product with the lowest price. Rather, it is the product that will provide the greatest satisfaction for the cost.

Other factors can make the purchase decision more emotional than rational. Fear, guilt, excitement, or emergency situations may be reasons for selecting a certain product. Personality and self-image have a strong influence on consumer behavior. Also, the social groups to which a person belongs or with which a person wants to identify will affect purchase decisions. Emotional motives are more difficult to predict than rational motives. As you examine everything from a brand's package design to advertising messages, you can see the power of emotions on purchasing decisions.

FEATURES AND BENEFITS

Businesses offer products with a number of features. A **feature** is a specific characteristic of a product. Examples of features for a shirt are the fabric, style, and color. Some features of a product may be quite similar to those of other products. Other features are unique. Businesses design products with features that they believe will best meet customer needs.

Features have little value to consumers unless they see the associated benefits. A **benefit** is the advantage gained from a product feature. Have you ever read the technical descriptions of several computers and wondered what each meant and whether it was important to you? Until you understand the benefit of each feature, it is difficult to choose the computer that is best for you. Businesses must understand customer needs and how their products' features benefit the customer. Then they must communicate those benefits in a way that the customer understands.

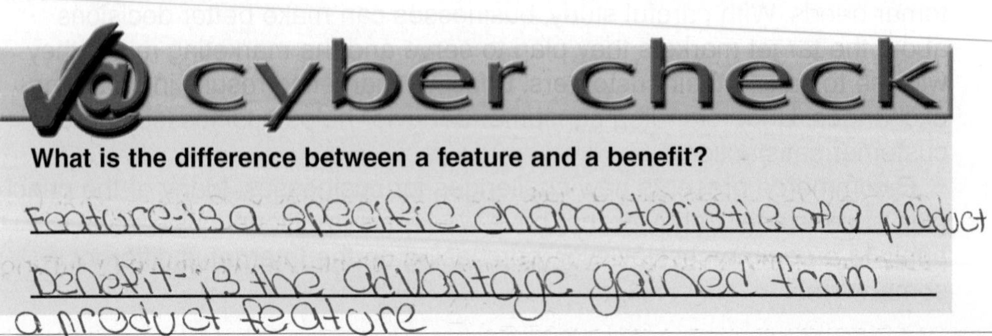

What is the difference between a feature and a benefit?

Feature-is a specific characteristic of a product

benefit- is the advantage gained from a product feature

CONSUMER DECISION MAKING

Consider the most recent product or service that you purchased. How did you decide when and where to make the purchase? What information did you gather? What or who influenced your choice of product and brand? Did you take a long time to reach a decision, or did you make up your mind quickly? Was it a product or service you purchase frequently, infrequently, or once in a lifetime? Consumers follow a consistent five-step sequence when making a purchase decision. Those steps are shown in Figure 7.2.

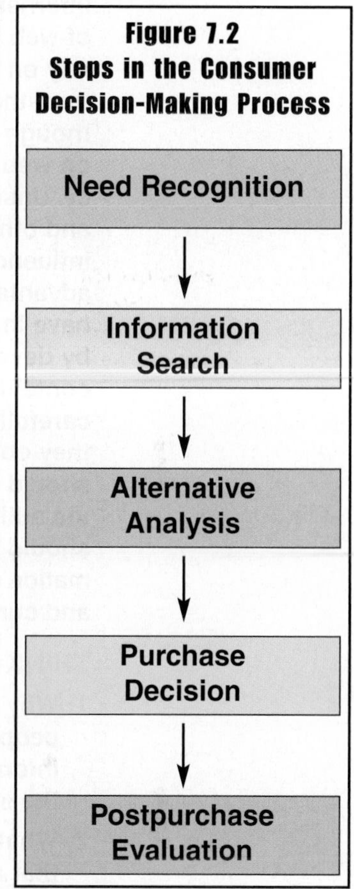

Figure 7.2
Steps in the Consumer Decision-Making Process

1. **Need Recognition** People do not actively look to purchase products or services until they recognize a need for them. You may view many advertisements and not be influenced to make a purchase if the advertised products or services are of no use to you. Yet if the fuel gauge on your car is nearing empty or if you don't have an appropriate outfit to wear to a job interview, you will begin searching for products to meet that need. The importance of the need will determine whether you will immediately begin or delay the search.
2. **Information Search** Once a need is recognized, you will want to find a product or service that meets the need. Information regarding possible choices is necessary. You must determine the sources to use for gathering the needed information. If this need occurs regularly, memory of previous purchases may be all that is required. For a new or significant need, you may look at several sources. You may seek advice from friends and family, review advertisements, and search the Internet. The goal at this stage is to identify possible choices and determine which choices will likely satisfy your need.
3. **Alternative Analysis** Information regarding alternative choices is compared to determine which product or service best meets your need. You will compare features, benefits, availability, cost, and other factors. The evaluation period may take moments, days, or even weeks.
4. **Purchase Decision** Once you are satisfied with the information and evaluation, you will make a choice. You will then complete the steps to purchase your choice if it is available. It is possible that your decision will be to refrain from buying if a good choice or adequate resources are not available.
5. **Postpurchase Evaluation** Once the purchase is made, the decision-making process does not stop. You will continue to evaluate the product or service while it is being used. Does it satisfy your need? If you are satisfied, it is likely that you will purchase the same product or service the next time the need arises. If the purchase isn't as satisfying as expected, it is likely that you will make a different choice the next time. You will also question the information sources and the evaluation process that led to the poor purchase decision.

Dissonance arises after a major purchase, such as a car, when alternatives are recommended or dislikes emerge with the choice. To eliminate the discomfort of dissonance, the consumer will rationalize the choice by finding positive information and ignoring the negative.

E-MARKETING MYTHS

A growing concern with the Internet relates to the credibility of web information. Many people rely on information they obtain from the World Wide Web even though there are few controls on web content and its accuracy. Unscrupulous businesses and others often attempt to influence opinions. They take advantage of the trust people have in Internet information by developing biased or false content. Web users need to carefully evaluate information they obtain from the Web. They should consider the source and the authority of the source. They should also examine the information's accuracy, objectivity, and currency.

THINK CRITICALLY

1. **Why do you think many people trust the accuracy of information they obtain on the Internet?**
2. **What evidence might indicate that an information source is not reliable?**

TYPES OF DECISION MAKING

The consumer decision-making process is followed for all purchase decisions. People will spend different amounts of time moving through each step. Those differences result from the importance of the need and the availability of product choices and information. The costs of the choices and the risk felt by the consumer in making the decision are also factors. Decisions may be divided into three types—routine, limited, and extensive.

Routine Decisions For products that are purchased frequently and require little information, consumers move through the decision-making steps quickly and with little thought. The consumer will often choose the same brand again and again. Likewise, the consumer may find several brands satisfying and pick the one that is readily available. Examples of routine purchases are groceries, gasoline, fast food, and newspapers.

Limited Decisions If a product is more expensive or complex, the consumer may take additional time and be more thoughtful in reaching a decision. An extensive information search and evaluation will occur. Products that require limited decision making are those purchased infrequently or those unfamiliar to the consumer. Examples of products requiring limited decision making are jewelry, cellular telephones, Internet service providers, and meals at expensive restaurants.

Extensive Decisions When an important or first-time purchase is made, extensive decision making will usually occur. The consumer will carefully go through each step of the decision-making process. The consumer may thoroughly gather information. The consumer may then discuss alternatives with others or seek expert advice. Much time may be spent considering the final choices before making a purchase decision. Postpurchase evaluation will be important as the consumer decides if the correct decision was made. People use extensive decision making when buying a home, selecting a college, or purchasing an expensive automobile.

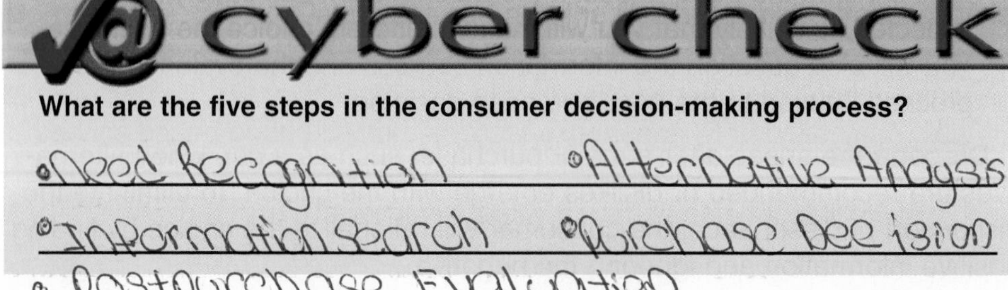

What are the five steps in the consumer decision-making process?

- Need Recognition
- Alternative Analysis
- Information Search
- Purchase Decision
- Postpurchase Evaluation

LOGGING OFF

UNDERSTAND MARKETING CONCEPTS

Circle the best answer for each of the following questions.

1. Which of the following is a benefit rather than a feature?
   a. leather interior
   b. six-speaker stereo system
   c. added safety from side-impact air bags
   d. full-size spare tire
2. Which type of decision making will be used by a consumer who is satisfied with a regularly purchased product?
   a. extensive
   b. routine
   c. limited
   d. repeat

THINK CRITICALLY

Answer the following questions as completely as possible. If necessary, use a separate sheet of paper.

3. **Research** You are gathering information about possible colleges to attend after graduating from high school. Identify five information sources you could use to help analyze your choices. For each source, describe the type of information available and where you can access it. Also, explain why it would be a good source of information.

4. For each type of decision making, identify one product you might purchase. Create a table that lists each product as a column heading. List each step in the consumer decision-making process as a row heading. Within the table cells, explain how you would complete each step in the decision-making process for each product. When you have completed the table, develop a summary that illustrates the differences among the three types of decision making.

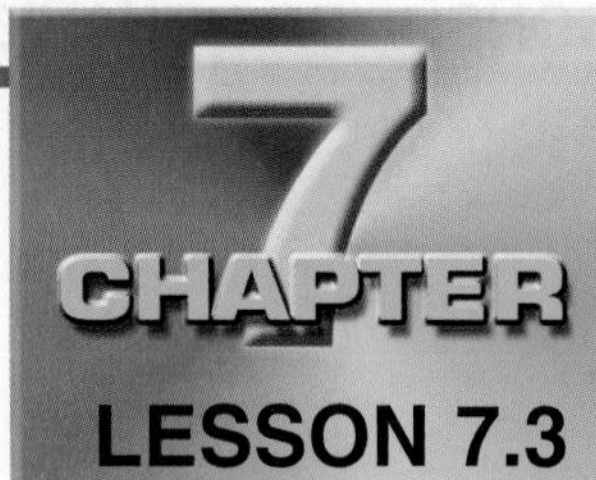

BUILDING VIRTUAL CUSTOMER RELATIONSHIPS

Describe how e-commerce businesses can apply knowledge of consumer behavior.

Identify tools and resources used in e-commerce to build customer relationships.

LOGGING ON

America Online is the world's largest Internet service provider. However, in recent years it has been losing both customers and money. Other online content providers and ISPs have gained strength. AOL is fighting back. Rather than cutting prices, it has decided to improve its software and add specialized services. AOL 9.0 was introduced in 2003 offering better firewalls, virus protection, spam filters, and parental content control. It even offers voice conversation through its instant messaging service. In addition, AOL negotiated deals with entertainment companies. AOL will offer exclusive online performances by musical artists. It will provide previews of upcoming movies and special productions of popular television shows. It also is planning specially designed access areas for children and teens. The areas will include games, chat areas, and music and video clips.

Work with a partner. Discuss why AOL faced increasing competition from other companies. Do you believe the changes AOL is making will result in more customers and higher profits? Why or why not?

SELECTING AND SATISFYING CUSTOMERS

It is important for all businesses to identify prospective customers, understand consumer behavior, and recognize how customers make decisions. Business consumers and final consumers with common characteristics and needs make up target markets. All consumers are attempting to satisfy needs with the purchases they make. They will follow the steps in the consumer decision-making process. They will also use each of the three types of decision making from time to time.

©GETTY IMAGES/PHOTODISC

Principles of consumer behavior can be applied to all businesses and types of products and services, including those on the Internet. E-commerce businesses may find that their target markets are different. Thus, the types and sources of information used by their consumers will vary. Even so, consumer behavior is somewhat predictable. Understanding consumers and their needs allows e-commerce businesses to attract customers and aid them in the decision-making process. The results are satisfied customers and a successful, growing business.

CHARACTERISTICS OF E-COMMERCE CUSTOMERS

The Internet is still an innovative technology. While the number of people using the Internet grows each day, only a small percentage of businesses and final consumers use the Internet for shopping. Of those who do, most do not actually complete the entire purchasing process online. Even people who buy products on the Internet make only a small percentage of their total purchases online.

If you started an e-commerce business, what would be the characteristics of your target market? Do you know the demographic and psychographic descriptions of people who use the Internet and those who don't? How would you decide whether to attempt to serve international markets rather than just those in your own country? What information would you provide? Which communication methods and tools would be most effective for helping customers through the decision-making process?

MARKETING INFORMATION MANAGEMENT

Abundant research has been completed in the attempt to understand who is using the Internet. Much of that research is available on the Internet. It can be used by businesses to make segmenting decisions about their customers.

Would you buy a used car on the Internet? eBay not only is one of the top 15 retailers in the United States but surprisingly is the largest used-car dealer as well.

Internet Consumers The typical U.S. Internet user is young, Caucasian, employed, well educated, and a suburban dweller with above-average income. Almost as many females as males regularly use the Internet. African-American and Hispanic usage rates are lower than average. However, they are increasing at a faster rate than that of Caucasian users. The lowest participation rates are found in the youngest (under 13) and oldest (over 65) age groups.

Internationally, the United States currently has more Internet users, but U.S. growth is much slower than in many other countries. People in Sweden, Hong Kong, the Netherlands, and Australia have the highest level of computer ownership and usage. They also have the greatest percentage of computers connected to the Internet. Spain and the countries of central and eastern Europe are viewed as high-potential Internet markets for the next ten years.

People who purchase online are characterized as innovators and risk takers. They are interested in new products, services, and ideas. They want to be viewed by others as trend setters and opinion leaders.

People who are less likely to purchase products online have greater needs for safety and security. They take longer to complete the decision-making process. They want to be viewed as making good economic decisions.

Decision-Making Process Today, the majority of Internet users are online for the purposes of gathering information, communicating with others, and enjoying entertainment. This scenario suggests that most Internet shoppers are in the second step of consumer decision making—the information search. However, their interest in communicating with others online can be helpful in the later steps of alternative analysis and postpurchase evaluation.

Fewer Internet shoppers are in the purchase decision step because they are uncomfortable with making online purchases. They may want an alternative method of purchasing. They also may need support and confidence in completing an online purchase. The average online consumer makes a relatively small number of purchases, spends less than $100 online per year, and is most likely to purchase familiar, low-cost products. People with annual incomes exceeding $100,000 purchase more than five times as much online per year and usually buy more expensive items.

Why are the majority of Internet users online today?

for gathing information, communicating with others and enjoying entertainment

VIRTUAL TOOLS AND RESOURCES

E-commerce businesses must choose appropriate tools and resources to gather consumer information and provide information to potential and current customers. The right tools are needed to interact with customers and provide easy and secure online shopping. An understanding of consumer behavior is critical in order to make these choices.

Target Markets Businesses need information to identify the best market segments for their products. Companies can purchase research from other businesses or can conduct their own marketing research. Online surveys and other marketing research tools will help to gather needed information. Additionally, businesses can use software to track consumer interactions, such as customer purchases and customer service requests, with their web sites. The data will help to identify the best market segments for the companies' e-commerce activities.

Consumer Decision-Making Steps Many people are active Internet users. E-commerce companies can help them move through each step of the decision-making process.

1. **Need Recognition** Carefully placed advertising, the development of information portals, and effective use of search engines will help consumers clarify needs and connect products and services to those needs. Internet businesses should develop sponsorships of frequently visited web sites that are related to their products.

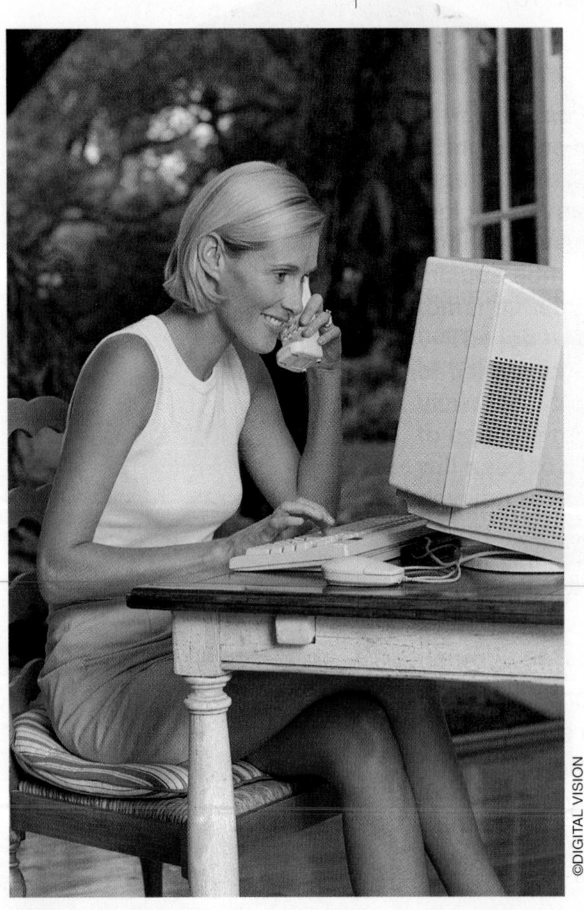

©DIGITAL VISION

2. **Information Search** Well-organized web sites and answers to frequently asked questions are useful to consumers as they gather information. E-mail access and live chats with customer service representatives are also helpful. Carefully prepared communications using understandable language will make the information more meaningful. Relationship sites and online communities allow interested customers higher levels of involvement when gathering information. The sites might provide chat groups, interactive product demonstrations, streaming video, and testimonials from satisfied customers.

3. **Alternative Analysis** E-commerce businesses can aid in the evaluation of alternatives by providing brand comparison information. Comparisons should include important features and benefits as well as price information. Favorable product evaluations and tests that have been completed by government agencies or consumer groups can be incorporated into or accessed from the businesses' web sites.

4. **Purchase Decision** The most critical step in consumer decision making for e-commerce businesses is the purchase decision. Most Internet users do not make purchases online. Even when customers begin an online purchase, over half end the process before completing the order. The purchasing procedure must be quick and easy. Incentives such as coupons or free shipping may be offered to encourage purchase completion. Above all, customers must be assured that the company is a legitimate business and that all personal information submitted is protected. Orders must be processed and delivered efficiently. Adequate customer service and support should be readily available.

5. **Postpurchase Evaluation** An important method of satisfying customers and building long-term loyalty is postpurchase support. Customers should be sent confirmations that their orders were received and are being processed. If there are any delays due to backorders, customers should be notified and given estimated availability times. When orders have shipped, customers should be alerted to expect delivery. After product delivery, businesses should make contact to ensure that the products met the customers' needs. Customer databases should be maintained to allow for periodic follow-up. Follow-up may include tips on product maintenance and use, information on new products, and encouragement for customers to stay in contact.

VIRTUAL VIEWPOINTS

The Internet can do more than offer a new way for businesses to sell products. It can also improve customer service. One company that sells medical equipment links each machine sold to one of its own computers via the Internet. Its computers monitor the performance of each customer's machine. Equipment problems can be spotted and a repairperson sent out before the machine actually breaks down. Customer satisfaction has never been higher. The high level of customer service has saved the company over $1 million annually.

THINK CRITICALLY

1. **Why would customers want a monitoring service such as the one described above when purchasing medical equipment?**
2. **What security concerns or other issues might customers have if a company has continuous Internet access to their equipment's performance? Would you be willing to give a company that sells you a computer or cell phone this type of access? Why or why not?**

List three tools and resources that e-commerce businesses can use to help build customer relationships.

• need Recognition • Alternative Analysis

• Information Search

WORKING ONLINE

Jasahn is an *online community facilitator* for a consumer products company. He is responsible for developing and managing a web site that will attract the interest of potential and current customers for one of the company's product categories. The main goal of the online community site is to increase product sales and customer loyalty for the company's brands. Another important goal is to encourage loyal users to recommend the company and its products to others.

Jasahn works with the company's product managers to gather information. He reviews product advertisements and helps develop special offers and incentives available only to online community members. An important early activity that Jasahn completed was to serve as an advisor to the web design team that developed the community web site. Several unique technologies were used to offer audio and video content to visitors. Jasahn helped create an interesting and easy-to-use chat room. He developed ways to deliver online surveys and to maintain a database that tracks web site participation. Along with several assistants, Jasahn manages the online community web site. He posts questions to customers, asks for product feedback, and encourages discussions. He seeks and provides information to community members. He also keeps the web site up to date and interesting.

To prepare for his career, Jasahn completed a communications degree with an emphasis in technical writing. He also took several marketing courses while in college. As a college student, he held a part-time job as a telephone survey specialist for a marketing research company. After graduating, Jasahn accepted an entry-level position in the advertising department of his current employer. After two years, he became a copywriter for Internet advertising. When the company decided to develop several online communities, Jasahn was asked to head the development and management of one of them.

THINK CRITICALLY

1. **Why would a company spend the time and money to develop and manage online communities rather than let consumers develop their own online interest groups?**
2. **What do you believe are the most important skills needed by an online community facilitator to ensure that a company's goals for an online community are met?**

LOGGING OFF

UNDERSTAND MARKETING CONCEPTS

Circle the best answer for each of the following questions.

1. Which of the following does *not* apply to the average U.S. Internet user?
   a. middle income
   b. higher-than-average education
   c. suburban dweller
   d. young
2. Which is the most critical step in the consumer decision-making process for e-commerce businesses?
   a. information search
   b. alternative analysis
   c. purchase decision
   d. postpurchase evaluation

THINK CRITICALLY

Answer the following questions as completely as possible. If necessary, use a separate sheet of paper.

3. Identify three products that you believe would be more likely purchased by active Internet users than by people who do not regularly use the Internet. Use demographic and psychographic information to describe why frequent Internet users would be a better target market for the three products.

____

____

____

____

____

4. **Communication** Choose a product that you believe could be sold effectively using the Internet. Using a word-processing program, create a two-column, six-row table. Label the left column "Product Features." Label the right column "Customer Benefits." Complete the table by listing five important features of the product in the left column. For each feature, use the right column to write a description of how the feature benefits the customer.

____

____

____

____

CHAPTER 7 REVIEW

REVIEW E-COMMERCE MARKETING CONCEPTS

Write the letter of the term that matches each definition. Some terms will not be used.

- a. benefit
- b. business consumers
- c. consumer behavior
- d. dissonance
- e. emotional decisions
- f. feature
- g. final consumers
- h. innovation
- i. market segment
- j. needs
- k. rational decisions
- l. wants

K 1. Based on facts and logic

A 2. The advantage gained from a product feature

E 3. Based on feelings, beliefs, and attitudes

H 4. A new and unique product, process, or idea

I 5. A group of individuals within a larger market who share one or more important characteristics resulting in similar purchasing needs and behaviors

J 6. Those things that are required for you to live

L 7. Unfulfilled desires

F 8. A specific characteristic of a product

C 9. The study of how people make decisions about the purchase and use of products and services

Circle the best answer.

10. The lifeblood of a business is
    - a. new products.
    - b. competition.
    - c. customers.
    - d. sales.
11. Final consumers are more likely than business customers to make
    - a. emotional decisions.
    - b. innovative decisions.
    - c. rational decisions.
    - d. economical decisions.
12. The first step in the consumer decision-making process is
    - a. alternative analysis.
    - b. postpurchase evaluation.
    - c. information search.
    - d. none of the above
13. The last step in the consumer decision-making process is
    - a. alternative analysis.
    - b. postpurchase evaluation.
    - c. information search.
    - d. none of the above

THINK CRITICALLY

14. What are the advantages of a business focusing its efforts on a smaller target market whose members have similar characteristics and needs? How is this better than targeting a much larger, unsegmented market that has a variety of characteristics and needs?

15. If a business has a large number of satisfied customers prior to e-commerce expansion, do you think those same consumers will become satisfied e-commerce customers? Why or why not?

16. Do you believe it is important to differentiate between prospective customers' needs and wants? Justify your answer. If consumers have both unsatisfied needs and unsatisfied wants, which do you think they will be most concerned about satisfying? Explain.

17. Using your own experience with purchasing products and services, do you believe that people follow all the steps outlined in the consumer decision-making process? Support your answer by describing a recent purchase you made in which all of the steps were or were not followed.

MAKE CONNECTIONS

18. **CRITICAL THINKING** Choose a product that is commonly purchased by many consumers. Develop three distinct target markets for the product. Describe each target market as completely as you can. Identify demographic and psychographic characteristics and product usage differences. Specify important wants and needs related to the product. Indicate the features and benefits that would appeal to each market.

19. **RESEARCH** Many sources of information exist on the Internet that help businesses identify characteristics and purchasing behaviors of prospective business customers and final consumers. Use an Internet search engine to locate three web sites that provide such information. Develop written descriptions of each site, including the URL, the name of the organization that owns the web site, and the type of information available.

20. **DECISION MAKING** The same products can be sold to both final consumers and business customers. The products will have different uses, and different reasons for purchasing will exist. Use word-processing or spreadsheet software to prepare a chart that lists five products purchased by both types of customers. For each product, describe an important use each customer group would have. Then develop one rational reason and one emotional reason that a customer might have for purchasing the product. Identify the type of customer most likely to use each reason to support the purchase decision.

21. **MARKETING MATH** Through its research, a company has identified 895,500 potential customers for one of the products it plans to market using the Internet. Using the percentages listed in Figure 7.1, calculate the number of potential customers that would be in each of the adoption categories for the product. Prepare a chart to illustrate your results.

22. **COMMUNICATION** Visit a business web site for a product you might be interested in purchasing. Review the information provided, the design, and the tools and resources available. Evaluate the web site based on the steps in the consumer decision-making process. Write a report of your evaluation. Describe the strengths and weaknesses of the web site in helping customers complete the decision-making process.

This part of the project will focus on how your business plans to identify its target markets and apply its understanding of consumer behavior.

Work with your team members to complete the following activities.

1. Using available information from the Internet and other sources, develop complete descriptions of at least three possible target markets for your product. One of the target markets should be a business market. Identify which target market is your priority for Internet sales.
2. Complete a features/benefits description for your product. List the important product features and the benefits that customers will obtain from each feature.
3. Identify several rational and emotional reasons people might use to justify the purchase of your product. Determine if your product is likely to be a routine purchase or will require limited or extensive decision making.
4. For each step in the consumer decision-making process, develop one communication resource that can be used on your business's web site to help a customer successfully move through that step. Resources might include an advertisement, a picture or graphic, written information, audio, or video.

CASE STUDY

UPSCALE RESORT PARKS ARE NOT FOR EVERYONE

Southern California's newest luxury resort has palm-lined boulevards, a perfectly manicured golf course in the desert, and six beautiful tennis courts. Five swimming pools, hot tubs, a corral for horses, and hiking trails to the mountains make Rancho California a traveler's paradise. The location offers everything for a perfect getaway—except rooms where guests can sleep. Rancho California is a park for vacationers who travel by recreational vehicle (RV).

Rancho California caters to the wealthiest of RV lovers. Only the best motor homes are allowed to partake in the park's country-club atmosphere. Campsites cost $49 per night. This is more than double the standard rate. Campers get the straightest, cleanest, 18-by-60-foot concrete pads for the $49 rate. Pads are wide and long enough for the largest RVs on the market. Pads are equipped with all the standard hookups and more. Water, sewer, electric, telephone, and cable television are all provided. Twenty feet of perfectly manicured grass separate each of the 594 lots. Winter refugees who want to stay for longer periods of time can rent space by the month for $1,100. Lots also may be purchased for $59,900 to $119,900, depending on location.

The developer, Outdoor Resorts, has built Rancho California for a small but growing subculture of wealthy RVers who break the camping stereotype. This target market drives the most expensive, custom motor homes made by Prevost, the Rolls-Royce of the RV world, and expensive rivals such as Monaco and Country Coach. The RVs cost anywhere from $300,000 to $1.5 million. The rolling suites are fitted with lavish bedrooms, designer kitchens, on-board navigation computers, and satellite televisions that cost $3,500.

The $10-billion RV industry is still growing. RV sales jumped 21 percent in 2002. High-end motor coaches are drawing more customers and more attention from RV-park companies. Luxury retreats are opening near Naples, Florida and Hilton Head, South Carolina.

Not all vacationers with money to burn want the formality of a high-end hotel like the Ritz-Carlton. There are increasing numbers of people who prefer the freedom of wandering America's byways and camping under the stars, even if it means bringing their own king-size bed covered with 300-thread-count linens.

Many of the upscale visitors are older couples who grew up vacationing by camper. Although these individuals have earned large sums of money, they don't want to trade the travel style they know for the expensive resorts of the old-money crowd. Many of the guests are small business owners who worked hard for years to succeed.

Think Critically

1. Why are upscale RV parks becoming increasingly popular?
2. Describe the target markets for upscale RV parks.
3. What special technologies should be offered at these upscale RV parks? Why?
4. How can these properties be effectively marketed over the Internet?

VEHICLES AND PETROLEUM MARKETING ROLE PLAY

Snowbirds flock to Rancho California RV Park. It caters to the needs of wealthy travelers who choose not to stay at luxury hotels. The well-maintained resort includes a golf course, horse stables, hot tubs, tennis courts, paved bike trails, and swimming pools. Rent for RV pads is $49 per night, almost double the amount charged by other RV parks. RV lots can be purchased for approximately $60,000 to $120,000.

You have been hired by Rancho California to help design a service station with all of the latest technologies needed by RV travelers. The service station must be physically attractive for the pristine RV park. You must describe all of the features of this service station. You have also been asked to determine what should be included on a web site for upscale RV travelers.

You have ten minutes to review and determine how you will handle the role-play situation. You will have up to ten minutes to role-play your situation with the park's owner.

Performance Indicators Evaluated

- Define the target market for Rancho California RV Park.
- Understand the importance of Rancho California's RV park's image versus camping stereotypes.
- Describe how a service station can be incorporated into the park, and explain its importance.
- Define the features that should be included on the park's web site.
- Describe how customers will learn about the web site.

Go to the DECA web site for more detailed information.

1. Why is an upscale service station relevant for the Rancho California RV Park?
2. What image must the upscale RV park overcome?
3. Why might it be economically feasible to design a web site for the Rancho California RV Park?
4. What technological services should be offered at the service station? Why?

www.deca.org/publications/HS_Guide/guidetoc.html

CHAPTER 8 PRODUCT AND SERVICE PLANNING

8.1 Traditional and Digital Products
8.2 Product Design and Development
8.3 Legal Protection

©GETTY IMAGES/PHOTODISC

HOW MANY MOVIES CAN YOU WATCH?

What company rents more movies to consumers than either Blockbuster or Hollywood Video? Netflix has been offering videos for rent over the Internet since 1998. Today, it provides videos from its list of 15,000 movie titles to over one million customers each month. Netflix offers the same products as local movie rental stores. However, Netflix provides the videos in a unique way.

Netflix customers pay $19.95 per month. Customers visit the Netflix web site, review movie titles, and select those they would like to order. The company mails up to three movies to a customer at a time. Customers can keep each movie as long as they choose. They can view the movie as many times as they want. When a customer returns a movie, Netflix sends the next movie on the customer's list. Along with each movie, customers are provided a prepaid mailer. The movie can be dropped in the nearest mailbox and returned at no cost.

Netflix says it offers customers more than five times as many video titles as the typical movie rental store. The company also promises to always have the latest video titles as well as classic movies. Over 50 percent of Netflix customers receive their video choices within one day of order placement. Orders are shipped from one of 20 shipping centers the company maintains.

THINK CRITICALLY

1. What advantages and disadvantages does Netflix have compared to a local movie rental store?
2. Assume you own a local movie rental business. How will you compete with Netflix to attract and keep customers?

LESSON 8.1

TRADITIONAL AND DIGITAL PRODUCTS

List the possible unique elements of a product.

Identify examples of digital products and services used in e-commerce.

LOGGING ON

Digital photography has reshaped the market for cameras and film. Companies such as Kodak and Fuji were leaders for many years in the film and photo processing markets. Since the introduction of digital cameras, they have had to rethink the products and services they sell.

A Kodak subsidiary has helped the company transition to the digital market. Ofoto is a full-service, online photographic services company. It was recently named one of the top 50 web sites and also was named "Best Photo Service." Ofoto offers film processing for traditional cameras. It converts the pictures to digital images. The images are placed in an online "photo album" for customers to view.

Customers with digital cameras can use Ofoto software to upload pictures from their computers. The pictures are placed in customers' personal photo albums on the company's web site. Ofoto offers image editing tools so customers can improve colors, crop photos, and add borders and captions. Photos can be shared with family and friends through online access. Customers can convert their photos into calendars, cards, and posters. They can also order film, frames, and photographic gifts from the company.

Work with a partner. Discuss the impact of digital photography on companies such as Kodak and Fuji. What do you believe has made Ofoto a successful e-commerce business? Visit the Ofoto web site. What features have made it one of the top 50 web sites?

DEVELOPING PRODUCTS AND SERVICES

If you are planning to establish an e-commerce business, one of the first questions you must answer is, "Why will customers want to purchase from my business?" In the first years of e-commerce, innovators likely purchased products from an Internet business because of the novelty or convenience. Those reasons are not enough to keep customers returning to a business again and again. The primary reason people purchase from a business is directly related to its products. If a business does not offer products that meet market needs, there will be no reason for customers to purchase from or even visit the business.

To maintain long-term, satisfying relationships with customers, a business must provide a distinct value. A **value** is a business offering that is unique and superior in important ways from similar offerings of other businesses. A value is composed of all elements of the marketing mix. Value begins with the product or service offered by the business.

THE COMPONENTS OF A PRODUCT

The product is one of the four components of the marketing mix. A **product** is all of the tangible and intangible attributes that customers receive when they make a purchase. Most businesses offer products for which there are many substitutes. Competing companies offer the same basic product. If the basic product were all that customers could purchase, it would be difficult to differentiate one company's product from another. Each business provides enhancements to a basic product to make it different from competitors' products and more appealing to customers. Unique elements of a product can include the following.

How do older Americans get online? Through the help of their children! A survey by the American Association of Retired Persons (AARP) found that 78 percent of people surveyed had helped their parents learn how to use a computer. Eighty-seven percent had taught them how to find information online. Nearly 75 percent had helped their parents learn to use e-mail.

THINK CRITICALLY

1. **What are the most important Internet skills you would teach a novice computer user?**
2. **List the steps you would use to teach a first-time computer user how to find a particular web site.**

- **Features** are additions to the basic product that make it more usable. Examples of features for a bicycle are the number of speeds, tire size, frame construction, weight, seat style, and type of brakes.
- **Uses** are alternative ways the product can be utilized. For example, instant messaging software can be used as an alternative to long-distance telephone service. It also can be used for online meetings and discussions by a virtual business team.
- **Brand and image** offer a unique identification for a company's product. The brand's name and artistic treatment can communicate a meaningful image to customers that reminds them of the value of the product. What image do you have of brand names such as Lexus, Microsoft, or Disney?
- **Product quality** is the composition and construction of the product that makes it durable and free of defects. Quality is a particular concern for customers who are spending a great deal of money. Quality is also important to customers who expect to use the product for a long time.

Over 22 million people used online tax-service sites in 2003 to help prepare their tax returns. That was an increase of 15 percent from 2002. The most visited tax-service site was the U.S. Internal Revenue Service, followed by TurboTax and H&R Block.

- **Packaging** consists of the container and materials in which the product is shipped and stored. Packaging provides protection. It enhances the image of the product with its composition, design, and colors. It also is a communication tool. Packaging conveys information to the customer through words, pictures, and symbols. A package can attract attention. It can even be an important attribute of the product's use. For example, a resealable food container keeps unused portions of a product fresh after the package has been opened.
- **Guarantees** offer protection to the customer in the event the product is defective or fails during use. Companies may refund money, provide a new product, or make repairs as part of the guarantee.
- **Customer service** involves after-sale support. This support includes delivery, setup, training, technical help, and repair services.

OFFERING SERVICES

In addition to or instead of products, some companies offer services to customers. **Services** are activities of value that do not result in the ownership of anything tangible. They are exchanged directly between the producer and consumer. Services are consumed at the time they are produced. Examples of traditional service businesses are banks, travel agencies, lawn care businesses, vehicle repair centers, hospitals, schools, and legal firms. Entertainment, transportation, and public utilities are all services with high consumer demand.

Some of the most successful e-commerce businesses are service providers. eBay offers an auction service. Expedia is a travel planning and purchasing site. Lending Tree connects consumers interested in borrowing money with preselected lenders.

©GETTY IMAGES/PHOTODISC

As with products, companies must find ways to make services unique and valuable for their customers. People perform services or operate and maintain the equipment and other resources used to produce and deliver the services. The preparation, skill, and commitment of service personnel are essential to the businesses' success.

Some services are **homogeneous**, meaning they are offered in the same way each time a customer orders them. The same procedures are followed each time a movie is shown in a theater, a customer uses a bank's ATM, or an airfreight company delivers products for a business. Other services are **heterogeneous**, meaning there might be significant differences in the type of service and method of delivery for each customer. Examples include legal services, medical services, architectural design, and repair services for complex equipment.

One of the most difficult issues facing service businesses is the ability to match availability with customer demand. A company can produce a large number of products in advance and have them on hand to meet customer needs. However, personnel must be available to produce services at the exact time customers have a need for them. Depending on the service, demand may fluctuate greatly from day to day or throughout the day. If more personnel are available than needed to meet customer demand, business costs will be excessive compared to revenues. If customer needs exceed the resources of the service business, the demand cannot be met and business will be lost. If customers contact a helpdesk and have to wait 30 minutes for service, they will likely be quite dissatisfied. Service businesses must balance resources with demand at all times in order to be successful.

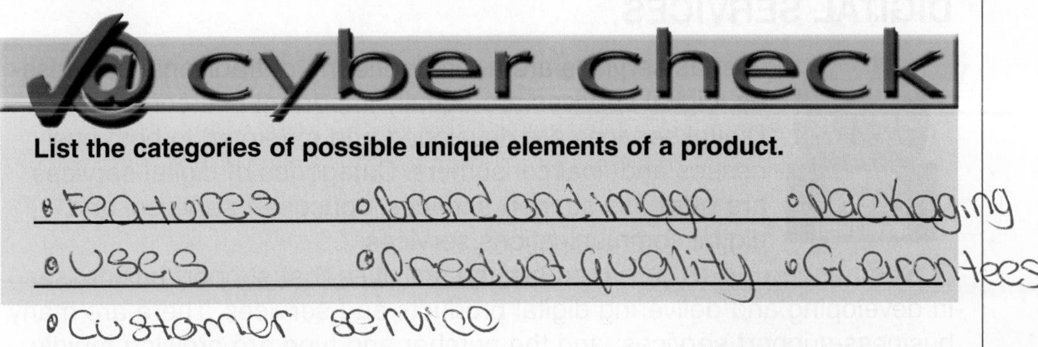

List the categories of possible unique elements of a product.

• Features • brand and image • packaging
• Uses • Product quality • Guarantees
• Customer service

DIGITAL PRODUCTS AND SERVICES

Digital technology has allowed businesses to develop a new generation of products and services. Digital technology allows the conversion of data, graphics, text, sound, or video into electronic signals that can be transmitted and stored. The digital data can then be consumed through technologies such as digital television, cellular telephones, or computer monitors. They also can be converted back into nondigital products such as photographs and printed text.

The conversion of traditional products into digital formats allows for easier and more rapid distribution. Customers can access and use those products through computers and other digital technologies. Movies, audio recordings, photographs, and documents such as tickets for entertainment and travel are now being digitized. Consumers can read newspapers and magazines online, review bank records, and send electronic copies of resumes for job applications.

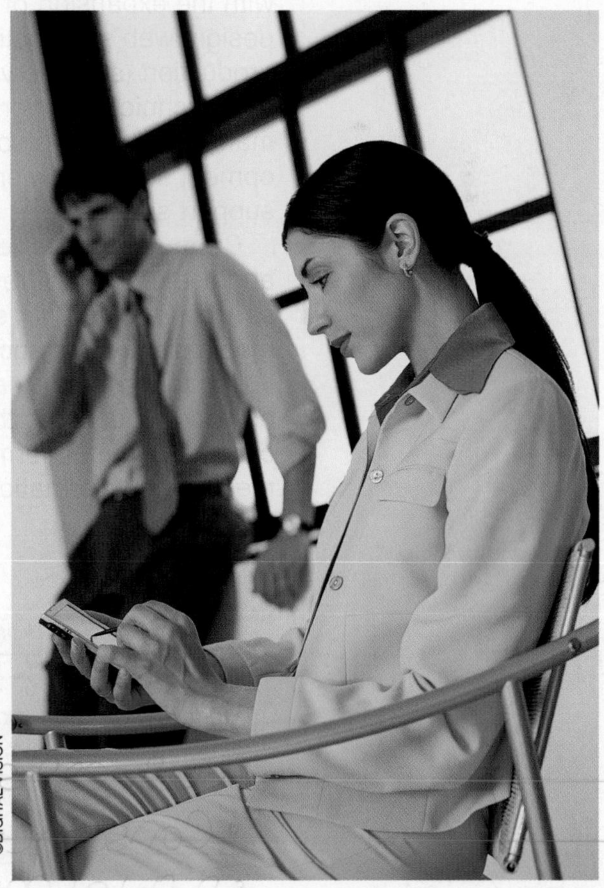
©DIGITAL VISION

DIGITAL PRODUCTS

Companies develop and market a variety of digital products. Those products are designed for both business and consumer markets. Two categories of digital products are content and technology.

Digital content consists of information in digital format including video, audio, text, and graphics. The content is converted to business and consumer products such as newspapers, magazines, online games, photos, graphics, and videos.

Digital technology is the equipment used by businesses and consumers to develop, store, distribute, and use digital content. The technology ranges from digital video and audio equipment to cellular telephones, personal digital assistants (PDAs), and computer software.

DIGITAL SERVICES

Just as services are a major offering of traditional businesses, digital services are equally important in e-commerce. Digital services are developed and marketed to both businesses and final consumers. Categories of digital services are business-support services, consumer services, and digital communications services.

Business-support services are the activities that support businesses in developing and delivering digital products and services. There are many business-support services, and the number and type are growing rapidly with the expansion of e-commerce. Business-support services include web design, web site hosting and management services, and digital content production (such as video, audio, and multimedia development). Data storage, technical support services, and online order processing and payment management are also examples of business-support services. The development and placement of digital advertising is an important business-support service.

Consumer services are the activities that support consumer access to and use of Internet resources and digital information. Common consumer services are Internet service providers (ISPs), information portals, and media distributors such as digital television and radio stations.

Digital communications services provide management of the technology and procedures that support business and consumer virtual communications. Common forms of virtual communications include e-mail, instant messaging, information centers, and online communities.

Describe several examples of digital products and services.

- Business-support services
- Consumer services
- Digital communications services

LOGGING OFF

UNDERSTAND MARKETING CONCEPTS

Circle the best answer for each of the following questions.

1. When developing a value for its customers, a business begins with
   a. the product or service.
   b. a low price.
   c. e-commerce.
   d. all of the above

2. E-mail, instant messaging, information centers, and online communities are examples of
   a. digital products.
   b. business-support services.
   c. virtual communications.
   d. online advertising.

THINK CRITICALLY

Answer the following questions as completely as possible. If necessary, use a separate sheet of paper.

3. Identify three brands of the same product. Prepare a chart that compares the brands using each of the categories of possible unique elements. These categories include features, uses, brand and image, product quality, packaging, guarantees, and customer service. What do you believe is the distinct value offered by each brand?

4. **Communication** It has been suggested that digital technology has increased the quality of and consumer access to products and services while reducing their costs. Develop a one-page analysis of the impact of digital technology on consumers. Provide examples of digital products that support your analysis.

PRODUCT DESIGN AND DEVELOPMENT

Discuss the procedures for new product development.

Identify examples of products and services used by e-commerce businesses.

LOGGING ON

Security of customer information on the Internet is a major issue for businesses, consumers, and the government. People are shopping, banking, and submitting personal information online at an ever-increasing rate. These consumers need assurance that their personal information and online accounts are secure. One method of added security is unique user IDs and passwords for each customer. A drawback to this method is that customers transacting with many businesses must remember multiple names, characters, and numbers. Also, hackers are often still able to illegally obtain customer information.

Companies are developing advanced technologies that provide higher levels of identity security for Internet users. One exciting, new technology is a personal fingerprint scanner that attaches to the user's computer. The scanner looks like a small mouse pad. Rather than typing in an ID and password, the user places his or her index finger on the scanner. Using installed software, the scanner recognizes the user's fingerprint. It then communicates the correct ID and password to the Internet site being accessed.

Work with a partner. Discuss whether you believe consumers will accept this type of identity security. What are the advantages and limitations of this technology for consumers and for businesses?

NEW PRODUCT DEVELOPMENT

Thousands of new products are introduced by businesses each year. Only a limited number are "new to the world." **New-to-the-world products** are being offered for the first time and have never been seen by consumers. When the first personal computer was introduced, it was new to the world, as was the first television set. New-to-the-world products often are widely publicized because they are innovative and unique. For example, the personal transporter is a two-wheeled mobile transportation device developed by Segway. It has been featured in various news articles on television and in magazines since its introduction in 2003.

Most new products are "new to the company." **New-to-the-company products** are offered for the first time by a company but are familiar to consumers. When Sony introduced its first cellular telephone and Handspring offered its first personal digital assistant (PDA), each of the products was a new model of already-existing technology familiar to many consumers.

NEW PRODUCT SUCCESS

The success rate for new products is low. As few as ten percent of new products introduced ever become profitable. The cost of new product development is high. It is not unusual for a company to invest several million dollars to develop a new product and bring it to market. Those millions are lost if the product is not successful. Companies search for ways to improve the chances of new product success.

Companies face increasing time pressures to develop and market new products. In the past, companies may have taken several years to study and plan for a new product introduction. Today, companies must complete new product development activities in well under a year. Otherwise, they will risk losing out to competitors who are able to get the new product to consumers much faster. Speed must be balanced with attention to quality. If consumers purchase a new product and find it to be problematic, they will likely turn to a competitor for their next purchase. It is important for companies to follow a product development procedure that will result in a successful new product introduction in a timely fashion.

3M has been an innovative company since it started in 1902. It has introduced hundreds of new products including sandpaper, cellophane tape, and Post-it® Notes. To encourage innovations, employees are allowed up to 15 percent of their work time to experiment with new ideas.

PRODUCT DEVELOPMENT PROCEDURE

Product development is a complex process involving all aspects of a business. Once a product idea is developed, the company needs to determine if it can be produced. If production is possible, the company must gather the resources needed and develop financial and marketing plans. The company must then coordinate all of the activities and people involved.

A product development procedure should be in place to ensure that proper steps are coordinated and completed. The procedure should include checkpoints when the project is assessed. At those times, decisions are made whether to continue development or stop the process before additional time and resources are used. The major steps in the new product development procedure are outlined in Figure 8.1.

1. **Generate Innovative Ideas** New product ideas come from many sources. The two primary sources of ideas are research conducted by scientists and engineers within the company and input gathered from current and prospective customers. Businesses can also study competitors' products to obtain new ideas.

©DIGITAL VISION

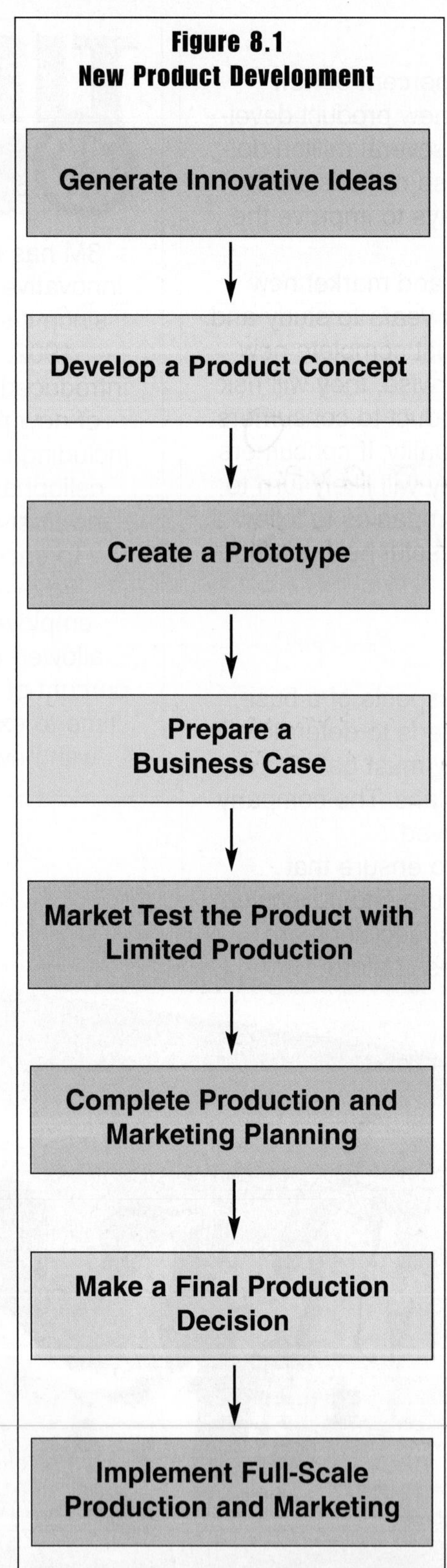

Figure 8.1
New Product Development

2. **Develop a Product Concept** Not all ideas become products. It may not always be possible to develop an actual product from the research of scientists or the needs of customers. Moving from an idea to an actual product requires a combination of creative planning (What would the new product do?) and engineering planning (Could an actual product really do that?).
3. **Create a Prototype** When a product concept has been approved, a *prototype* or product model is created. Creation of a model allows the company to determine the actual design, materials, and production processes required. The prototype is tested to determine its quality and durability. It may be used in consumer research to determine customers' reactions to the new product.
4. **Prepare a Business Case** Before going forward with production, a company needs adequate evidence that the product can be financially successful. Company experts in production, marketing, and finance must work together to prepare a business case. A **business case** is an objective analysis that determines if projected sales and profits justify the estimated expenses of the new product.
5. **Market Test the Product with Limited Production** Prior to full-scale production, the company may market test the new product. The actual product is produced in limited quantities. The test run confirms the time and cost of production, and the production process is refined as necessary. The product is then offered for sale in a small market area. A market test helps to determine customer response to the marketing mix, including the product's price.
6. **Complete Production and Marketing Planning** Based on the market test, final production and marketing planning are completed. Personnel are prepared for full-scale implementation.
7. **Make a Final Production Decision** The company uses all of the information collected to this point to decide whether to move forward with the product. While a great deal of information is available to aid in the decision, there is still some risk involved with any new product.
8. **Implement Full-Scale Production and Marketing** If all planning and testing are successful and the production decision is positive, the company moves the product into its product line. Production and sales may be small at first. The company must be prepared to increase production and marketing efforts as the market grows and competition increases.

Each step of the process is important to the development of a successful new product. At the completion of each step, a company may assess the information gathered and make a decision to halt development. For example, the company may realize that it cannot produce the envisioned product at a cost below what customers are willing to pay. If a product successfully passes each step in the process, the chances of financial success are greater.

List the steps in the new product development procedure.

- Generate innovative ideas
- Develop a product concept
- Create a prototype
- Prepare a business case
- Market test the product with limited
- Complete production and mar
- Make a final production
- Implement full-scale

DEVELOPING PRODUCTS FOR E-COMMERCE

The development of personal computers, the Internet, and digital technology has generated opportunities for new products. Many existing products can be marketed more widely to prospective customers. Additionally, many new-to-the-world products have been developed as a result of recent technologies. As with traditional products, the success rate of new technology products has been low. As new e-commerce products failed, many of the e-commerce businesses developed to produce and market those products failed as well. Most companies that successfully moved through the first decade of e-commerce have identified activities important for developing digital products and services. The companies have also mastered the use of digital technologies that support effective e-commerce.

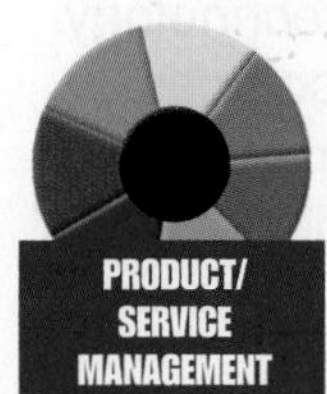

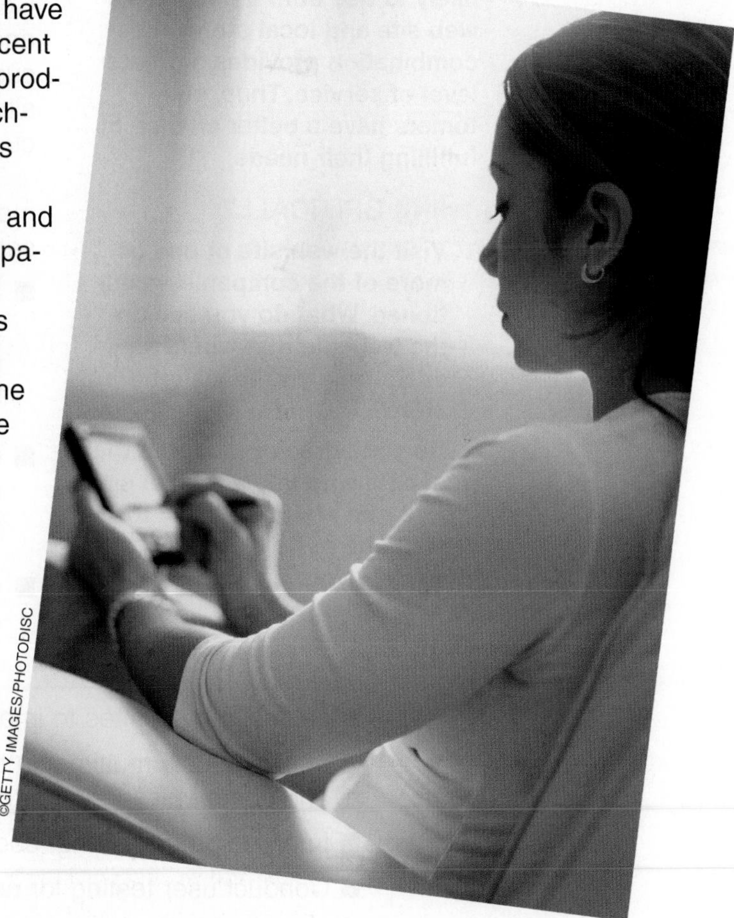
©GETTY IMAGES/PHOTODISC

DIGITAL TECHNOLOGIES

Many new products and services exist as a result of the development of digital technologies. The products replace or improve on traditional technologies. They provide support for and improve the use of the Internet and wireless communications. There are a number of areas of digital technology product and service development.

- Digital hardware development
- Network systems design

E-MARKETING MYTHS

Some traditional retailers are concerned that offering online sales through an Internet site will reduce sales in their stores. However, if managed well, Internet sites can actually increase in-store traffic. A report by Nielsen Research rated the retailers who had successfully integrated online and in-store shopping. Coach led the list. Consumers who visited the Coach web site were 27 times more likely to visit a Coach store than the average Internet user. Coach was followed by Neiman Marcus, J. Crew, Bloomingdale's, and Williams-Sonoma. The research concluded that consumers are more likely to use both a business's web site and local store. The combination provides a greater level of service. Thus, customers have a better chance of fulfilling their needs.

THINK CRITICALLY

1. **Visit the web site of one or more of the companies mentioned. What do you see on the web site that would encourage you to visit the store?**
2. **Do you agree or disagree that people who use a retailer's web site are more likely to visit one of its stores? Explain your answer.**

- Database development, management, storage, and analysis
- Web design, authoring, and programming
- Visual, graphic, audio, and multimedia technology and design
- Security systems and security services
- Systems management services
- Customer support services

IMPROVING E-COMMERCE SERVICES

Many consumers are slow to complete online purchase transactions because the web sites of some businesses are hard to navigate and the technology used is unreliable. Individuals are reluctant to buy a new product using an unfamiliar procedure on the Internet. First, the customer must trust the company. Second, the customer must believe the product is better than those available from traditional sources. Third, the customer must feel comfortable and secure with the purchasing procedures and technology. Companies devote a great deal of resources and expertise to understanding and meeting customers' needs. Companies must design web sites that are user-friendly with procedures that customers can trust.

There are several important product development activities that can improve e-commerce services for customers.

- Study average consumer technology skills and Internet usage experience. Avoid using complex technologies that are beyond the average customer's ability and comfort level.
- Gather customer input about current web design, usage problems, and ideas for improvement of the web site.
- Organize development teams that combine expertise in hardware and software, production, marketing, finance, and customer service.
- Redesign web sites to improve access, reliability, and security.
- Integrate new multimedia technologies into web sites to improve interest and communication and to provide more realistic product models.
- Improve programming, coding, and technology integration for web sites.
- Conduct user testing for new technology and web site modifications.

Figure 8.2 E-Commerce Products and Services

E-Commerce Business Type	Important Products and Services
Brokers—bring buyers and sellers together to facilitate exchanges. Examples—auctions, product distributors, search agents.	Databases, search engines, search robots, payment systems, security systems, customer communications, helpdesks
Promotion and Communication Services—provide media advertising and develop content and customer communications. Examples—portals, classified advertising, user registrations, paid search placement, web-based advertising technology	Banner ads, animation, interactive advertising, customer registration, pop-up technologies, search robots, web usage analysis technology, portal management
Manufacturers—provide the company's products directly to consumers. Examples—product sales, leasing, software licensing	Digital and traditional products, mass customization, product content, sales services, customer support
Retailers—accumulate the products and services of many manufacturers for sale to customers. Examples—virtual malls, e-tailers, mail-order and catalog sales	Web catalogs, sales and customer management systems, supply-chain management technology
Subscription Services—offer access to digital products and content on a subscription or pay-for-use basis. Examples—online newspapers and magazines, relationship sites, music and video distributors, library services, ISPs, web-based software access, data storage	Audio, video, graphics and multimedia technologies, virtual communications tools, usage monitoring and management technologies

E-COMMERCE APPLICATIONS

Many types of e-commerce businesses have emerged as a result of digital technologies. Figure 8.2 describes these e-commerce businesses and the products and services they use.

Describe several ways that marketing activities are completed using the Internet.

•Database development, mangement, storage, and analysis •Web design, authoring and programing
•visual, graphic, audio, and multimedic technology and design
•security system and security services

LOGGING OFF

UNDERSTAND MARKETING CONCEPTS

Circle the best answer for each of the following questions.

1. New products that have never been seen by consumers are
   a. new design models.
   b. new-to-the-world products.
   c. e-commerce technology.
   d. new-to-the-company products.
2. The type of e-commerce business that accumulates the products and services of many manufacturers for sale to customers is a
   a. subscription service.
   b. broker.
   c. promotion and communication service.
   d. retailer.

THINK CRITICALLY

Answer the following questions as completely as possible. If necessary, use a separate sheet of paper.

3. **Technology** Use the Internet to locate at least three web sites that provide information on new digital products. Describe the type of information provided and the technologies used to communicate product information.

4. **Research** Use the Internet to locate a research report on the level of customer satisfaction with the Internet. Prepare a written summary of the findings. Include one table or graph.

LEGAL PROTECTION

LOGGING ON

Because of the digital technology on which the Internet is based, music files can be downloaded onto a personal computer and played in their original quality. Initially, the process of finding and downloading music files was not easy. Then Shawn Fanning, a college student, wrote a simple computer program that searched the Web for music files and indexed them.

Shawn's uncle helped him form a company. Through word of mouth, Napster was an immediate hit. The company attracted over $12 million in venture capital and over 80 million registered users. The recording industry was horrified, feeling that free music sharing would result in the end of music sales. The industry filed numerous lawsuits that ultimately resulted in a court order to stop Napster's activities. Napster subsequently filed bankruptcy. However, online file sharing continues today through individuals and other companies.

Work with a partner. Discuss the effects on industry professionals of unrestricted sharing of music and videos. If you made your living as a musician or an author, what protection would you want for your creative works?

Describe the legal protection available to creators of intellectual property.

Discuss recent laws and guidelines for e-commerce businesses.

INTELLECTUAL PROPERTY RIGHTS

A business invests months of time and many thousands of dollars to develop a new product. If that product could be immediately copied and marketed by competitors, there would be little incentive for the company to make the investment. Suppose you have an idea for a new product. You devote personal time and effort to develop the idea. You commit personal finances to open a business to market the new product. It would be unfair for a larger business to take the idea and use its size and resources to compete against you.

©GETTY IMAGES/PHOTODISC

Individuals and businesses have legal protection for intellectual property they create and own. **Intellectual property** results from creative thinking and may include products, services, processes, and ideas. Intellectual property is protected from misappropriation. *Misappropriation* is taking the intellectual property of others without due compensation and using it for monetary gain.

The U.S. Patent Office's web site provides weekly lists of patents that were granted. The lists give interesting insight into recent inventions and possible forthcoming products. Pictures of the inventions are shown.

FORMS OF LEGAL PROTECTION

Legal protection is provided for the owners of intellectual property. The three common types of legal protection are patents, copyrights, and trademarks.

Patents provide exclusive use of inventions. If the U.S. Patent Office grants a patent, it is confirming that the intellectual property is unique. The patent prevents others from making, using, or selling the invention without the owner's permission for a period of 20 years.

Copyrights are similar to patents except they are applied to artistic works. A copyright protects the creator of an original artistic or intellectual work, such as a song or a novel. A copyright gives the owner exclusive rights to copy, distribute, display, or perform the work. The copyright prevents others from using and selling the work. The length of a copyright is typically the lifetime of the author plus an additional 70 years.

Trademarks are words, names, or symbols that identify ownership of a product and distinguish it from the similar goods of others. A servicemark is similar to a trademark but is used to identify services. A trademark prevents others from using the identical or a similar word, name, or symbol to take advantage of the recognition and popularity of the brand or to create confusion in the marketplace. Upon registration, a trademark is usually granted for a period of ten years. It can be renewed for additional ten-year periods indefinitely as long as the mark's use continues.

OBTAINING LEGAL PROTECTION

Legal protection is offered at the state, federal, and international levels, depending on where the product, service, or idea is developed and used. For the greatest level of protection, the creator and owner should apply through the appropriate government office.

A patent is obtained from the U.S. Patent and Trademark Office. When an application is filed, it is reviewed by the Office to determine if the item submitted is patentable. The item must meet the definition of invention included in patent law. There cannot be an existing patent for the same type of product, service, process, or idea. Once the patent is granted, the U.S. Patent and Trademark Office maintains a record of the patent. Records can be searched by individuals and businesses who want to avoid legal problems with a new product or service idea.

A trademark or servicemark to be used in interstate or international business should be registered with the U.S. Patent and Trademark Office. A business with a registered trademark uses the symbol ®. A trademark does not have to be registered in order to provide legal protection. However, failure to register may result in using an already registered mark. It also may make a legal claim more difficult against those who misuse the mark.

A copyright registration is obtained from the Copyright Office of the Library of Congress. The symbol for a registered copyright is ©. The author or publisher typically identifies the date of copyright registration on the publication, such as "Copyright © 2005 South-Western." As with trademarks, a work does not have to be registered for legal copyright protection. However, obtaining and publishing the registration makes the owner's rights easier to enforce.

What are the three types of legal protection available to the creators of intellectual property?

• Patents • Copyrights

• Trademarks

PROTECTING LEGAL RIGHTS IN E-COMMERCE

The creators and owners of products, services, and artistic works have the right to dictate how their efforts are distributed and used. They also have the right to be compensated for their efforts if others find that the works have value.

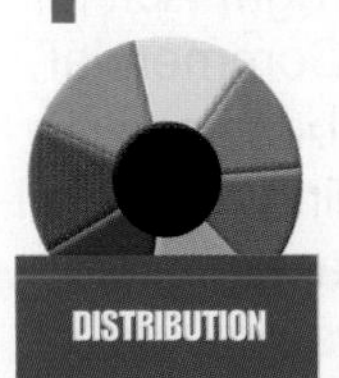

Those rights have been recognized through the development of procedures to obtain protection and laws to provide remedies for violation. The protection of the intellectual property of individuals and businesses is never easy. Owners must be aware if others have misused their property for personal gain. Intellectual property owners must then use the legal system to end the misuse and to gain compensation for any losses.

Digital technology has resulted in the creation of a new generation of products and services. It has made copying of existing products such as books, documents, photographs, videos, and artwork much easier. The duplicates often have the same quality as the originals. The Internet allows instant contact among millions of people, access to thousands of web sites, and relatively easy transfer of digital data. Intellectual property can quickly be accessed, distributed, and used throughout the world.

VIRTUAL VIEWPOINTS

Many people believe that Internet users expect to access music, videos, books, and newspapers at no cost. However, research shows that some consumers are willing to pay a reasonable amount for products and services they consider valuable. The biggest complaint of consumers regarding fees for online content is that there is not an easy, reliable, secure way to make payments.

The prices for online content such as music, articles, or videos often range from less than a dollar to a few dollars for each item purchased. These small fees make it difficult to find an effective way to make online payments. If companies can convince customers that they offer a valuable product with an understandable and safe payment method, they will be able to sell online content.

THINK CRITICALLY

1. **For what types of online content would you be willing to pay? What types of online content do you believe should be free? What are the differences between the types of content you identified?**
2. **What do you believe will happen to the Internet if consumers are unwilling to pay for most online content?**

HISTORIC U.S. LAWS

While the Internet is relatively new, much of the communication and commerce activities on the Internet are not. Historic laws regulating those activities apply to Internet usage and e-commerce.

The original rights for protection of intellectual property were recognized in the U.S. Constitution. Article 1, Section 8 stated, "To protect the progress of science and useful arts, by securing for limited times to authors and inventors the exclusive right to their respective writings and discoveries." The U.S. Congress enacted both the Patent Act and the Copyright Act into law in 1790. The modern patenting process was enacted in the Patent Act of 1952. Current copyright procedures are regulated through the 1976 Revision of the U.S. Copyright Act.

©GETTY IMAGES/PHOTODISC

The Uniform Commercial Code regulates business practices, including the development of contracts, sales, and leases. Laws provide protection for individual privacy and restrict a business from releasing customers' personal information to others without permission. There are also laws protecting the freedom of speech and expression.

CYBERLAW

Some Internet users are not familiar with the forms of legal protection for intellectual property. They may have the impression that if something is placed on the Internet, it is available for the unrestricted use of anyone who can access it. Laws have not kept up with technological changes, so it is not always clear what types of protection are available. There are many pertinent questions related to the legal use of the Internet.

- Can you use the name of a company or product as a domain name on the Internet if you do not own the trademark?
- Can you share any information you find on the Internet with others without the permission of the information's originator?
- Can you hyperlink from your web site to someone else's web site without permission?
- Can a search engine collect information from other sources and provide that information to you?
- Can you print and display graphics and pictures obtained from the Internet?
- Can you copy the program code from an Internet site and use it in the development of your own web page?

Under current law, the following actions are illegal.

- Using a registered trademark you do not own as a domain name for your web site
- Using copyrighted material including text, sound clips, and graphics on your web site without permission of the owners
- Using the web site of another company as a target so visitors to that site will receive a popup of your advertisement
- Downloading copyrighted music, video, or graphics files from a web site for re-use or resale
- Using copyrighted materials that have been illegally obtained by others from the World Wide Web
- Publishing personal information of other individuals on the Web without their permission

Technologies are being developed that help protect businesses from illegal uses of their intellectual property.

- **Encryption software** and other copy protection technologies make it more difficult for Internet users to illegally use programming code or online content.
- **Digital watermarking** embeds owner/author information into video, audio, and graphics files.
- **Secure containers** hold content that can be opened only with electronic keys sent to purchasers of the information.
- **Tracking software** allows information obtained from a web site to be monitored, following the trail of the information from computer to computer.

Digital Millennium Copyright Act Recent laws were passed to respond to issues raised by the development of the Internet. One of the most comprehensive laws is the Digital Millennium Copyright Act of 1998. The act recognizes the importance of copyright protection for information distributed on the Internet. It provides liability protection to Internet service providers if their subscribers violate copyright laws. The act requires ISPs to remove content from users' web sites that clearly violates copyright laws. The act requires anyone who webcasts copyrighted music to pay a licensing fee to recording companies. A controversial part of the law makes it illegal to manufacture equipment or software that can disable or bypass copy protection technologies such as encryption codes and passwords used on software, music, and videos.

Millennium Digital Commerce Act Another important law related to e-commerce is the Millennium Digital Commerce Act of 1999. The act recognizes that electronic signatures are a legitimate way to complete a business agreement or contract. Printed contracts with handwritten signatures are no longer required to complete a business transaction. The provisions of a contract are enforceable when the parties agree to use electronic content and electronic signatures.

Identify two practices of Internet users that are illegal.

using a registerd trademark you donot own as a doman name. • downloading copyright music, video or graphic files

WORKING ONLINE

Jorge opened the envelope from the Product Development & Management Association (PDMA). He was excited about the information in the letter. He had passed the NPDP certification exam and was now a *Certified New Product Development Professional.* The certification qualifies him to apply for a product manager position in his company.

Since graduating from high school eight years ago, Jorge has worked for a national wireless data and telephone company. He worked in telephone sales for three years. Jorge then joined a product development division and participated as a member of several new product teams. For the last year, he has been a team leader reporting directly to a division manager. While continuing to work full time, Jorge completed a number of community college courses in marketing and finance. He recently completed a diploma program in digital technology.

To qualify to take the four-hour, written NPDP exam, Jorge needed five years of professional product development experience in addition to his high school diploma. He was tested in areas such as product development tools and metrics, market research, product development processes, and team and interpersonal skills. The NPDP exam is detailed and technical to ensure that people who are awarded certification are fully qualified to lead product development in their companies. Jorge studied for six months prior to taking the exam and was pleased that all of the hard work paid off. He couldn't wait to share the good news with his family and plan a celebration!

THINK CRITICALLY

1. **What value do certifications offer to people who want to advance in their professions?**
2. **If you were responsible for hiring a new product manager in Jorge's company, would you require applicants to have the NPDP certification? Why or why not?**

LOGGING OFF

UNDERSTAND MARKETING CONCEPTS

Circle the best answer for each of the following questions.

1. A word, name, or symbol that identifies ownership of a product and distinguishes it from the similar goods of others is
   a. a patent.
   b. a copyright.
   c. a trademark.
   d. intellectual property.
2. The rights of individuals to have their inventions and artistic works protected under the law were first recognized in the
   a. U.S. Constitution.
   b. Millennium Digital Commerce Act.
   c. Digital Millennium Copyright Act.
   d. Uniform Commercial Code.

THINK CRITICALLY

Answer the following questions as completely as possible. If necessary, use a separate sheet of paper.

3. **Research** Use the Internet to locate examples of trademarks and copyrights currently used by e-commerce companies. Identify those that use the legal symbol for each and those that do not. Are you able to identify any examples that appear to be illegal uses of names or symbols?

4. **Communication** Consider the statement, "All content on the Internet should be available for free use and distribution by anyone with Internet access." Decide if you agree or disagree with the statement. Prepare a two-page essay stating your position and presenting your reasons for agreement or disagreement.

CHAPTER 8 REVIEW

REVIEW E-COMMERCE MARKETING CONCEPTS

Write the letter of the term that matches each definition. Some terms will not be used.

- a. business case
- b. heterogeneous
- c. homogeneous
- d. intellectual property
- e. new-to-the-company products
- f. new-to-the-world products
- g. product
- h. services
- i. value

C 1. Services offered in the same way each time a customer orders them

G 2. All of the tangible and intangible attributes that customers receive when they make a purchase

E 3. Are offered for the first time by a company but are familiar to consumers

D 4. Results from creative thinking and may include products, services, processes, and ideas

B 5. Services in which there might be significant differences in the type and method of delivery for each customer

F 6. Are being offered for the first time and have never been seen by consumers

A 7. An objective analysis that determines if projected sales and profits justify the estimated expenses of the new product

I 8. A business offering that is unique and superior in important ways from similar offerings of other businesses

Circle the best answer.

9. Services are different from products in that they do not offer ownership of anything
   - a. of value.
   - b. permanent.
   - c. tangible.
   - d. new.
10. Legal protection is provided to owners against the misuse of
    - a. intellectual property.
    - b. digital technology.
    - c. business services.
    - d. none of the above
11. Which of the following provides exclusive use of an invention?
    - a. trademark
    - b. copyright
    - c. patent
    - d. business case

THINK CRITICALLY

12. Do you believe that consumers who are new to buying online are more likely to purchase new, innovative products or common products they have frequently purchased in the past? Justify your answer.

13. The primary reason many consumers buy some types of products is the brand and image. For others, it is the products' features. Describe some products that you believe fit into each of the two categories. What are the differences in the two categories that might affect how people make purchasing decisions?

14. List reasons why new product success rates are low. What should businesses do to increase their success rates for new products?

15. The development of the Internet has made the protection of intellectual property rights more difficult. Provide some reasons that support this statement. Do you believe new laws are needed to increase protection of intellectual property for businesses and individuals? Why or why not?

MAKE CONNECTIONS

16. **MARKETING MATH** The Oldhymer Company is concerned about its new product success rate. In the past three years, the company introduced 83 new products. Only 12 of the products are still being sold, and only 7 are profitable. The average new product success rate in Oldhymer's industry is 18 percent. Calculate the percentage of Oldhymer's products that are still on the market and the percentage that are profitable. How many of Oldhymer's 83 products would need to be successful in order to meet the industry average?

17. **TECHNOLOGY** Use the Internet to locate an example of each of the types of digital products and services—digital content, digital technology, business-support services, consumer services, and digital communication services. For each example, write a short description that identifies why it fits into the specific category.

18. **HISTORY** Conduct research on a product that was new to the world 50 years ago and is still being produced today. Determine who was responsible for its creation. Find information on how the product was developed. Using the Internet or library, locate a drawing or photograph of the original product as well as a photograph of the product as it is currently produced. Identify important ways the product has changed since its invention. Prepare a written report of your research.

19. **DESIGN** Choose a company that sells products and services online. Visit its web site and study it thoroughly. Identify the elements of the site's design that you believe are effective for customer service. Recommend ways the company could improve its site's design. Prepare a poster that illustrates the effective and ineffective features of the web site.

20. **BUSINESS LAW** Search business magazines and newspapers to identify articles and reports on three legal cases related to intellectual property rights. One of the cases should relate to intellectual property rights and the Internet. For each case, prepare a written "brief" that summarizes the reason for the lawsuit, the important facts of the case, the opposing arguments, and the decision of the court.

This part of the project will focus on your business's new product development procedures.

Work with your team members to complete the following activities.

1. Identify five prospective customers for your business. Bring them together as a group for a 30-minute meeting. Have the prospective customers discuss the types of products your company plans to offer, their views of competing products, and their likes and dislikes. Based on the discussion, ask them to offer suggestions for new products they would like to see. If possible, audiotape the meeting. Prepare a written summary of the group's suggestions.
2. Select one new product idea from the customer discussion group. Prepare a detailed outline of the procedures your company will follow to study the feasibility of developing the new product.
3. Using either craft materials or a computer drawing or design program, develop a model of the proposed new product.
4. Develop a chart in which you describe the new product and its major features, possible uses, and product guarantee. Include a description of customer services to be provided, if appropriate. Indicate the brand name you will use. Include an image of the product and its packaging.
5. Complete a study of possible competitors for your new product. Identify similar products and brand names. Ensure that the product you have chosen for your business is not protected by patents, trademarks, or copyrights as the intellectual property of others.

CASE STUDY

DECA PREP

An Association of Marketing Students

EARNING COURSE CREDIT AND COLLEGE DEGREES WITHOUT LEAVING HOME

A competitive workplace that requires continuing education combined with universities faced with budget cuts creates the perfect opportunity for online courses and college degrees.

Students who take online courses pay tuition and purchase books, but they don't attend a traditional class on campus. Online courses allow students to earn college credit and degrees from the comfort of their homes. Students are required to e-mail assignments on time to college instructors. Interactive quizzes may be taken online. Once students hit the submit button, the results are e-mailed to the instructor. Immediate feedback is given to the student.

Students of online courses have the opportunity to communicate with the instructor during scheduled times and days of the week. Chat rooms are set up to allow students to communicate with and learn from one another. Successful online courses require timely feedback from instructors to students.

Most students like the idea of taking classes from home. The flexibility allows students to complete their class work anytime during the day. In many cases, employers encourage the courses and allow employees to access the classes at work.

Not all individuals have the discipline to successfully participate in online courses. Students must take a disciplined approach to complete all tasks on time. Because most online students have busy work schedules, flexibility is generally built into the course structure. Many courses allow automatic grace periods of up to two weeks from the original deadlines for lessons to be completed. After a grace period has passed, the lesson and associated assignments and quizzes are no longer available online.

Instructors enjoy the convenience of teaching classes online. The classes eliminate the need for instructors to get dressed up, drive to campus, and present lessons multiple times in classrooms with limited capacity.

Sometimes universities are tempted to enroll too many students in an online course. Overenrollment makes it difficult for the instructor to communicate with all students and to keep up with all of the assignments.

Think Critically

1. **Why are online college courses and degrees becoming increasingly popular?**
2. **What is one disadvantage of taking an online course?**
3. **What is one advantage of taking an online course?**
4. **Why are more universities turning to online courses?**

FULL-SERVICE RESTAURANT MANAGEMENT ROLE PLAY

Southwest Steakhouse, a major national restaurant chain, has an excellent web site. It includes locations of the restaurants, the complete menu with prices, and hours of operation. The menu prices are in the middle to upper range. Average meals cost $18 to $25 per person for the finest steaks and seafood. Southwest Steakhouse has predominantly operated as a dinner restaurant open from 4 P.M.–12 A.M.

Southwest Steakhouse has decided to expand its market. Two major changes will include offering a lunch menu and an expanded children's menu. Both menus will include smaller portions and lower prices of the same items found on the dinner menu. With the expanded children's menu, the restaurant hopes to attract large families on a budget. Southwest Steakhouse does not want to compromise the high quality of its food or trivialize items offered on the menu.

Southwest Steakhouse has reached a niche market through the Internet. Now the company wants to expand into related markets. You are challenged to develop strategies to catch the attention of an expanded customer base with the information included on the web site. You have been asked to describe the new web site for the restaurant. Further, you must explain how the new hours of operation and the new menu items will be incorporated without compromising quality.

You will have ten minutes to present your recommendations to the restaurant owner, who will begin the meeting by greeting you and asking to hear your thoughts. After you have given your presentation and have answered the owner's questions, the owner will conclude the meeting.

Performance Indicators Evaluated

- Understand the opportunities and challenges that Southwest Steakhouse faces.
- Define the current target market for the restaurant.
- Explain a strategy for expanding the customer base.
- Develop an expanded menu that does not compromise the quality of food.
- Describe promotions that can be effectively included on the restaurant's web site.
- Describe the restaurant's Internet advertising campaign.

Go to the DECA web site for more detailed information.

1. Describe the competition faced by major restaurant chains.
2. Why would a successful restaurant change its menu?
3. What marketing strategies would attract new customers to Southwest Steakhouse?
4. What features would you recommend adding to the restaurant's web site?

www.deca.org/publications/HS_Guide/guidetoc.html

CHAPTER 9
E-COMMERCE DISTRIBUTION

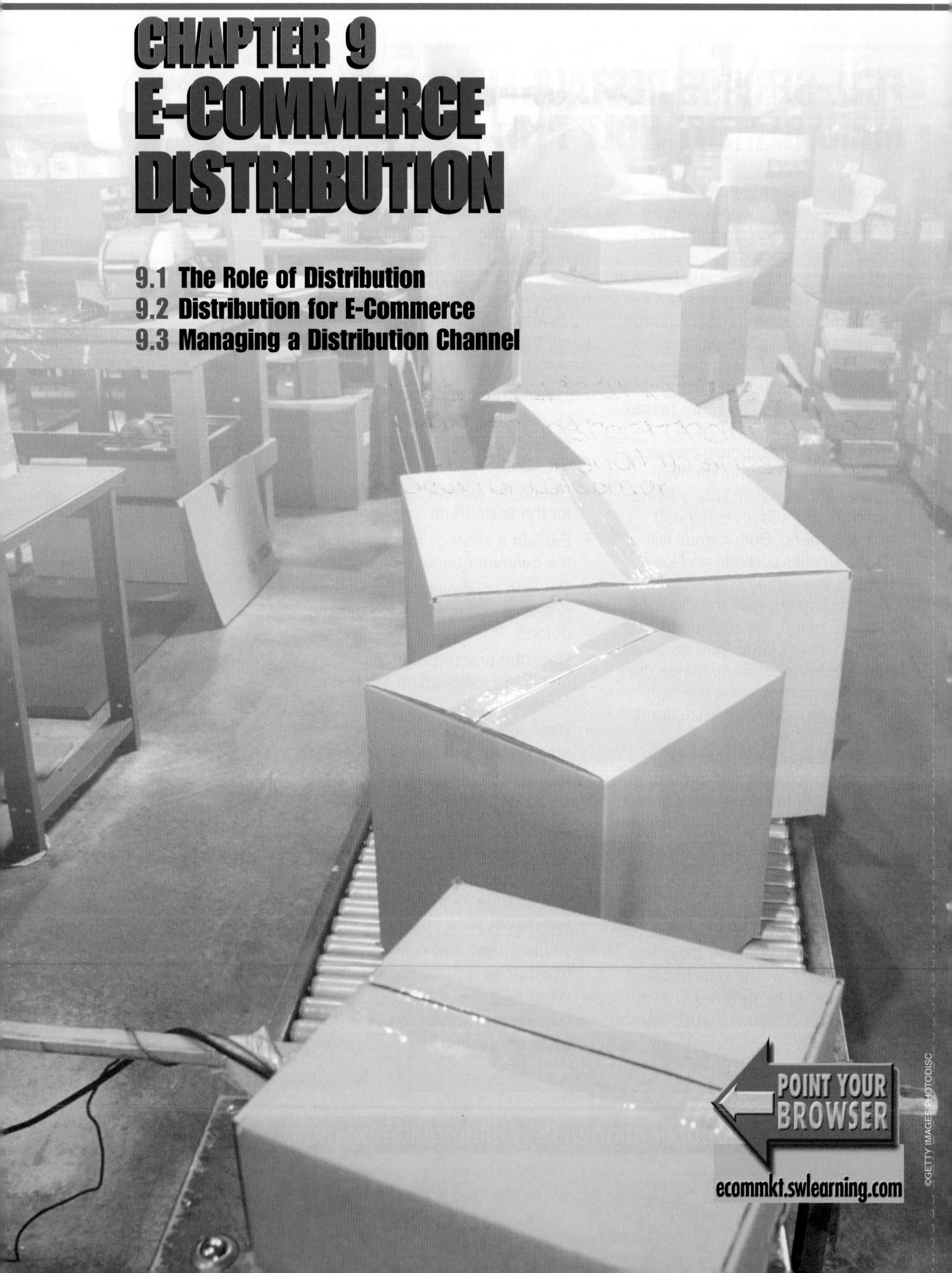

POINT YOUR BROWSER

ecommkt.swlearning.com

SINDBADMALL.COM

A new shopping mall recently opened in the Middle East. However, customers can't walk into any of its stores. It is a virtual mall named Sindbadmall.com. International Media Production Corporation of the United Arab Emirates owns the mall. An Egyptian company, Sahm Advanced Systems, manages it. In just two years of operations, the mall attracted thousands of customers from over 30 countries. Sindbadmall.com offers a virtual marketplace where customers can search for products that meet their needs. It is now the most visited Arabic online shopping web site.

Just like traditional malls, Sindbadmall.com's products are produced and distributed by many companies. The mall started with books, cassettes, CDs, and videos. It expanded into many other product categories based on customer requests. In just three months, the number of new products more than quadrupled to over 3,000 products.

The mall is promoted through relationships with well-known Arabic web sites. The mall's e-marketing supervisor coordinates continual public relations and publicity activities. Through routine surveys, the company encourages word-of-mouth promotion from satisfied customers.

The mall's products are sold to customers in many countries. Thus, a common form of payment is an issue. In ten countries, customers pay cash in their own currencies to the delivery service when products are received. In other countries, acceptable forms of payment are credit cards, bank transfers, and Western Union money orders.

THINK CRITICALLY

1. Why has Sindbadmall.com grown so rapidly, both in number of products offered and number of customers?
2. At this point, the web site is only in Arabic. Do you think it should be translated into other languages? Why or why not?

LESSON 9.1

THE ROLE OF DISTRIBUTION

LOGGING ON

Explain the importance of distribution in successful marketing.

Identify major activities that are a part of the distribution function.

Product recycling is a well-accepted way to reduce landfill waste. It is also an effective way to preserve natural resources. Recycling is difficult because of the high cost. Collecting materials and returning them to manufacturers for use in new products is expensive.

Global Recycle Ltd. manages an online trading exchange. The site allows companies to buy and sell recyclable materials. It works with businesses from small one-person salvage yards to large multinational firms. Global Recycle's web site introduces buyers and sellers to each other. It assists in transactions so the materials can be obtained and reused in manufacturing. Global Recycle charges a one percent commission on each exchange made through its site. As the business grows, its owners would like to manage the entire exchange process. This would include the delivery of products from seller to buyer.

Work with a partner. List the activities needed to successfully recycle products. How do both buyers and sellers benefit from Global Recycle Ltd.'s services?

THE IMPORTANCE OF DISTRIBUTION

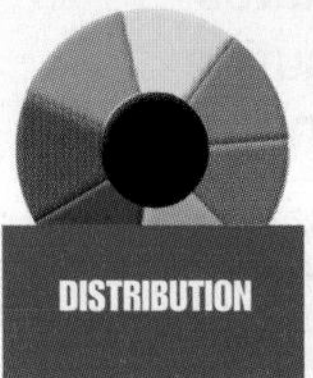

Today, businesses operate on a worldwide stage. Large businesses often have operations in many countries. Even the smallest businesses are often involved in international trade. They may purchase goods produced in other countries. Their products may be distributed to international customers.

©GETTY IMAGES/PHOTODISC

E-commerce has rapidly expanded global business opportunities. Both businesses and customers have instant access to almost any location in the world via the Internet. Worldwide interaction puts a priority on effective distribution. If a product is not available, arrives late, or is damaged in transit, there will not be a successful customer exchange. Distribution is an important marketing function for all businesses. It is especially important for e-commerce businesses.

SATISFYING EXCHANGES

The goal of marketing is to create satisfying exchanges between businesses and their customers. Good economic utility is key to a satisfying exchange. *Economic utility* is the need- and want-satisfying power of a good or service. It includes the *form* of the product at the time of consumption, the *time* and *place* the customer can obtain it, and the ability of the customer to take *possession*. Taking possession includes the ability to afford the product. Improving economic utility increases the chances that a business can sell its product or service to prospective customers.

Distribution is almost totally responsible for time and place utility. It also is important to form and possession utility. Distribution includes the locations, organizations, and methods used to make the product available to customers. Distribution activities must be completed in a careful and timely manner. Otherwise, the product's form may not be of the same quality as when it was produced. Customers may not be able to purchase the product when needed. The product may be difficult to locate or expensive to ship. The cost of the product may increase to a point where the customer no longer considers it a value.

The days of the home telephone may be numbered. People are moving toward wireless communications. The prices of cellular telephones and service continue to drop. Some people are wondering if two phone services are needed. There are nearly 150 million U.S. cell phone users. Many are giving up their home phones wired through the walls. That change is particularly true for 18–24 year olds. Of that age group, 12 percent use only a cell phone. Just 4 percent of those over age 24 use only a cell phone.

THINK CRITICALLY

1. **Why might people need both a home phone and a cell phone?**
2. **Why are younger people more willing to use only a cell phone?**

EFFECTIVE DISTRIBUTION

Many activities must be completed in order to distribute products and services to consumers. A **distribution channel** includes organizations and individuals that physically move and transfer ownership of a product from producer to consumer. A distribution channel that involves only the producer and the consumer is a **direct channel**. A distribution channel that involves additional businesses between the producer and consumer is called an **indirect channel**. With an indirect channel, businesses with expertise in an area of distribution are used to complete those activities.

Developing an effective distribution channel is an important part of marketing. A business must determine when, where, and how customers would like the product to be available for purchase and use. It is important to learn if customers are willing to complete any distribution activities themselves in order to speed the process or reduce the cost. The company must perform the remaining activities or locate other businesses to participate in the distribution. No matter who performs an activity, it is the business's responsibility to ensure that distribution is effective and efficient.

@ cyber check

What is the difference between a direct and an indirect distribution channel?

Direct-a channel that involves only the producer. indirect-channel that involves additional business between a product or consumer

DISTRIBUTION ACTIVITIES

You walk into a store to purchase a new pair of shoes. You select a pair that was manufactured in Chile. How did the shoes get from Chile to the store? What businesses were involved? What activities were completed in the process? How will the money you pay be divided among the participating businesses? Who will take responsibility if you have problems with the shoes? The answer to each of these questions represents an organization participating in a distribution activity.

The worldwide cost of cyber attacks is growing rapidly. In 1997, the cost was $3.3 billion. The cost for 2003 was estimated at $12 billion.

CHANNEL PARTICIPANTS

Organizations that participate in the distribution process are known as **channel members**. In addition to the producer and consumer, the most common channel members are retailers and wholesalers. Those companies participate in indirect channels. **Retailers** accumulate manufactured products and sell them to final consumers. **Wholesalers** support the distribution of products from manufacturers to retailers or other businesses. Other types of specialized businesses also may participate in the exchange process.

DISTRIBUTION ACTIVITIES

Channel members perform three types of activities—exchange, physical distribution, and information management.

Exchange activities consist of purchasing and selling as well as providing customer support. Exchange activities include providing locations and procedures for product returns if customers are not satisfied with their purchases. Independent sales companies, purchasing cooperatives, and businesses specializing in customer service complete exchange activities in indirect channels.

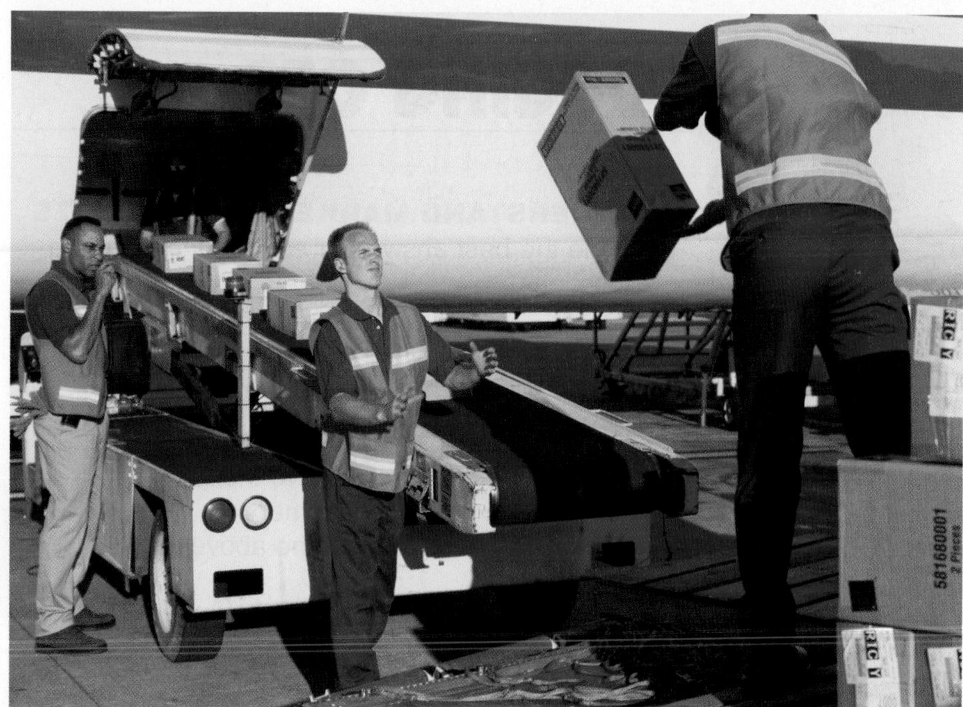

Physical-distribution activities involve product handling. Typically, product handling requires temporary storage in a warehouse or distribution center. Orders are filled and transported to the next channel member or the final consumer. Trucking firms, small parcel shippers, railroads, shiplines, airlines, and pipelines move products around the world each day. Some channel members will package products for storage and shipping. Products might range from small, fragile items to hazardous materials. Warehouses, distribution centers, and storage facilities hold products until needed.

Information-management activities help to record, organize, transmit, store, and update the information needed to buy, sell, and distribute products. The activities include providing product information to customers, completing order forms, and maintaining inventory and shipping records. Receiving and processing payments and making information available to channel members are also important information-management activities. Many distribution channels include businesses that specialize in order processing, data processing, and financial transactions management. Other businesses might focus on information storage and security and customer support.

In addition to the producer and consumer, what are the two major types of businesses involved in indirect distribution channels?

• Exchange activites
• Physical-distribution activites

LOGGING OFF

UNDERSTAND MARKETING CONCEPTS

Circle the best answer for each of the following questions.

1. All four forms of economic utility are affected by
   a. product.
   b. distribution.
   c. price.
   d. promotion.

2. Both direct and indirect distribution channels involve the
   a. retailer.
   b. wholesaler.
   c. consumer.
   d. all of the above

THINK CRITICALLY

Answer the following questions as completely as possible. If necessary, use a separate sheet of paper.

3. Develop a chart that lists the four forms of economic utility. For each form, describe two ways that distribution can be used to increase customer satisfaction.

4. Use an Internet search engine to locate an online business directory. For each of the three categories of distribution activities, identify at least three businesses that could participate in an indirect channel of distribution. Give a brief description of the distribution activities each business provides.

DISTRIBUTION FOR E-COMMERCE

LOGGING ON

Publix Supermarkets recently shut down PublixDirect, a web-ordering and home-delivery grocery service. Other companies' early attempts at online grocery services had failed. However, many in the industry had hopes for Publix's success. The web-based operation was built on Publix's already successful brick-and-mortar business. It did not require large investments in facilities and workers. It was hoped that existing Publix customers would have the confidence to try the new online service.

Customers who used the online alternative experienced high levels of satisfaction. However, the company did not attract enough customers to survive. Each Publix warehouse had the capacity to process 14,000 orders per week. Only about 4,000 orders per week were processed. Just 9,000 products were available online. This number was about one-fourth of the total items in a Publix brick-and-mortar store. After only two years of operation, the service suffered a $30-million loss. Currently only Tesco, a British supermarket chain, has been able to develop a profitable e-commerce grocery business.

Work with a partner. List activities that PublixDirect needed to complete in order to fill and deliver a customer order. List advantages and disadvantages to customers of an online grocery service.

Compare distribution in e-commerce businesses with that in traditional businesses.

Describe major e-commerce distribution activities.

DISTRIBUTION PLANNING

Distribution is an important part of any marketing transaction. It usually involves several businesses. It may take many days or weeks of numerous activities. Distribution is expensive. It can account for 50 percent or more of a product's final price. Distribution activities do not disappear when a business moves to an e-commerce strategy. In fact, these activities may become more complex and more critical. Many of the early dot-com businesses failed because of distribution problems.

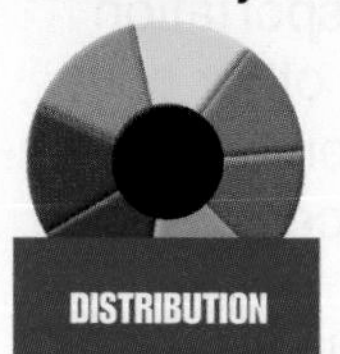

©GETTY IMAGES/PHOTODISC

COMPARING TRADITIONAL AND E-COMMERCE DISTRIBUTION

How does product distribution typically occur in traditional businesses such as Wal-Mart? Large quantities of products are shipped from manufacturers to Wal-Mart's distribution centers. Wal-Mart trucks move the products to individual stores. Customers visit the stores to select the products they need. Sales are completed at a checkout area with a computerized cash register. Customers pay with cash, personal check, or credit or debit card.

Because most products purchased at a Wal-Mart store are small, customers usually take the products home. If purchases are bulky or require special handling, such as large appliances from Sears, the company may provide delivery and setup, often for an additional fee. If there is a problem with a product, a service person can make repairs at the customer's home or the product can be returned to the store where it was purchased.

Business-to-business distribution usually involves products purchased less frequently. For example, salespeople who make regular contacts with business customers sell Xerox copiers. Upon receipt of an order, the salesperson checks inventory at the closest distribution center to determine availability. Then the order is placed and shipped to the purchaser. Some manufacturers have their own storage facilities and transportation equipment. Many use other companies for those activities. Order processing, billing, and payments are completed after the sale. These activities often involve mailed invoices, checks, or electronic funds transfers.

VIRTUAL VIEWPOINTS

Darknets **are private groups of Internet users that exchange information secretly and securely. The secret exchange prohibits cyber criminals and hackers from accessing the information. Darknets were first used to share illegal copies of music and video files.**

Darknet users set up a network by installing special software that can be accessed only with a digital key. The software and key are shared with only a few people. Data are encrypted before being sent over the network. The darknet has a short life, often a few days or even hours. At that time, the darknet is closed, and a new one is started at a different web location. Darknets are being formed by businesses. They are used to privately share software code and to conduct important negotiations.

THINK CRITICALLY

1. **What are other possible uses of darknets?**
2. **Do you think there should be controls placed on the use of darknets? Why or why not?**

When companies move to e-commerce strategies, some distribution processes change. Wal-Mart's customers no longer must physically visit a store. Customers can search for products on Wal-Mart's web site. Customers can place orders, make payments, and check order status using the Internet. With digital products such as music, the actual possession transfer of the purchase occurs electronically when the customer pays for the music and downloads it.

Many e-commerce businesses sell the same products offered by brick-and-mortar businesses. In this case, the distribution process may be similar to that for traditional products. The products may be stored, transported, installed, serviced, and, if necessary, returned by the customer to the seller.

When consumers become regular Internet purchasers, their perspectives regarding distribution often change. Consumers use the Internet to reduce costs, find products otherwise unavailable, or increase their shopping convenience. Internet customers typically expect service 24 hours a day, seven days a week. Quick access to customer-support information regarding products, prices, and shipping options is expected. Because the speed of the Internet is almost immediate, customers tend to expect the speed of distribution to be fast as well. Customers may be unwilling to wait days or weeks for product delivery. Online consumers expect easy, understandable, and secure ordering and payment systems. Customers want assurance that orders will be filled immediately. They want an easy, low-cost way to return a purchase if it does not meet their needs.

Ninety percent of manufacturers and distributors do not currently sell their major brands directly to consumers through their own web sites. The primary reason is fear that it will cause competition and ill will among the retailers that sell the products.

How do customer expectations regarding distribution change for e-commerce businesses?

____

____

CYBER CHANNELS

It is more typical to use indirect distribution channels in e-commerce than direct channels. Several businesses are involved in order processing and fulfillment. Businesses may be involved in building and managing the web site, processing data, and completing financial activities. Companies that participate in a distribution channel to facilitate exchanges between the producer and consumer are known as **intermediaries**. **Cybermediaries** are companies that facilitate exchanges in an electronic market.

E-COMMERCE EXCHANGE

E-commerce buying and selling occur through a web site. Web site design, management, security, and maintenance may be handled by the producer or outsourced to a web-hosting business. The producer may choose to have its products marketed through an e-retailer that promotes the goods of many businesses. Another option is to use an electronic mall. An electronic mall provides one location where many related businesses are represented on the Web. The mall promotes the products of each business. It may also provide information to help customers make purchase decisions. The information may include price comparisons, product reviews, and customer-service ratings.

E-COMMERCE PHYSICAL DISTRIBUTION

Products must be available at the time they are ordered. They must be shipped to customers quickly and safely. Customer choices increase with e-commerce. E-commerce businesses must meet specific customer needs in order to be competitive. For businesses that customize, production must be set up to complete the products and ship them quickly after orders are placed.

To speed order delivery, e-commerce businesses frequently establish large distribution centers. These centers are located in several centralized areas throughout the businesses' markets. Distribution centers are linked electronically. They often use satellites to transmit information.

Sometimes a producer or retailer is not prepared to manage some or all distribution activities. In this case, a fulfillment company is selected to handle those activities. A **fulfillment company** offers complete distribution services for other businesses. The fulfillment company handles the products and distribution activities of many companies. It uses the client's name on all packing and shipping materials and customer correspondence. Thus, the customer is unaware that a fulfillment company is involved.

A distribution challenge facing e-commerce businesses is providing an easy, inexpensive way for customers to return products. With traditional businesses, customers simply take the product back to the seller for an exchange or refund. If the e-commerce business does not have a physical location close to the customer, the return can be more difficult and frustrating. Brick-and-click businesses have an advantage because a customer that makes an online purchase may be able to return the product to a local store.

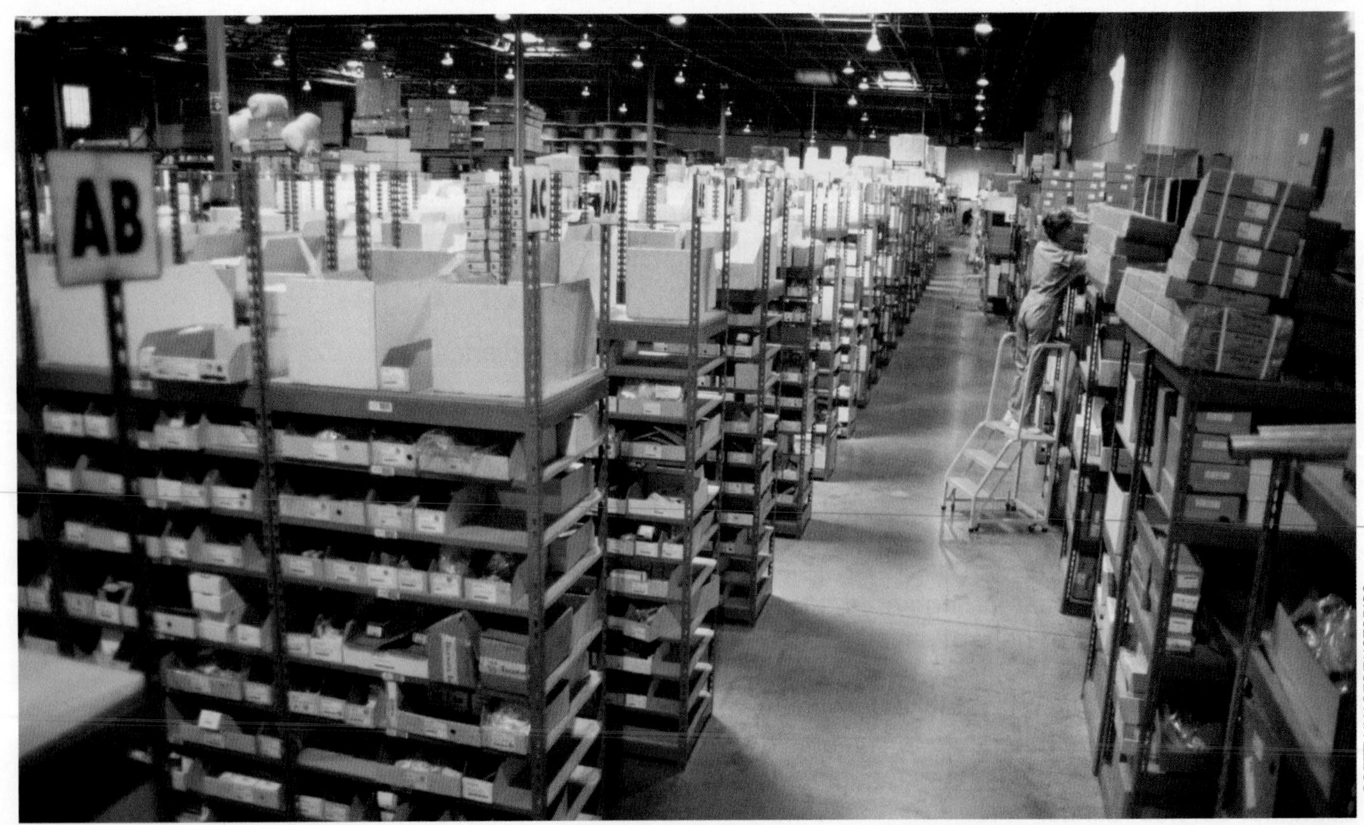

E-commerce companies have followed the lead of catalog and telemarketing businesses to process returns. The business ships a return address label and product return directions with the order. The customer repackages the product to be returned, applies the supplied address label, and notifies the company. A parcel delivery service such as FedEx or UPS picks up the package at the customer's home or business for return to the seller. Some e-commerce businesses have developed agreements with supermarkets or packing and mailing stores to serve as local product-return sites for their customers.

©GETTY IMAGES/PHOTODISC

E-COMMERCE INFORMATION MANAGEMENT

E-commerce relies on effective communications and information exchanges. Most communications with e-commerce businesses are transmitted electronically. Digital communications make it easier to capture and use the information throughout the distribution process.

A complete e-commerce information system should include the following components.

- customer database
- updated product inventory
- order processing
- order filling and customer notification
- sales by product and customer
- customer–business interactions
- product catalog
- online ordering
- payment processing
- shipping information
- order tracking
- channel member interactions

The information system should be integrated so that information collected in one component can be used in other components. Information must be accessible by channel members, including the customer, who need the data to successfully complete their activities. The information should be secure. Those who should not have access to it should be restricted.

What is a cybermediary?

are companies that facilitate exchang in an electronic market

LOGGING OFF

UNDERSTAND MARKETING CONCEPTS

Circle the best answer for each of the following questions.

1. Which distribution activity is eliminated when a company sells a digital product?
   a. order processing
   b. product storage
   c. possession transfer
   d. customer service

2. An organization that offers complete distribution services for other businesses is a
   a. fulfillment company.
   b. distribution company.
   c. full-service company.
   d. shipping company.

THINK CRITICALLY

Answer the following questions as completely as possible. If necessary, use a separate sheet of paper.

3. **Technology** Locate the web sites of two companies that describe their product return procedures. Prepare a chart that compares the procedures of the two companies. Which company do you believe has the better procedures? Why?

4. **Communication** Many e-commerce retailers offered free shipping to customers for a number of years. Today, more and more companies add shipping costs to orders. Write a short memo to an e-commerce business owner. Recommend whether the owner's company should or should not have a free shipping policy.

MANAGING A DISTRIBUTION CHANNEL

LOGGING ON

Manufacturers can now work with distributors to manage online sales of their products. New software makes it appear to customers that orders are being sent to the distributor. Actually, the manufacturer manages the catalog and order processing. Products are shipped from the manufacturer's distribution center. However, the distributor's name and address are printed on the shipping label.

The manufacturer's order-processing system is integrated into the distributor's web site. The integration maintains the unique look and feel of the distributor's business. The advantage is that, at almost no cost, the distributor now has an efficient e-commerce strategy. The manufacturer instantly receives and processes all orders. The distributor is credited with the sales. The manufacturer relies on only one ordering and order-processing procedure.

Work with a partner. Discuss why distributors may not want to participate in this type of online ordering partnership. How can the manufacturer ensure that customer questions are answered and problems are solved?

Explain how channel management supports e-commerce.

Describe important tools for channel management.

CHANNEL MANAGEMENT

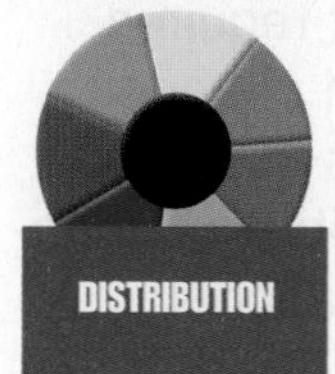

Almost every product that reaches a consumer moves through several organizations. Each organization is responsible for a specific activity or set of activities that supports the exchange of products between the producer and the customer. Each activity must be provided at the appropriate time. The activity must be performed effectively in order for the entire distribution channel to work properly.

©GETTY IMAGES/PHOTODISC

AN E-COMMERCE CHANNEL

Assume you are a member of a band that performs at theme parks and fairs during the summer. Based on fan interest, your group has decided to sell its CDs, posters, and t-shirts online. Several companies produce the products for your band. The band has designed a web site and operates it through an Internet service provider.

The ISP provides a secure shopping cart for ordering and processes credit card payments for merchandise. Your group contracts with a fulfillment center that accepts the orders. The center obtains the required merchandise from the manufacturers. It then ships the orders to customers using a parcel delivery company. Upon shipment, the parcel company generates a product tracking number. The number is sent to your office, the fulfillment center, and the customer. Using this number, the delivery can be traced from shipper to customer's door. The fulfillment center provides a customer helpdesk that resolves any problems with orders. The helpdesk responds to customer questions that are submitted via e-mail, web forms, or toll-free telephone number.

This is an example of a small-scale distribution channel. Although it is for a small business, it still has several participating members. The channel involves many activities. It requires careful planning and management. Consider the complexities of channel management for a large company with suppliers and customers throughout the world. What challenges would you face if you were responsible for channel management of either a small business or a complex international company?

Will online sales result in businesses reducing their number of brick-and-mortar locations? Evidence suggests that those who purchase online continue to purchase from the same businesses using other methods as well. Up to 78 percent of online shoppers also buy at the same merchants' physical stores. Forty-five percent also buy from the companies' catalogs using telephone or mail order. As many as 23 percent of catalog shoppers also use the Internet. Only six percent of in-store shoppers also purchase a company's products via the Internet.

THINK CRITICALLY

Why do you believe Internet buyers continue to purchase from the same businesses using other methods?

DEVELOPING SUPPLY CHAINS

In the past, businesses produced or purchased large quantities of products. The products were stored until ordered by customers. Businesses would then fill and ship customer orders as a separate process. Today, most businesses operate on a *just-in-time* basis. To reduce costs and to meet specific customer needs, companies keep only small inventories of products on hand. The products are quickly shipped to customers when orders are received. When possible, businesses customize the products to meet individual customer needs.

A company's distribution activities and distribution channel are seen as part of a longer channel known as a supply chain. A **supply chain** is the flow of products, resources, and information through all organizations involved in producing and marketing a company's products. A supply chain accumulates raw materials from suppliers for production as well as distributes manufactured products through channel members to the customer. A supply chain is responsible for

- **Products**—raw materials from suppliers and finished goods sold to customers.
- **Resources**—production and distribution, including money and people.
- **Relationships**—interactions among the participants involved in the channel, including the customer.
- **Information**—data needed by all channel members to complete their responsibilities.

A supply chain is complex. It must work well in order to result in satisfying exchanges. Just as a business needs a chief executive, a supply chain needs one business to manage the channel. A **channel captain** is a channel member that organizes and controls a supply chain. Often, the channel captain is the manufacturer. Large retailers may also fill the role. The company that develops the e-commerce business sometimes serves in the role of channel captain. In the example of the band with a web site, your group could serve as the channel captain. The group would carefully plan and coordinate the activities and organizations within the supply chain.

Compare a distribution channel and a supply chain.

• supply-is the flow of products, resources and information
channel-is a channel member that organizes and controles a supply chain

TOOLS FOR CHANNEL MANAGEMENT

The channel captain is responsible for organizing the supply chain. The work begins with identifying the activities needed and possible channel members to participate in the supply chain. The channel captain works with each channel member to develop a plan that identifies roles, responsibilities, and standards. The plan ensures that each activity in the supply chain process is effective. In today's era of digital technology, a number of tools are available to help channel captains manage the supply chain.

SUPPLY-CHAIN MANAGEMENT

MARKETING INFORMATION MANAGEMENT

Supply-chain management (SCM) software is used to manage the information needed by the channel captain. SCM software also allows sharing of that information among channel members. The software maintains records of raw materials suppliers, supply schedules, the manufacturing process, and finished-product inventory and storage. It also records information on shipping and delivery, financial transactions, and returns. Data must be collected at various points in the manufacturing and distribution processes and entered by each channel member. Technology such as barcode systems, global-tracking hardware, and SCM software support data collection, analysis, and exchange.

CUSTOMER-RELATIONSHIP MANAGEMENT

Customer satisfaction and business profits are the goals of a successful supply chain. Success requires that businesses track information related to target markets and customers. The information is used to match the right products with each customer. The information helps to ensure that each part of the marketing mix is implemented as planned. The information is also used to control expenses and track customer satisfaction. The channel captain and other channel members use *customer-relationship management (CRM) software* to manage customer relationships.

The types of data collected and analyzed using CRM software include specific information about individual customers, their needs, and their purchasing histories. The software tracks product requests, returns, and complaints. It also aids in identifying new customers and marketing opportunities.

CRM software and hardware collect information when a customer's purchases or returns are scanned into a computer terminal. Customer-service representatives and repair personnel enter information into records each time they interact with a customer. Online purchases and payments are recorded by shopping-cart software. Delivery and return records are entered into the CRM database by shippers and customer-service personnel.

Junk e-mail now accounts for almost half of all information transmitted over the Internet. Thirty-four states now have anti-spam laws. These laws attempt to reduce the amount of junk e-mail. However, it is easy for those sending the messages to hide their identity.

IMPROVING SUPPLY CHAINS

Competition requires businesses to be quicker, more efficient, and better at completing the activities for which they are responsible. Customers have more and more choices. They are quick to switch to competitors if their needs are not being met or if prices are too high. All businesses in a supply chain need to cooperate to ensure that the chain works efficiently.

Supply-chain cooperation is improving in e-commerce businesses. Many previous efforts in e-commerce failed because parts of the distribution system did not work well. Customers did not receive what was promised. Identifying a channel captain is an important step in improving the effectiveness of distribution. The channel needs to adopt software that can be accessed and used by all channel members. When all members are interconnected with common software, it allows information to be collected, analyzed, and shared. Problems can be quickly identified and corrected. Each channel member works to improve the speed and quality of the activities it performs. Improvement allows for just-in-time manufacturing, customization of products, and quick distribution.

Recent evidence shows that companies now spend over $21 billion each year on supply-chain management technologies. As a result of those investments, delivery performance has increased by over 25 percent. Companies have reduced their inventory levels by as much as 50 percent. At the same time, they have seen a 30 percent increase in the number of customer orders filled.

©GETTY IMAGES/PHOTODISC

Identify two types of software used to manage supply chains. Explain the function of each.

WORKING ONLINE

Alisha finishes her breakfast, turns on her computer, and accesses her e-mail. It is early morning in Japan, but she knows she will have a number of messages waiting from her manager Jerico. His office is in Cleveland. There is more than a half-day's time difference, so Jerico has finished his business day and has sent work for Alisha to complete. By the time he is back in the office tomorrow, she will have finished the tasks and returned them to him.

Alisha used to work with Jerico in Cleveland. She relocated two years ago when her husband's company transferred him to Osaka. Alisha was able to continue her work by becoming a virtual assistant. *Virtual assistants* are home-based workers who efficiently handle administrative tasks for business owners and managers. They complete their work using computers, the Internet, telephones, and fax machines. The work tasks may include responding to e-mail, preparing correspondence, editing reports, arranging meetings and travel, or conducting research. Depending on the level of skill and the work provided, virtual assistants can earn $25–$75 per hour. The work of virtual assistants frees up the time of their managers. The managers can then concentrate on planning, decision making, meeting with clients, and leading their companies.

Employing virtual assistants has several advantages to a business. Highly qualified people can be retained without limiting where they must live. There are often cost savings since no office space is required. If working as a private contractor, the virtual assistant is responsible for many typical employee benefits. In Alisha's case, the time difference allows work to continue almost 24 hours a day. Some employers hire two or three virtual assistants on a part-time basis, each of whom has specialized skills.

THINK CRITICALLY

1. Other than location, for what other reasons might Alisha want to be a virtual assistant?
2. What are possible disadvantages of the position for the virtual assistant? for the manager?
3. What duties other than those listed might be appropriate for a virtual assistant to complete?

LOGGING OFF

UNDERSTAND MARKETING CONCEPTS

Circle the best answer for each of the following questions.

1. Which of the following is a responsibility of supply-chain management?
   a. products
   b. resources
   c. relationships
   d. all of the above
2. Software used to manage the information needed by the channel captain and to allow sharing of that information among channel members is called
   a. customer-relationship management software.
   b. electronic data processing.
   c. supply-chain management software.
   d. distribution-management software.

THINK CRITICALLY

Answer the following questions as completely as possible. If necessary, use a separate sheet of paper.

3. **Research** Use the Internet to locate reports of several e-commerce businesses that have failed in recent years. Determine the reasons for the failures. Make a list of the distribution activities that were not completed effectively. Classify each one as an exchange, physical-distribution, or information-management problem.

4. **Technology** Use the Internet to identify vendors of SCM and CRM software. Analyze one software package using the information provided on the vendor's web site. Prepare a list of the types of information that the software collects and manages. Compare your list with the lists of other students.

CHAPTER 9 REVIEW

REVIEW E-COMMERCE MARKETING CONCEPTS

Write the letter of the term that matches each definition. Some terms will not be used.

- a. channel captain
- b. channel members
- c. cybermediaries
- d. direct channel
- e. distribution channel
- f. fulfillment company
- g. indirect channel
- h. intermediaries
- i. retailers
- j. supply chain
- k. wholesalers

E 1. Organizations and individuals that physically move and transfer ownership of a product from producer to consumer

H 2. Companies that support the distribution of products from manufacturers to retailers or other businesses

G 3. A distribution channel that involves additional businesses between the producer and consumer

A 4. A channel member that organizes and controls a supply chain

I 5. Companies that accumulate manufactured products and sell them to final consumers

D 6. A distribution channel that involves only the producer and the consumer

B 7. Organizations that participate in the distribution process

C 8. Companies that facilitate exchanges in an electronic market

F 9. A business that offers complete distribution services for other businesses

J 10. The flow of products, resources, and information through all organizations involved in producing and marketing a company's products

Circle the best answer.

11. Which of the following is *not* one of the major classifications of distribution activities?
    - a. exchange
    - b. physical distribution
    - c. information management
    - d. manufacturing

12. A major distribution challenge faced by e-commerce businesses that is easier for brick-and-mortar businesses to manage is
    - a. getting information to prospective customers.
    - b. communicating a product's price to customers.
    - c. providing an easy, efficient way for customers to return products.
    - d. providing an easy means by which customers can contact the business.

THINK CRITICALLY

13. Why is it not enough for a business to offer a good product in order to provide satisfying customer exchanges?

14. It is easier for a company to control a direct channel of distribution. Why would businesses choose to use indirect channels for some or all of their products?

15. Why might consumers be more willing to complete some of the distribution activities for local brick-and-mortar businesses than for e-commerce businesses?

16. Do you believe a fulfillment company could effectively serve as a channel captain in an e-commerce channel of distribution? Why or why not?

MAKE CONNECTIONS

17. **COMMUNICATION** You work for an e-commerce company that sells sports memorabilia. The company is concerned that customers will be reluctant to purchase its products based on time, place, or possession utility. Create a one-page advertisement that communicates how customers will be satisfied by purchasing from the company. Use illustrations and graphics to enhance communication. The ad will be inserted into sports magazines.

18. **TECHNOLOGY** Locate the web site of a brick-and-click retail business with which you are familiar. Review the procedures described on the site for product distribution to e-commerce customers. Using your experience with the company, develop a chart that compares the business's e-commerce distribution with its brick-and-mortar distribution. Point out the similarities and the differences.

19. **MARKETING MATH** Access a web site that provides comparison pricing of products. Select one product that has price comparisons for at least three businesses. Using a computer spreadsheet program, create a table that compares the prices of the product from the three companies. Go to each company's web site and determine how much the company charges for shipping and handling of the product. Enter those charges into your table. Calculate the total costs including shipping and handling for each company. Compare the results with your original price comparisons.

20. **COMMUNICATION** Locate the web site of a cybermediary. Read the information on the services it provides to businesses. Prepare a one-page sales letter to persuade a prospective e-commerce business to use the cybermediary's services.

21. **DEBATE** "A manufacturer should never use e-commerce to sell its products to customers in direct competition with the company's local distributors." Take a position in support of or in opposition to this statement. Develop written reasons for your position. Participate in a small-group or full-class debate of the issue.

This part of the project will focus on your business's distribution strategy.

Work with your team members to complete the following activities.

1. Prepare a chart that compares the use of a direct and an indirect distribution channel for your company. For each channel, identify the organizations involved in the distribution process. Also identify the distribution activities each organization would provide.
2. Use the Internet to identify a fulfillment company you could use to assist in the distribution of your company's products. Identify the range of services the company offers. Briefly explain the services you would ask the company to provide for your business.
3. Use poster board to prepare an illustration of a plan for your complete supply chain, from the sources of raw materials and finished products through the distribution to customers. Be sure to illustrate all products, resources, relationships, and important information that will be a part of your supply chain. On the illustration, identify the organization you believe should be the channel captain. Include a short statement describing why it is the best choice.

E-COMMERCE: THE EQUALIZER FOR THE BANKING INDUSTRY

Several decades ago, the banking industry was a 9-to-5 business. Drive-through banking and increased hours of service significantly changed the industry. Deregulation of the banking industry was responsible for numerous changes. In 1999, the Financial Modernization Act was passed. Banks began to offer securities investment and insurance products, which they were once prohibited from selling. With the deregulation, larger banks began to expand services.

Smaller local banks were purchased by larger national banks. With the new bank names came new checks, credit cards, and rules. Customers no longer experienced the comfort of knowing their banker. Frequently, customers were forced to use larger national banks that they previously had avoided. Banks merged, expanded into new areas such as insurance, and developed relationships with other businesses. Consumers became concerned about how their private information was being shared. Most consumers wanted a long-lasting relationship with a bank they could trust. The smaller community banks provided a personal touch sought by many customers.

The banking industry has offered electronic funds transfer and direct deposit for several decades. E-commerce allows customers to pay bills, apply for loans, check account balances, and transfer funds online anytime, day or night. Convenience factors include not having to make a trip to the bank and maintaining a banking relationship from any distance. Customers can apply for loans at home. They can pay bills on time without depending on postal delivery. With e-banking, location is no longer an issue. A small local bank can serve many people outside of the community.

Security is a major issue for the online banking industry. Customers want assurance that their money is secure. Since only 50 percent of the population uses the Internet, not all bank customers have access to the latest technology. Even individuals who do have access are somewhat hesitant about managing their finances online. Some people still want to receive a paycheck instead of having money directly deposited into their bank account. Growth of e-banking will depend on convenience, confidentiality, consistency, and consumer confidence.

Think Critically

1. **How has e-commerce made banking more convenient?**
2. **Why are some customers hesitant to use e-banking?**
3. **List three marketing strategies a bank can employ to encourage customers to use e-banking.**
4. **What additional services can a bank offer to online customers?**

BUSINESS SERVICES MARKETING ROLE PLAY

U.S. banks are able to serve customers throughout the country with online banking. Even banks in small towns can now retain customers who move to other parts of the country. Automatic deposit of paychecks, electronic withdrawal of funds, and online bill paying are some of the features that allow a small-town bank to retain customers near and far.

You have been hired by First Local Bank, located in a community of 2,000 people. The bank wants to retain customers who move to other parts of the state and country. First Local Bank takes great pride in knowing all of its customers by first name. The bank offers a toll-free telephone number for long-distance customers who have questions or concerns during regular business hours.

You have been asked to develop a promotional campaign to retain bank customers who will be attending colleges out of the area. The campaign must assure customers that they have instant control of their checking and savings accounts. The bank wants to emphasize its friendly, small-town hospitality that is not available with big chain banks. You must present your promotional strategy and ideas for the bank's web site to the president of the bank.

You will have ten minutes to review this information and to determine how you will handle the role-play situation. You will have up to ten minutes to present your ideas to the bank president. The bank president then will have five minutes to ask questions.

Performance Indicators Evaluated

- Define the benefits of a small-town bank.
- Explain how businesses in small communities can effectively compete with businesses in much larger cities.
- Explain why a bank in a small community would want to retain customers.
- Describe how a small business can expand with e-commerce.
- Explain a marketing strategy to retain customers leaving the community to attend college.
- Describe the information to be included on First Local Bank's web site.
- Describe how customers will learn to use online banking services.

Go to the DECA web site for more detailed information.

1. How can a small-town bank effectively compete with national banks in larger cities?
2. What are the advantages of banking with a financial institution in a smaller community?
3. What marketing strategy should be used to retain the business of college students?

www.deca.org/publications/HS_Guide/guidetoc.html

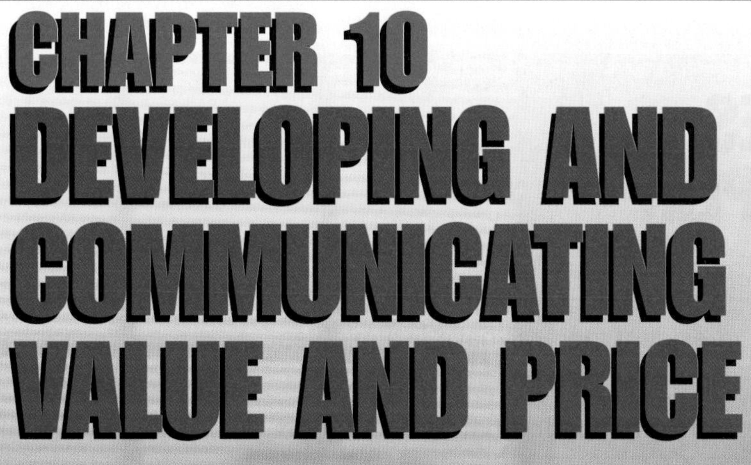

CHAPTER 10
DEVELOPING AND COMMUNICATING VALUE AND PRICE

10.1 Value in an Electronic Marketplace
10.2 Competitive Advantage and Value Chains
10.3 Customer and Price Strategies

POINT YOUR BROWSER
ecommkt.swlearning.com

©THINKSTOCK

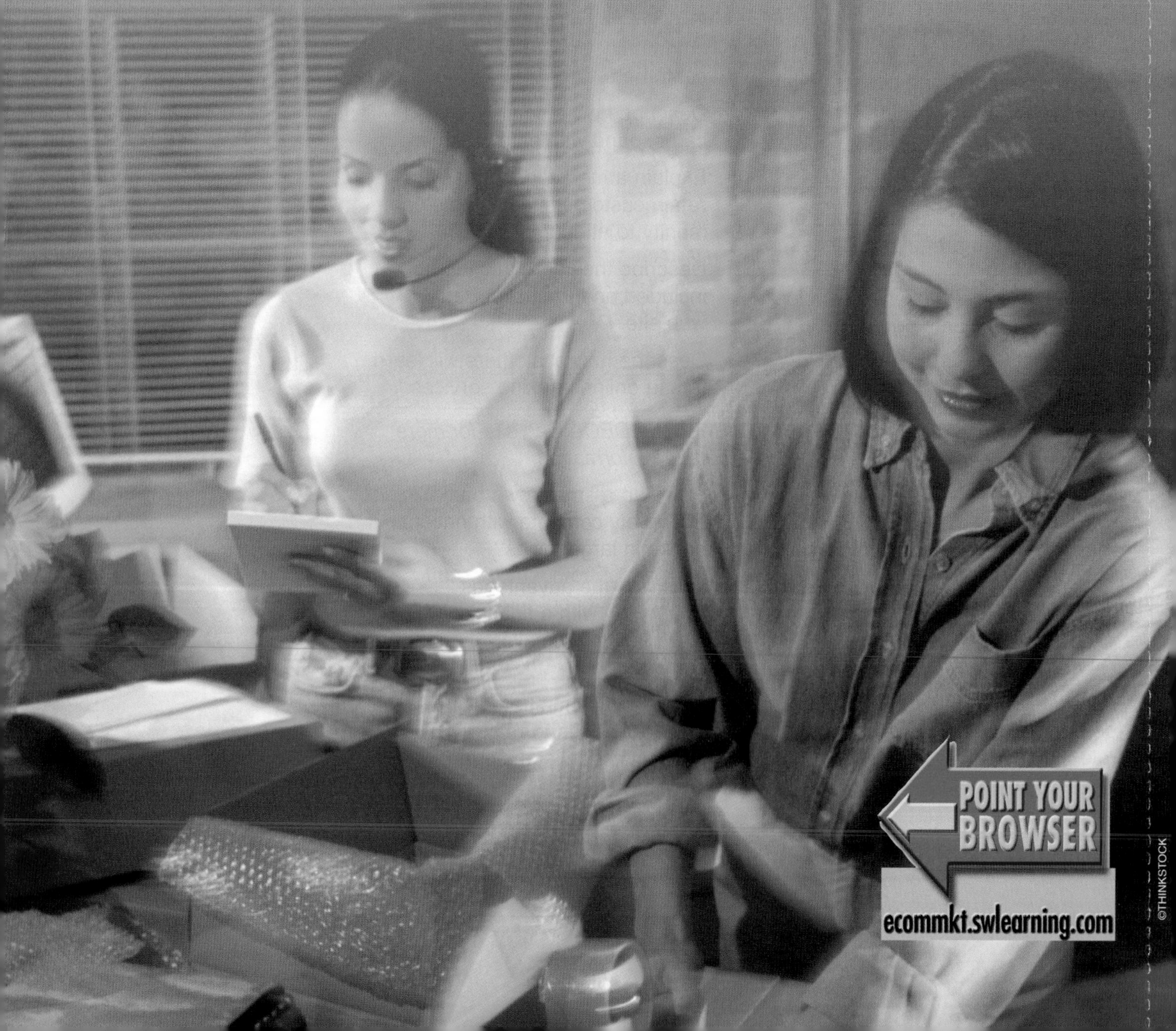

DELL'S VALUE SYSTEM

Michael Dell started Dell Inc. in his college dorm room. He placed ads and sold computers over the phone. As his business grew, he continued to advertise and began to use catalogs to drive sales. In 1996, Dell expanded his computer sales to the Internet. Dell's online sales increased from $5 million per day in 1998 to $50 million per day by 2000.

Michael Dell started his company with $1,000. Today, he is worth more than $8.5 billion. It takes more than just a good idea to be that successful. Dell had to develop a highly efficient company and reach a global market. Dell's web site allows shoppers to customize their computer orders. Companies use Dell's web site as a purchasing portal for technology equipment, automating the buying process. This efficiency allows Dell to sell at low prices.

Dell's customers can place orders via the telephone or the Internet. Dell's suppliers are linked electronically. Suppliers are located close to Dell's factories to ensure quick shipment of products. As Dell receives orders, it sends online requests to suppliers who deliver the products "just in time."

Michael Dell saw an industry with poor service and high prices. By having a vision of delivering value to customers, Dell has transformed the computer industry.

THINK CRITICALLY

1. Why do you think Dell Inc.'s multichannel approach is successful?
2. Explain why Dell does not sell its products through traditional retail stores.
3. Compare and contrast Dell's retail approach to those used by other computer and technology equipment companies.

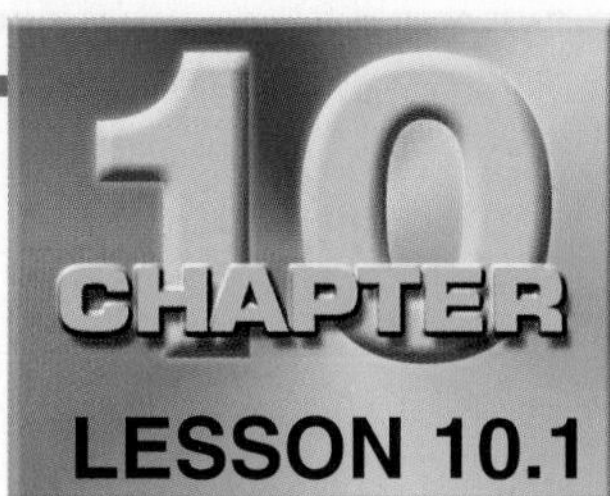

LESSON 10.1

VALUE IN AN ELECTRONIC MARKETPLACE

Discuss strategies that help e-commerce businesses provide value to customers.

Explain why satisfaction levels are higher for online businesses.

LOGGING ON

Amazon.com has built an online-only business based upon maximizing customer value. Once a consumer develops a relationship with Amazon.com, he or she is treated as a unique customer. The customer can access a personalized web site. The site offers book and product suggestions. The site also allows the customer to sample books and music selections. The customer can read reviews and obtain service information.

Amazon.com creates value by offering online purchasing, individualized customer service, and digital communication. It provides online auctions, low prices, and an efficient business process. Other businesses, such as Toys "R" Us and Target, use Amazon.com's site to sell their products. Amazon.com effectively delivers value to customers. It constantly rates at the top of customer satisfaction studies.

Work with a partner. Determine how customers receive value from Amazon.com. Find someone who has a relationship with Amazon.com's web site. View the personalized content. Determine how this personalization adds value.

DELIVERING E-COMMERCE VALUE

©GETTY IMAGES/PHOTODISC

Consumers make decisions about value based on how they will use available resources to satisfy their needs and wants. At its most basic, value is the benefits that customers receive given the costs (in money, time, and energy). E-commerce businesses must create value for their customers. Businesses create value by providing quality goods and services at acceptable prices.

VALUE STRATEGIES

E-commerce businesses use technology-based strategies to develop alliances with customers, employees, and suppliers. E-commerce impacts product, distribution, communication, and pricing strategies. Businesses need an advantage over their competitors in order to survive. E-commerce businesses must use value strategies to gain these advantages.

E-commerce is a tool used by both online-only and brick-and-click businesses. Many technology-based strategies have emerged that allow these businesses to enhance customer benefits. The ability to gather information from numerous competitors via the Internet gives customers many more product and price options than in the past. Increased competition forces businesses to become more creative and efficient in order to survive. Seven strategies help e-commerce businesses provide value to customers.

1. **Online-purchasing strategy** focuses on increasing sales by offering customers the convenience of finding information and making purchases over the Internet.
2. **Digital-communication strategy** focuses on organizing the delivery of digital information, products, services, or payments.
3. **Business-process strategy** seeks to gain advantages through efficient, streamlined business processes. Efficiency is generally increased through technology that automates business transactions and workflows.
4. **Market-of-one strategy** focuses on customizing products for the single customer with costs similar to mass production.
5. **Service strategy** seeks to gain advantages by reducing the cost, improving the quality, and increasing the speed of services.
6. **Pricing strategy** focuses on gaining market share by selling at low prices or at prices that fluctuate with market demand.
7. **Auction strategy** focuses on gaining sales through online bidding for products.

Each of these strategies can be used to enhance customer value. Businesses can offer these advantages through efficiencies from technology and streamlined business processes.

Customers can purchase online, but more often they use the Internet for information. For every $1 spent online, the Internet influences $1.50 in brick-and-mortar sales.

ONLINE-PURCHASING STRATEGY

An **online-purchasing strategy** focuses on increasing sales by providing customers the convenience of finding information and making purchases over the Internet. Retail e-commerce is expected to grow and change over the next few years. The number of consumers shopping online is estimated to increase. Product information delivery is expected to change due to broadband connections. Americans with at-home broadband connections have a greater ability than dial-up users to research products and shop online. Broadband users tend to spend more money because they are a wealthier market.

Another impact of an online-purchasing strategy is the movement toward multichannel purchasing. Most consumers use a mixture of shopping sources. Customers may shop and view products in one channel and then purchase in another. For example, customers may look for products online and then purchase in brick-and-mortar stores. Or, they may look in stores, order online, and have the products shipped to their homes.

VIRTUAL VIEWPOINTS

When copyrighted work exists in digital form, it can be easily copied. This ease of duplication is a problem for the music and movie industries. More people download music than pay for CDs. Most of them don't care that they are stealing copyrighted material. The movie industry experiences losses ranging from $1.3 billion to $4 billion annually from online file sharing of movies.

THINK CRITICALLY

1. **Assume you are a creative artist. How would you feel if someone copied your work online? Would you continue to create work if you weren't paid for it?**
2. **Explain how the theft of copyrighted work could endanger the music and movie industries. Infer how broadband access will impact copyright theft.**

DIGITAL-COMMUNICATION STRATEGY

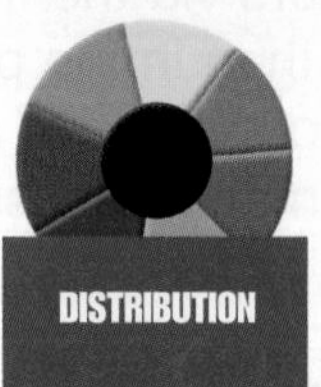

A **digital-communication strategy** focuses on organizing the delivery of digital information, products, services, or payments. Digital products include entertainment (such as music, movies, multimedia, and games), online information services, and published documents. Customers may access digital products and download them immediately.

Broadcast media use the Internet to deliver their own rich content. This content includes news and radio broadcasts and special programming. Hollywood uses the Internet to promote movies. Smaller, independent movie producers deliver motion picture and television-type entertainment to users via the Internet. One of the greatest benefits of online movies is the low cost of delivery. The Internet allows for a publish-once, view-many-times environment.

List at least five strategies that e-commerce businesses use to create customer value.

• online-purchasing strategy • digital-communication
• business-process strategy • market-of-one-strategy
• service strategy

SATISFACTION

The American Customer Satisfaction Index evaluates customer satisfaction within industries and a variety of individual businesses. For 2002, the average satisfaction level for brick-and-mortar retailers was 74.6 (out of an index of 100). The highest-ranking store was Kohl's with a score of 84. The average satisfaction level for e-commerce retailers was 83. Amazon.com ranked the highest of all businesses, both online and offline, with a score of 88. It was followed by Barnes & Noble with a score of 87.

Amazon.com is scoring satisfaction levels never before seen in a service industry. Amazon.com is applying its value-creation process used with books to many other products. Amazon.com's e-commerce applications set value levels so high that customer expectations are increasing not only for Amazon.com but for all businesses.

©GETTY IMAGES/PHOTODISC

The main technologies that e-commerce businesses use to add value are the Internet and databases. The Internet allows access to e-commerce communication platforms. Databases allow products to be searched and viewed, questions to be answered, and products to be ordered, all in a fast and convenient timeframe. At one time, online-only companies were the only businesses using these technologies. Today, traditional businesses are adding e-commerce strategies to their marketing mixes. When e-commerce is combined with popular brand names and high levels of service, traditional businesses achieve competitive advantages.

The most important value for many online shoppers is convenience. One study found that consumers saved almost 64 hours per year by shopping online.

List the two technologies that e-commerce businesses use to deliver value to customers.

• online-purchasing strategy
• Digital-communication strategy

LOGGING OFF

UNDERSTAND MARKETING CONCEPTS

Circle the best answer for each of the following questions.

1. A strategy that focuses on organizing the delivery of digital information, products, services, or payments is
   a. an online-purchasing strategy.
   b. an online-couponing strategy.
   c. a digital-communication strategy.
   d. a market-of-one strategy.
2. In 2002, the retail business with the highest customer satisfaction rating was
   a. Amazon.com.
   b. Dell Inc.
   c. Kohl's.
   d. Wal-Mart.

THINK CRITICALLY

Answer the following questions as completely as possible. If necessary, use a separate sheet of paper.

3. This textbook expands on many areas related to value creation. Determine which chapters relate to each of the seven value strategies. Explain why you chose these chapters.

4. **Technology** Visit an e-commerce site other than Amazon.com. Identify which of the seven value strategies the e-commerce business employs. State how these strategies improve a customer's satisfaction rating of the business.

COMPETITIVE ADVANTAGE AND VALUE CHAINS

LOGGING ON

The airline industry has changed how customers purchase and receive airline tickets. At one time, almost all customers contacted a travel agent for airline schedules and price information before they purchased tickets. It was inefficient for the airlines to interact with customers for ticket sales. Today, most airline tickets are purchased online.

Online ticketing is more efficient. Since travel agents were not adding value, airlines stopped paying them for ticketing services. The airlines found that they could use technology to provide these services. As a result, they added online ticket sales to their value-delivery processes.

Work with a partner. Determine why customers receive greater value by purchasing tickets online rather than from travel agents. Identify a function that a specific business does better than its competitors. Explain why this business gains an advantage in this area.

Explain how a business can gain competitive advantage.

Describe the e-commerce value chain.

COMPETITIVE ADVANTAGE

Providing something of value to customers better than the competition or at lower costs over the long term is known as **competitive advantage**. Lower costs allow a business to sell at lower prices or receive a higher profit at the same selling price. Technology alone may not grant a competitive advantage. It is merely a tool that must meet the needs of the company and its customers. However, both brick-and-click companies and online-only e-commerce businesses are learning how to use technology to improve customer value.

BUSINESS-PROCESS STRATEGY

A **business-process strategy** is designed to obtain efficiencies in the way a particular business activity is performed. Extranets allow businesses to connect electronically for business-to-business transactions. Remote employees can use an intranet to work on research and development projects, attend virtual meetings, and provide customer and employee support.

Service businesses have gained competitive advantage through process improvements. For example, the medical industry uses the Internet to help lower costs, improve patient care, and enhance caregiver skills. Over 55 percent of physicians use the Internet to search for information,

©GETTY IMAGES/PHOTODISC

communicate with colleagues, and e-mail patients. Governments use the Internet to lower costs and improve services offered to citizens, such as access to publications and databases. The U.S. government has automated online filing of federal tax forms. More than 47 million taxpayers submitted their forms online for the 2002 filing year. Businesses can save billions of dollars per year by cutting waste from inefficiency and duplicated paperwork.

Improved business processes allow the economy to operate more efficiently. One study projected that Internet-based business practices could account for up to 40 percent of the estimated increase in U.S. productivity between 2001 and 2011.

cyber check

Explain how e-commerce is affecting business-process strategies.

is designed to obtain efficiencies in

the way a particiular business

TIME OUT

Over half of all Internet users use the Web to meet their travel needs. Three-quarters of this group buy airline tickets online, and half rent cars online. The most popular travel sites are Expedia, Travelocity, and Orbitz.

E-COMMERCE VALUE CHAIN

Businesses create value for customers in different ways. The value-creation process differs by industry and among competitors. For example, a bookstore in your local mall does not have Amazon.com's personalization process or variety of books. However, it does offer a number of bestsellers and other books that you can browse and purchase immediately. The values that these two businesses offer to customers are different from those a wholesaler offers to its customers.

A business can be viewed as a number of unique functions that work together to create value. A **value chain** divides a business into functional areas. Each link in the value chain shows how the business acquires materials; produces, distributes, and markets its products; and provides customer support. All links work together to create strength. To gain an advantage, a business must be able to perform some function in its value chain better than its competitors. It must also effectively perform all other value-chain functions while maintaining its competitive advantage.

Figure 10.1
Generic E-Commerce Value Chain Supported by E-Commerce Communication Platforms

Distribution	Value Production	Marketing and Sales	Customer Targeting and Support	Management	Competitive Advantages Through Stronger Customer Relationships
Inbound shipments *Extranets:* Lower costs, increase speed	Advantages through customization and pricing	*E-Commerce:* Lowers costs, provides greater variety and promotion	Databases, CRM, and service *Internet:* Lowers costs, speeds service	*Leadership:* Management and knowledge workers *Intranets:* Lower costs, improve communications *Innovativeness:* Speed, flexibility	

E-commerce has added a new standpoint to the value chain. The **e-commerce value chain** views information technology as part of the overall value chain, adding to the competitive advantage of a business. Figure 10.1 shows how e-business technologies and techniques impact the e-commerce value chain. The delivery of value is supported by e-commerce communication platforms.

Figure 10.1 shows that businesses can gain cost advantages through the use of extranets, intranets, and e-commerce. Cost savings may give businesses only short-term advantages. Competitors can employ cost-saving technologies as well. Thus, businesses must focus on improving value delivery to customers through the marketing process. Many e-commerce businesses outsource key functions or form partnerships with other businesses to create the e-commerce value chain. Target and Toys "R" Us formed partnerships with Amazon.com to utilize its extranets, e-commerce, and service. These companies are taking advantage of Amazon.com's expertise in marketing, sales, and customer targeting and support.

Keys to an e-commerce value chain are a management team and employees who are willing and able to work in an e-commerce environment. Management and employees must understand and create the advantages of customer databases and online access to information between buyers and sellers.

E-MARKETING MYTHS

Many companies have attempted to compete in the grocery delivery business. Webvan chose an online-only e-commerce strategy. It built fulfillment centers to serve large markets. Webvan offered personalized web sites, low prices, and guaranteed delivery times. Webvan needed to achieve $1 billion in sales to support its strategy. In 2001, Webvan folded.

Successful multichannel grocers use brick-and-mortar stores along with web site sales to support customers. To lower costs, these online grocers fill customer orders from existing stores rather than build separate distribution centers.

THINK CRITICALLY

1. **Compare and contrast the strategy adopted by Webvan versus multichannel grocers.**
2. **Explain why multichannel grocers are succeeding while online-only grocers have not survived.**

Describe the role that a value chain plays in business strategy.

Divides a business into functional areas

LOGGING OFF

UNDERSTAND MARKETING CONCEPTS

Circle the best answer for each of the following questions.

1. Which of the following is true about a value chain?
   a. A value chain shows customers where to buy.
   b. A value chain divides a business into functional areas.
   c. All businesses have the same value chain.
   d. None of the above
2. Which of the following may be used as part of a business-process strategy?
   a. extranets
   b. intranets
   c. the Internet
   d. all of the above

THINK CRITICALLY

Answer the following questions as completely as possible. If necessary, use a separate sheet of paper.

3. Identify a business. Divide its processes into functions to create a value chain. Which functions can benefit from e-commerce strategies?

4. **Communication** Assume you are a consultant for the business you identified in Activity 3. Recommend how the business can use e-commerce strategies to improve its processes. Use the value chain you created to show where the business could improve.

CUSTOMER AND PRICE STRATEGIES

LOGGING ON

Lands' End uses the Internet to provide customer value. The company's web site features an online product search. Customers can use personalized virtual mannequins to try on clothes. They can receive customized notices about sales. If there is a problem with an order, customers can use the web site for service.

Lands' End customers have access to web-only discounts. The company can change the prices of overstock items without reprinting a catalog. Lands' End has one of the best online retail business models in the industry.

Work with a group. Visit the Lands' End web site. Determine how Lands' End adds customer value to its site. Describe the role that service plays in online clothing sales. Determine how the Lands' End site meets those service needs.

Describe customer-based value strategies.

Explain price-based value strategies.

CUSTOMER-BASED STRATEGIES

E-commerce creates value for customers in many ways. Customers are treated as a "market of one." Service businesses are enhancing how they deliver their services. Customers can access a greater variety of products, often at lower prices.

MARKET-OF-ONE STRATEGY

Serving customers on a personalized basis through online communication and in the product-development process is known as **market-of-one strategy.** Personalized web sites attract strong customer relationships. Databases target information to the specific needs of each customer. These data can be used to tailor web pages and target e-mail. The data also help to display products of special interest to the customer, personalize ads, and speed the purchasing process. Personalization can prevent customers from switching to other companies.

Customization of product development is achieved by linking the manufacturing process to customer-specific data. For example, Dell Inc. allows consumers to custom order computers. Order information is accessed on the factory floor where the products are manufactured and then shipped.

A study showed that 75 percent of respondents view personalization as a major contributor to a satisfying purchase experience. Online personalization includes e-mail, the ability to track purchases and requests, and service representatives who know a customer's history.

The Internet allows companies to mass customize a wide range of products. Examples of products that are being custom manufactured include eyewear, clothing, golf clubs, bicycles, fishing rods, and CDs. Smaller businesses use customization to gain competitive advantage. Larger businesses use customization to lower costs. Customers receive and pay for only the features they need. Building to order improves efficiency by lowering inventory costs for finished goods.

SERVICE STRATEGY

Service strategy seeks to gain competitive advantage by reducing the cost, improving the quality, and increasing the speed of services. Service strategy is notably important to businesses that provide a service. Service businesses include educational institutions, physicians, banks, realtors, insurance agents, and many others. Service businesses have four common factors.

1. **Intangibility** It is often difficult to see or feel what a service business does. The Internet allows customers to evaluate service offerings and compare service businesses. Evaluation includes the service product and price as well as its delivery.
2. **Perishability** Services usually cannot be placed in inventory or stored. Online services often can be delivered when and where they are needed more effectively than traditional brick-and-mortar services. This is especially true for information-based services such as those provided by educational institutions and the government.
3. **Inseparability** A service cannot be easily separated from its provider. The Internet allows service businesses to contact customers and to offer a variety of services online. Services as varied as realty and medicine use the Internet to reach out to customers. Medical doctors can even complete limited diagnoses over the Internet.
4. **Variability** Services often vary in their quality of delivery because of the human interface required. Databases and new production and distribution technologies are allowing businesses to deliver standardized services using the Internet. For example, in an online environment, all Lands' End customers receive the same level of service.

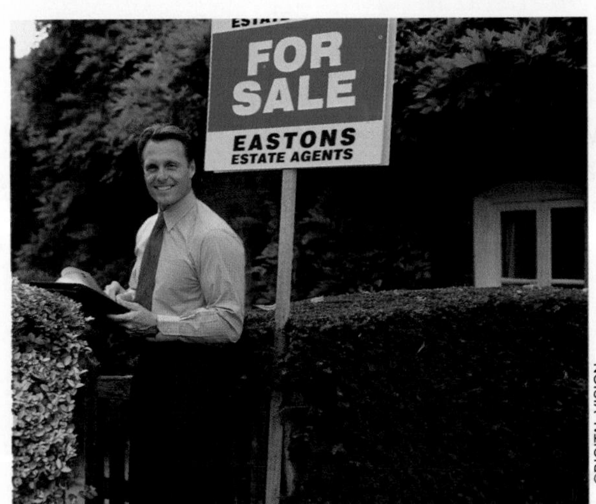

©DIGITAL VISION

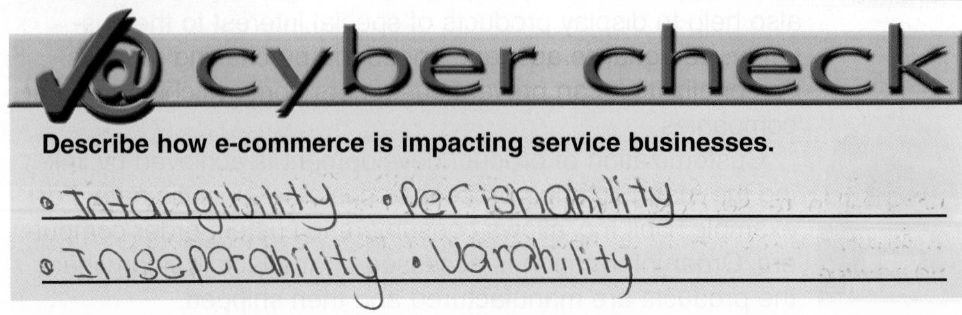

Describe how e-commerce is impacting service businesses.

• Intangibility • Perishability
• Inseperability • Varability

PRICE-BASED STRATEGIES

Businesses that focus on gaining market share by selling at low prices or at prices that fluctuate with market demand are using a **pricing strategy**. Greater efficiency allows some businesses to sell at lower prices because of lower overall costs. Cost savings result when a business does not need brick-and-mortar assets, when fewer employees are needed, and when technology is used to reach and serve customers. Customers save money, time, and energy when they can use the Internet to aid in the search and purchase process.

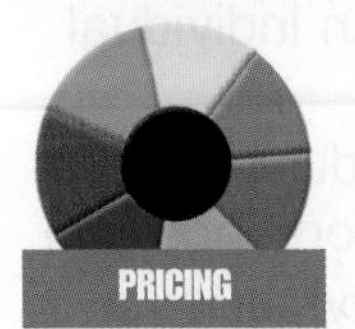

Examples of lower costs resulting from technologies can be found in three service businesses.

- Charges for telephone service can average $5 per call. Automated online service can cost $0.01 per call.
- A banking transaction with a live teller can cost $1.07. A web-based banking transaction can cost $0.01.
- Airline ticket processing can cost $8 per ticket. Web-based ticket processing can cost $1 per ticket.

When the cost differences are multiplied by the number of transactions handled each day, the cost savings are huge.

DYNAMIC PRICING

The Internet increases customer negotiation power. Customers can easily find and compare prices among suppliers. Customers can use software-based search systems called **intelligent shopping agents** that return product and price information. MySimon uses intelligent shopping agents to provide price and product comparisons. Intelligent shopping agents are useful for comparing products that have similar features and multiple vendors.

The Internet's ability to offer pricing information to all buyers and sellers at any place and at any time has led to dynamic pricing. **Dynamic pricing** means that selling prices may fluctuate above or below listed prices. Prices are adjusted based on market demand for the product. If demand is low, prices will drop in an effort to encourage sales. If demand is high, prices will increase. Businesses in the airline and hotel industries use dynamic-pricing software to match customer demand to available products and services. The software instantly adjusts prices to meet demand.

Online fraud occurs when individuals or businesses sell products they don't intend to deliver or purchase products without intent to pay. Fraud is a major problem in e-commerce. Over one percent of e-retail sales are lost due to fraud. This is 19 times higher than with offline sales. Retailers must ensure that orders are valid and payments are processed before they ship products. The highest category of online fraud is related to web auctions. The best way for consumers to safeguard against fraud is to use credit cards with online security guarantees.

THINK CRITICALLY

1. **What would allow fraud to be practiced online?**
2. **How can a buyer limit the prospect of online fraud?**
3. **How is fraud damaging to e-commerce?**

AUCTION STRATEGY

Auction strategy adds value by bringing together buyers and sellers who dynamically determine a market price online. Auctions can be business-to-consumer, business-to-business, or consumer-to-consumer. They are often hosted on auction sites such as the C-to-C industry leader, eBay. B-to-B auctions may be managed through industry exchanges or by an individual business.

eBay is the largest C-to-C web auction site. Sellers post product information on the site. Bidders place their bids online. When the auction ends, the top bidder submits an accepted form of payment. The seller pays eBay a commission and arranges shipment with the buyer.

Businesses use auctions to sell new products and excess inventory and to buy products. B-to-B online auctions work the same as C-to-C auctions. When a business wants to purchase inventory or services, it may set up a *reverse auction*. Several suppliers try to underbid each other to obtain the sale.

Explain how price can be affected in an e-commerce environment.

____

____

Barb is the *Internet marketing manager* for a large garden-supply business. Her business offers seeds, plants, gardening tools, advice, and service to numerous customers. Her job is to ensure that the Internet and technology provide value to customers and her business.

Barb manages inventory from suppliers. She also assures customers that they can engage in commerce easily and safely. Barb must guarantee that if someone wants information on products, they are able to find it. She must also ensure that customers are satisfied when they contact the business for service. She is in charge of developing and maintaining the customer database as a relationship tool.

Barb has a bachelor's degree in marketing. She has three years of previous experience as an Internet account manager. She is able to adapt quickly, prioritize jobs, and multi-task. Barb has strong organizational and communication skills. She is able to meet deadlines. Barb works independently but interacts with internal departments, third-party suppliers, and important customers.

THINK CRITICALLY

1. **Identify the skills for success as an Internet marketing manager.**
2. **Evaluate a number of garden-supply web sites. Determine the value strategies used in this industry. What must Barb do to maintain her business's competitive advantage?**

LOGGING OFF

UNDERSTAND MARKETING CONCEPTS

Circle the best answer for each of the following questions.

1. An online retailer allows a customer to use a personalized mannequin to view clothing. What type of value strategy is this business using?
   a. an online-purchasing strategy
   b. a service strategy
   c. a market-of-one strategy
   d. none of the above
2. Dynamic pricing implies that
   a. products will sell above or below listed prices.
   b. prices are not determined until the last minute.
   c. no one can predict the price of a product.
   d. none of the above

THINK CRITICALLY

Answer the following questions as completely as possible. If necessary, use a separate sheet of paper.

3. Personalization can form strong relationships with customers. List the types of products that you would like to have personalized. Explain why these products would create high levels of satisfaction for you.

4. Assume you work for a business that sells products to a large corporation. The corporation wants its suppliers to partake in a reverse auction. Explain how the reverse auction will affect your business.

REVIEW E-COMMERCE MARKETING CONCEPTS

Write the letter of the term that matches each definition. Some terms will not be used.

a. auction strategy
b. business-process strategy
c. competitive advantage
d. digital-communication strategy
e. dynamic pricing
f. e-commerce value chain
g. intelligent shopping agents
h. market-of-one strategy
i. online-purchasing strategy
j. pricing strategy
k. service strategy
l. value chain

K 1. Seeks to gain competitive advantage by reducing the cost, improving the quality, and increasing the speed of services

E 2. Allows selling prices to fluctuate above and below listed prices based on market demand

D 3. Focuses on organizing the delivery of digital information, products, services, or payments

C 4. Providing something of value to customers better than the competition or at lower costs over the long term

A 5. Brings together buyers and sellers who dynamically determine a market price online

I 6. Focuses on increasing sales by providing customers the convenience of finding information and making purchases over the Internet

H 7. Serving customers on a personalized basis through online communication and in the product-development process

B 8. Designed to obtain efficiencies in the way a particular business activity is performed

G 9. Software-based search systems that return comparative product and price information

Circle the best answer.

10. An online broadcaster sends movie clips to home Internet users. What type of value strategy is this broadcaster using?
    a. an online-purchasing strategy
    b. a service strategy
    c. a digital-communication strategy
    d. none of the above

11. Suppliers trying to underbid each other to obtain a sale are partaking in
    a. an auction.
    b. a reverse auction.
    c. a value chain.
    d. none of the above

THINK CRITICALLY

12. Choose a service business. Evaluate how the four service factors for this business could be impacted by e-commerce technologies. Would these changes increase your satisfaction with the business? Why or why not?

13. On poster board, diagram comparative value chains for Amazon.com and a local brick-and-mortar bookstore. From these value chains, determine where each business obtains its competitive advantage.

14. Choose two businesses that compete with each other. Prepare a chart with eight rows and three columns. Insert column heads of *Strategies, Business 1,* and *Business 2.* List the seven value strategies in the first column. Indicate for each business which of the strategies it is using. Determine the source(s) of customer satisfaction for each business.

MAKE CONNECTIONS

15. **MARKETING MATH** Use an intelligent shopping agent such as MySimon.com. Obtain various businesses' prices for a certain product. Compute and compare the percentage differences in price. Why do you think these differences in price exist for the same product?

16. **HISTORY** Education has changed its value delivery system minimally. Use the seven value strategies to propose an education model for the future. How would the new model impact student satisfaction?

17. **TECHNOLOGY** Define the technology that will be needed to execute the education model you proposed in Activity 16. Justify your choice.

18. **COMMUNICATION** Refer to Activities 16 and 17. Specify how your proposed education model will deliver service using the four factors of service businesses. Compare and contrast how the traditional education service model differs from your proposed model.

19. **COMMUNICATION** Managers and service providers are not often willing to change the way that they deliver value. Identify reasons why teachers may not want to adopt the education model you proposed in Activity 16. Develop proof to persuade teachers to use your model.

This part of the project will focus on your business's value strategies.

Work with your team members to complete the following activities.

1. Use poster board to develop a matrix showing how your competitors deliver the seven value strategies outlined in this chapter. Show where each of your competitors has an advantage. Specify the strategies your company must offer in order to compete. Identify where your company will have a competitive advantage.
2. Outline the details of how you will deliver each of the value strategies you adopt. For example, if you utilize the market-of-one strategy, will you use a virtual mannequin like Lands' End? Will you use databases to personalize content like Amazon.com?
3. Develop another poster showing the e-commerce value chain for your company. Specify which parts of the value chain your company will provide and which will be outsourced.

LEARNING FROM FAILED E-COMMERCE COMPANIES

What do Pets.com, Furniture.com, and Living.com have in common? All three companies no longer exist because they were trying to sell products that were not e-commerce friendly. Pets.com drew interest with commercials featuring a sock puppet. However, pet supplies that are readily available for reasonable prices at super retailers like Wal-Mart were not in high demand over the Internet. Poor business plans were the cause of many e-commerce disasters. Many early e-commerce businesses were poorly run, not well planned, and not a good fit for online business.

Be Realistic

Eager entrepreneurs frequently inflate the potential success of their ideas. Failed dot-com companies were set up with unrealistic hope that online sales would grow 100 to 200 percent each year. Most of the ambitious pioneers of e-commerce other than eBay and Amazon.com have disappeared. New online companies have learned from these mistakes.

Save Your Money

Failed dot-com companies often had eager owners who spent money without a strong financial strategy. Money spent on facilities, parties, and personal perks resulted in financial disaster. However, some firms did not get carried away with new wealth.

NetBank's frugal president opted to purchase used computer equipment and low-rent office space. Today, the company is one of the most successful Internet banks.

Have a Strategy

Successful companies must have strategies for selling merchandise online and offline. Online sales should complement traditional retail outlets and catalogs. Circuit City and Best Buy have successfully integrated their online and offline business operations.

Deliver the Goods

Successful e-commerce businesses offer reliable delivery of goods. E-commerce retailers should ensure that goods are always in stock to fulfill customer orders quickly. Customer service means fulfilling expectations and informing customers of delayed delivery if goods are out of stock. Poor customer service is the quickest turnoff for any retailer.

Price Appropriately

E-commerce businesses should not focus too much attention on low prices. Low-price strategies can quickly be undercut by competitors. Most customers are willing to pay higher prices for unique products and excellent service.

Consumers expect accurate information about the merchandise they are purchasing. Common sense and financial soundness are required elements for all types of business success. Early e-commerce enthusiasts frequently learned these lessons the hard way.

Think Critically

1. **Why did so many dot-com companies fail?**
2. **Explain how human nature was a factor in many dot-com failures.**
3. **What are customer expectations for dot-com companies?**
4. **Why is it important for retailers to have both online and offline outlets for their merchandise?**

E-COMMERCE MARKETING MANAGEMENT TEAM DECISION MAKING

You and a partner are marketing consultants hired by the owners of Vail Properties. Vail is located in the Rocky Mountains of Colorado. Vail is one of the premiere U.S. ski resorts.

Many townhomes and condominiums that rent for a premium during the skiing season are available for reasonable prices during the off-season months of May through September. Ski lovers who own vacation homes hire Vail Properties to rent out the units during the warm months. Vacation properties may be rented from one week to several months at a time. Vail Properties maintains the rentals during the off season. It also collects the rent from vacationers. Owners of the units pay Vail Properties 30 percent of the rent for its services.

Vail Properties' owners want advice about becoming a dot-com business. They want to advertise with virtual tours and accept online reservations. You must tell the owners why some companies have failed in the dot-com world. You must explain what Vail Properties can do to avoid failure. The owners also want to know what links should be related with the web site and why.

You have 30 minutes to plan your presentation. You will have ten minutes to explain your strategy to the owners and five minutes to answer questions.

Performance Indicators Evaluated

- Explain factors to consider when determining whether to open a dot-com business.
- Understand the value of advertising rental properties over the Internet.
- Explain the use of personalization strategies for current off-season resort customers.
- Describe the information to be included on the web page.
- Explain the value of virtual tours of rental properties.

Go to the DECA web site for more detailed information.

1. Why is the Internet a likely advertising medium for Vail Properties?
2. Why is it a good idea to have virtual tours of the rental properties?
3. Why would it be important to track visitors of the web site?

www.deca.org/publications/HS_Guide/guidetoc.html

CHAPTER 11
E-COMMERCE PROMOTION

11.1 The Promotional Process
11.2 AIDA in E-Commerce
11.3 E-Commerce Advertising

BMW'S ACTION PLAN

BMW is an international company that sells high-performance luxury cars. BMW owners are typically wealthier than the average car buyer. Over 85 percent of this affluent market uses Internet information to support the auto-buying decision before visiting a dealer. BMW uses traditional promotional media to inform people of its brand. The advertising sparks interest, prompting consumers to seek more information on the Web.

BMW's web site allows visitors to view the company's cars. Potential customers can use rich media to build their ideal BMWs on the web site. They can save their preferences or e-mail them to a dealer. The site also fosters relationships with customers by hosting chat rooms.

BMW developed a unique strategy to promote its cars online. It hired Hollywood directors such as Ang Lee (*Crouching Tiger, Hidden Dragon*), John Frankenheimer (*Reindeer Games*), and Guy Ritchie (*Snatch*) to showcase BMW cars in five-minute action films. The films featured stars such as Clive Owen, Mickey Rourke, and Madonna. The videos cost over $1 million each to produce. The videos were first posted on BMW's web site in April 2001. By December 2001, the videos had received more than 12 million hits. BMW also promoted the films in television commercials.

THINK CRITICALLY

1. Why do you think BMW uses the Internet to reach customers?
2. Explain why BMW includes product customization, chat rooms, and online videos on its web site.
3. List the advantages of BMW's online promotional strategy as compared to print and television advertising.

LESSON 11.1

THE PROMOTIONAL PROCESS

LOGGING ON

Car rental companies are extremely competitive. They must gain customers' attention and persuade them to rent from their agencies. Many customers use the Internet to research and make reservations for their travel needs. Knowing this, many car rental companies are shifting their advertising to an online environment.

Car rental companies use the Internet for promotions because it reaches customers efficiently and provides measurable results. Thrifty Car Rental spends 25 percent of its almost $10-million advertising budget on Internet promotions. Companies such as Thrifty are spending less on traditional national ads.

Work with a partner. Discuss how you would decide to rent from a specific car rental company. Would you rent from a company with which you were unfamiliar? Why or why not? Visit a car rental web site. Describe how it promotes its services.

Explain how the AIDA model fits into the promotional process.

Explain how hypermedia work in a promotional mix.

PROMOTIONAL GOALS

The Internet has opened a new set of communication channels. Businesses are using these channels to reach their target audiences.

Promotion is any form of communication that is designed to inform, persuade, or remind customers about a business's goods or services. The Internet can enhance traditional promotional goals such as informing customers about new products, persuading customers to visit a store, or reminding customers about a business location.

E-commerce businesses set promotional goals that include

- attracting visitors to a web site
- increasing the number of unique users to a site
- obtaining sales leads or opt-ins to e-mail lists
- collecting user data
- closing sales
- enhancing product and brand loyalty

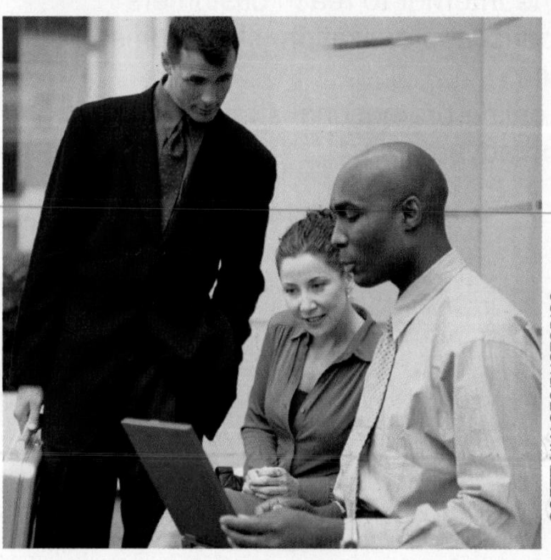

A traditional advertising industry model is called **AIDA** (for Attention/Awareness, Interest, Desire, and Action). The model states that customers must be made aware of a product or service. Attention will lead to interest. Interest will lead to desire, which will ultimately lead to action (such as making a purchase).

Businesses use a promotional mix to reach their objectives. A **promotional mix** includes advertising, personal selling, sales promotions, and hypermedia. Today, most e-commerce promotional campaigns require a combination of traditional methods and hypermedia. Reliance on hypermedia alone may not allow a company to reach its goals.

VIRTUAL VIEWPOINTS

Web sites must support themselves financially. One method of support is advertising sales. However, web surfers are growing intolerant of sites that have too much advertising. One study found that 63 percent of web surfers will leave a site that is cluttered with more than two ads per page. Teens are most likely to abandon a site if it is cluttered. This intolerance makes it difficult for advertising-supported sites to survive.

THINK CRITICALLY

1. **Explain why most people do not like to see more than two ads on a web page. Why will surfers leave a cluttered site?**
2. **Compare and contrast Internet advertising with ad clutter in magazines and newspapers.**

THE AIDA MODEL

Marketers use the AIDA model to guide strategies in the promotional process. Developing a strategy to gain the attention of the target audience helps to reach the promotional goal of informing. Creating interest and desire for the product or service helps to accomplish persuasion. Often, a company will set a goal to have the target audience take some type of action. In most cases, a single message or media will not move an audience through every stage of the AIDA process. A business can use several suggestions to improve the AIDA model.

- **Awareness/Attention** Use traditional media to create brand attention. Make the audience aware of the web site with offline advertising. Employ search engines to ensure that the web site is found. Place advertising and links to the site on other web pages. Send targeted e-mails, which can be used like direct marketing to gain initial attention.
- **Interest** Use personalized communication to meet individuals' needs. Use rich media. Send targeted, permission-based e-mails.
- **Desire** Develop a site design and content that appeal to the target audience. Include relationship-development components that will keep the audience at the site. Allow for feature comparison or personalized design of products.
- **Action** Use promotions to entice action. Use testimonials or show role models using the products. Design secure, user-friendly purchasing systems.

cyber check

List and explain the stages of the AIDA model.

Awareness/Attention-use traditional media to creat brand attention
Interest-use personalized communication to meet individuals needs
• Desire-Develop a site design and content that appeal to the target
• Action-use promotions to entice action

Customers have many media from which to choose. Often, they use more than one medium at a time. A survey of 25- to 34-year-olds showed that over 30 percent watched television while they surfed the Internet.

PROMOTIONAL MIX

Each element of the promotional mix has strengths for reaching specific communication goals. An **integrated marketing-communication strategy** brings together multiple media to reach desired goals. The strategy includes using hypermedia in promotional campaigns. Hypermedia enhance the visibility of firms and create new business opportunities. Hypermedia also save money and time and allow businesses to reach new customers.

Figure 11.1 shows how the components of a promotional mix, including hypermedia, influence the four stages of the AIDA model. The darker the area in the figure, the stronger influence the promotional mix element has on the AIDA stage.

Advertising is the most effective promotional mix element for gaining attention. It is strong in creating interest, less effective in creating desire, and least effective in obtaining action. Personal selling is not highly efficient in creating attention because of the high costs of using a sales force. Personal selling is more effective at creating desire and action (closing the sale). Sales promotions (such as coupons or point-of-purchase displays) are most effective in generating action. Hypermedia are strongest in the areas of creating interest and desire, but can also be used to facilitate action such as opting into a list or making a purchase.

Figure 11.1
Promotional Mix and AIDA Matrix

	Attention	Interest	Desire	Action
Advertising				
Personal selling				
Sales promotions				
Hypermedia				

HYPERMEDIA ELEMENTS

Traditional media use messages that attract and hold an audience's attention. Web sites differ from traditional media because customers must actively link to the company's site for information. Audiences are likely to view and interact with a hypermedia message only if they have given permission to the sender and recognize the brand name of the product or company. If customers are unaware of the web site, they will not visit. If customers don't know the company's brand name, they will not likely click on a related link.

Describe the role of hypermedia in a promotional mix.

traditional media use messagg that
attract and held an audience's attention

LOGGING OFF

UNDERSTAND MARKETING CONCEPTS

Circle the best answer for each of the following questions.

1. Any form of communication that is designed to inform, persuade, or remind customers about a business's goods or services is
   a. advertising. **c.** promotion.
   b. e-mail. **d.** none of the above

2. Which of the following is *not* part of the AIDA model?
   a. attention **c.** direction
   b. interest **d.** action

THINK CRITICALLY

Answer the following questions as completely as possible. If necessary, use a separate sheet of paper.

3. Choose a national restaurant chain you know well. Identify how this chain gains your attention. Specify how its promotions create interest and desire. Identify how this chain attempts to generate action from you.

4. Choose a national retail clothing chain. Specify the various media that this business uses. Do you feel the chain has an effective promotional mix with which to communicate? Make recommendations to improve the chain's promotional mix.

LESSON 11.2

AIDA IN E-COMMERCE

Explain how a marketer can attract audience attention.

Describe how interest is gained with hypermedia.

Discuss how a marketer can obtain customer desire and action.

LOGGING ON

Ford's Mercury division had its total advertising budget cut. The strategy devised to respond to the lower budget included various media. Mercury's target market was already aware of the brand. The division decided to use direct mail to reach the market with information. In addition, Mercury partnered with AOL for ad placement because their customer profiles were the same.

Mercury placed pop-up ads, banner ads, and a rich media video on AOL. It also sponsored some of AOL's lifestyle pages. Ford developed a promotional giveaway in which a Mercury Monterey was awarded. Participants had to opt-in by submitting their names and e-mail addresses to enter the drawing.

Work with a partner. Evaluate Ford Mercury's advertising strategy. Explain why Ford would use an online strategy. List the advantages of this strategy over a traditional media strategy. Explain why Ford required individuals to opt-in to the giveaway.

ATTENTION

©GETTY IMAGES/PHOTODISC

A marketer must first gain the attention of the audience before the audience can be informed or persuaded. The Internet is not necessarily the best medium for gaining audience attention. Traditional media such as television, magazines, and newspapers are often used to raise awareness of an e-commerce business and its web address. A business's web address should be included in advertising copy, business cards, direct e-mail, banner ads located on other web sites, and other media. Today, over 90 percent of print ads include a web address.

SEARCH ENGINES

Search engines are the primary tools that customers use to search for products online. **Search engines** examine databases for requested information and then provide links to that information. Search engines are a cost-effective means of raising awareness of a web site. However, they do not guarantee that people will choose to visit or even remember the site.

Many search engines, such as Google, use *web spiders* to collect information from sites. Spiders "crawl" through the Internet, capturing and returning information to the search engine. Search engines can return numerous hits (often several million), many of which do not fit the searcher's interests.

Search engines use specific criteria that determine which sites make the **top of the search**, or are listed at the beginning of the search results. Criteria may include the number of keywords at the site, the number of links to that site from other sites, and how often the site is updated. Criteria may also include the number of times the site has been hit, matches of certain text, and other factors known only to the management of the search engine. Sites that make it to the top of the search are often those of large, U.S.-based businesses that pay for the position.

Search engines may index over three billion web pages. This number is only a small percentage of the total web pages available. Most web users abandon search results after reviewing the first two pages of returns. For this reason, an e-commerce business should not solely rely upon search engines to gain attention. The site may be lost in the results list.

E-MARKETING MYTHS

Most people think search engines are like the white pages of a phone book. Instead, they are more like the yellow pages, where only paid placements are seen. Most Internet users are unaware that some search engines list paying clients' sites higher in the search results. Research has shown that consumers lose trust in search engines that do not clearly mark paid listings as advertisements. The Federal Trade Commission released a letter urging search engines to display "clear and conspicuous disclosures of paid placement" on results pages.

THINK CRITICALLY

1. **Is it fair to receive search results that show paid placements at the top of the search? Explain your view.**
2. **Consider this issue from the search engine sites' standpoint. Explain if the search engines exist to provide a public service or if they are designed to make money.**
3. **Would a notice of paid placement make you feel more comfortable about paid search results? Why or why not?**

HYPERMEDIA LINKS

Businesses often use links in hypermedia such as web sites or e-mail to gain attention. These links can be found in online ads, sponsorships, or affiliate marketing programs. A **sponsorship** integrates a company's brand into the editorial content of a web page. For example, a business may sponsor a news site or a community bulletin board.

By 2007, 12 percent of ads on the Internet are expected to include streaming video, 22 percent will include other rich media, and 66 percent will contain conventional ad formats.

Affiliate marketing programs include content sites that provide links to commerce sites. These programs usually charge performance-based fees, where the host site receives a percentage of sales or some other type of compensation for the click-through. Affiliate marketing programs can be a low-cost method for obtaining new customers.

Explain the role that search engines play in gaining audience attention.

many search engines, such as Google use web spiders to collect information from sites

INTEREST

Before customers take action, they must first have an interest in and a desire for a product or service. An e-commerce promotional strategy must give a site visitor a compelling reason to stay. Compelling reasons can be accomplished through both site design and content.

SITE DESIGN

Site designers must consider the communication goals of the business, the nature of the audience, and the technology the audience will be using. A visitor viewing a home page will decide quickly whether or not to explore the site.

SITE CONTENT

A web site must have well-organized content that allows visitors to easily find information. Many sites provide internal search engines. Individuals often leave web sites if unable to find the content they are seeking.

Site content should be continually updated. The type of content will depend on the browser used by prospective customers. For target markets with high-bandwidth connections, a site will often include rich media. For lower bandwidths, the content may be more text based.

Site content should appeal to the target audience. For example, children's sites are likely to be rich in animation. Business sites are usually information-based with designs that allow users to find information quickly.

Describe the role of site design in creating interest.

An ecommerce promotional strategy must give a site vistor a compelling reasen to stay

DESIRE

Personalization is one of the most effective tools for creating desire in e-commerce. A visitor who registers with a web site may provide personal information that the company can use for future personalized promotions. One study found that close to 75 percent of individuals stated personalization as a major contributor to a satisfying purchasing experience.

MARKETING INFORMATION MANAGEMENT

Web sites use cookies to track online behavior that can be used for personalization. A **cookie** is a short code that resides in the user's browser and tells a site who is visiting. The site sends the cookie to the browser the first time the user visits. A cookie does not identify an individual but rather identifies the computer being used. The recorded surfing behavior provides data to automated software. The software generates personalized content and design that are delivered back to the browser.

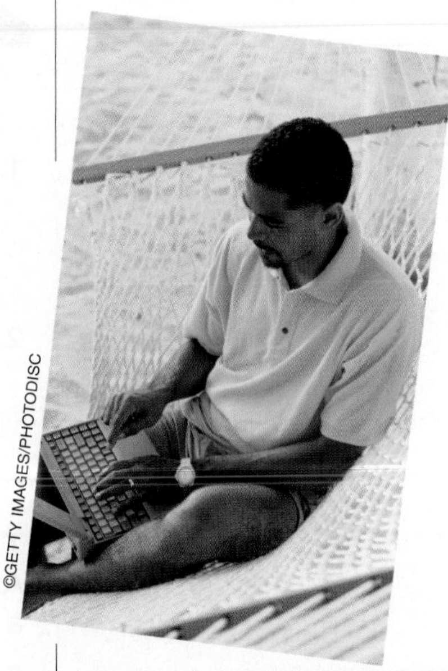
©GETTY IMAGES/PHOTODISC

One of the most effective promotional strategies for creating desire is e-mail marketing directed to existing customers. This strategy allows for specific targeting through personalized messages. E-mail marketing has a better return on investment than any other direct-marketing technique due to low costs. Average direct mail costs are $0.55 per contact, while average costs for an e-mail strategy are $0.09 per contact. Up to 40 percent of targeted e-mail gets opened. Nearly 9 percent of these e-mails reach the goal of having customers click through to web sites.

ACTION

Action does not necessarily imply a purchase. The action goal could involve having individuals visit a web site or obtaining a high **click-through rate** (CTR) (percentage of people who click through to another site). Or the goal may be receiving completed surveys, obtaining leads, or generating requests for information from potential customers. The closer a business meets the specific needs of its target market, the higher its chances of generating an action.

Rich media is effective in creating action. A study found that the CTR for rich media is 2.7 percent. The CTR for nonrich media is only 0.27 percent.

E-businesses can encourage action by offering incentives such as coupons or free shipping. Providing search engines that link a customer's desires to requested and similar products can generate action. Creating a forum for product reviews and testimonials can also influence action.

List five action goals that may be set in relation to e-commerce promotional campaigns.

or the goal may be receiving of people who click through to leads, or generating requests for information from potential customers

LOGGING OFF

UNDERSTAND MARKETING CONCEPTS

Circle the best answer for each of the following questions.

1. Which of the following is recommended to create interest in a web site?
   a. have well-organized content
   b. provide internal search engines
   c. update the site regularly
   d. all of the above
2. A short code that resides in the user's browser and tells a site who is visiting is called a
   a. spider.
   b. cookie.
   c. bot.
   d. search engine.

THINK CRITICALLY

Answer the following questions as completely as possible. If necessary, use a separate sheet of paper.

3. You are employed by a new e-commerce business. How will you inform your target market about your business? Specify both the goals and the media you plan to use.

4. You have set a promotional goal for your new e-commerce business of obtaining a high click-through rate. Design an online ad (banner, pop-up, or something similar) that you believe will get results. Justify your use of the ad type and design.

E-COMMERCE ADVERTISING

LOGGING ON

Advertisers are always looking for the best return on their investments. *Advertising Age*, a leading trade magazine for the advertising industry, conducted a study and found that some media advertising provides a poor return on investment. The medium providing the worst return was network television. It was also the most difficult medium to measure.

The top-rated advertising medium was direct mail. The second best medium was the Internet. Other studies have found that targeted e-mail is even better than direct mail at providing returns. Success rests on a business's ability to identify the needs of specific customers and to target the audience with an effective message.

Work with a group. List reasons why the effect of television advertising is difficult to measure. Then list the measurement advantages of online advertising. Speculate on the future allocation of advertising dollars between these two media by various businesses.

Describe the types of ads used online.

Explain how advertising effectiveness is measured in an e-commerce environment.

ONLINE ADVERTISING

Promotional placement in a medium is known as **advertising**. The Internet is the fastest-growing advertising medium. It took only five years to reach 50 million users. To reach this level of growth, radio took 38 years, television took 13 years, and cable took 10 years. Online advertising revenue was over $6 billion in 2003. However, this was only around 3 percent of overall ad spending.

PROMOTION

Online advertising has some unique differences from traditional advertising. Differences are found in advertising design and in the ability to track the effectiveness of campaigns.

BANNER ADS

Banner ads are the most common method of web advertising. **Banner ads** act like placement ads in print media. They are usually rectangular messages that come in different sizes. Small banners are called *buttons*. Tall and narrow banners are called *skyscrapers*. To catch a viewer's eye, banner ads are now using animation, Java programming, and multimedia. Banner ads are useful in creating awareness of products and in communicating information about them. They are not highly effective in achieving click-through. The Internet Advertising Bureau has set standards for online ad sizes. These standards allow for price comparisons across web sites.

POP-UPS

Pop-up ads automatically load and display content as a web site is brought up. Pop-ups are also called *interstitials*. Interstitials include pop-ups (in front of a web page), pop-unders (behind a web page), or floating ads (move over a web page). Interstitials are much more effective in delivering rich media content than banner ads.

Well-designed pop-up advertising can be effective. However, many consumers consider pop-up ads extremely annoying. A number of sites, including AOL and Ask Jeeves, have restricted pop-up ads. Web users can install software on their computers to block pop-ups.

CPM rates for online advertising will vary based on a number of measures. Example rates include

- $8 for no preferred placement
- $15 for a preferred placement
- $35 for placement based on targeted keywords
- $200 for opt-ins

cyber check

Describe the different types of online advertising.

Pop-up ads-automatically load and display as a web site is brought up Banner ads- act like placement ads in print media

ADVERTISING MEASURES

Advertisers are always interested in the effectiveness of their advertising dollars. The ideal measurement system for advertisers would show how many people see the ad (reach), how many times they see the ad (frequency), when they view the ad (timing), and if the ad achieves impact on promotional goals (to inform, persuade, or remind).

With traditional media, there is almost always a lag between the placement of an ad and measures of effectiveness. Advertisers must complete research to determine if traditional ads were seen and if there was any result from the ads. The Web can instantly track actual exposure to an advertisement. Because of this instant feedback, advertisers are changing how they pay for web ad placement. They are demanding *pay for performance* based on some type of advertising measure.

PERFORMANCE MEASURES

Advertisers want to determine the most cost-effective way to get their messages out to their target audiences. **Cost per thousand (CPM)** is the traditional payment measure used by advertisers. With CPM, the cost is based on the total number of users that can be reached with the medium. CPM can act as a standard of comparison across media outlets.

$$\text{CPM} = \frac{\text{Cost of creating the ad + Cost of placement in the medium}}{\text{Number of viewers in thousands}}$$

Traditional media report audience size based on internal or external *audits*, or examinations. Web sites are automated to report total and unique audiences. Web CPM rates are often higher than those for other media. However, ability to reach a target market can make the Web cost effective.

Online advertisers can link consumer actions to ad viewing. This ability has brought about new payment systems based on performance. Pay for performance shifts the risk of advertising to the medium. If the medium cannot provide results, it does not get paid. In 2002, 45 percent of ad campaigns used cost per thousand, 21 percent used performance-based measures, and 34 percent used a combination of measures. Online advertising pay-for-performance options include

- **Cost per click (CPC)** With CPC, charges are based on the number of viewers clicking through from a hypermedia page.
- **Cost per action (CPA)** With CPA, the cost is based on the number of viewers taking some specific action, such as making a purchase.
- **Cost per lead (CPL)** With CPL, the cost is based on the number of leads that register with the site because of seeing the ad.
- **Cost per acquisition (CPA)** With CPA, the advertiser pays only when a customer makes an acquisition (or purchase).

DVRs (digital video recorders) are replacing VCRs in the home. A DVR allows a viewer to pause a live broadcast, record to a hard drive, and eliminate TV commercials. It is expected that 20 percent of homes will have a DVR by 2007. This will dramatically change the effectiveness of TV commercials and the revenue system for television broadcasts. The television advertising industry could lose $5.5 billion in revenue.

THINK CRITICALLY

1. **Speculate on the future of traditional television advertising if ads can be skipped.**
2. **Devise a strategy to advertise your product on television when the audience can skip ads.**
3. **Recommend replacement media for television advertisements.**

AD BLOCKING

A shift in power from businesses to consumers is aided by *ad-blocking software*. Consumers can buy filters that check files and file types against a list to block ads, interstitials, or animated banners. Businesses often use ad-blocking software to improve network speed and performance. Some advertisers have retaliated by blocking individuals who use ad-blocking software.

While ad-blocking software may be appealing to some web surfers, they must keep in mind that advertising supports many sites. Without users viewing ads, the sites will not get paid and may be forced to close.

CAMPAIGNS

An advertising campaign combines strategy and media to reach goals. One study investigated how companies develop advertising campaigns. The study looked at how companies build awareness and enhance learning and how their customers make purchase decisions. Television and word of mouth were strongest in building awareness for most products. Hypermedia had the greatest impact on learning and purchase decisions.

The Interactive Advertising Bureau reported on a study that tested the effectiveness of two ad formats—floating ads and standard banners. The campaign was for McDonald's. It was developed by the media agency of Bandy·Carroll·Hellige Advertising. The campaign was entitled "Kentucky Derby Promotion." It included traditional media and had a goal of generating an opt-in e-mail list for future marketing efforts. The target audience was adults ages 18–49. Web results were tracked through web-tracking software. The floating ads received 48,872 total **impressions** (number of views) over three weeks with a 6.4 percent click-through rate. Of those who clicked through, 32.6 percent registered and 15 percent opted-in for future promotions. The traditional banner ads received 1,050,697 total impressions, but only a .01 percent response rate. Floating ads outperformed banner ads by 64,000 percent in obtaining click-throughs.

List and explain three online advertising performance measures.

•CPC-are based on the number of views

•CPA-is based on number of views taking some specific action

CPL- the number of leads

Elizabeth accepted an internship for the summer with an advertising agency in New York City. She is working for the Interactive Marketing Director. She assists advertising and marketing professionals with special projects. Her job duties include gathering information for evaluating the results of online campaigns, testing various search engine marketing alternatives, and assisting with proposals and presentations. Elizabeth is excited because she will also be making a sales presentation to a client in an attempt to land an online advertising account.

Eventually, Elizabeth wants a career as an *Interactive Marketing Director*. She is learning that the position involves more than just creating ads. The position involves developing communication strategies, recommending placement of ads, and evaluating the results of campaigns.

THINK CRITICALLY

1. **Evaluate the position of Interactive Marketing Director. Identify the skills that Elizabeth will need to develop in order to succeed in this position.**
2. **Assume that you are going to make the presentation to the client to land the online advertising account. Develop an outline of the major reasons why the client should hire your company as its advertising agency.**

LOGGING OFF

UNDERSTAND MARKETING CONCEPTS

Circle the best answer for each of the following questions.

1. Ads that automatically load and display content as a web site is brought up are called
   a. banner ads.
   b. pop-ups.
   c. auto ads.
   d. click-throughs.
2. The traditional payment measure used by advertisers is
   a. CPM.
   b. CPC.
   c. CPA.
   d. CPL.

THINK CRITICALLY

Answer the following questions as completely as possible. If necessary, use a separate sheet of paper.

3. **Communication** You are placing an ad for your business on a web site. Develop an argument to justify pay for performance instead of pay for placement. Specify advantages to both your business and the site.

____

____

____

____

____

____

4. Ad blocking can limit a business's ability to communicate with its target audience. Compare and contrast the pros and cons of ad blocking for the advertiser, the web site that hosts the ads, and the customer.

____

____

____

____

____

____

REVIEW

REVIEW E-COMMERCE MARKETING CONCEPTS

Write the letter of the term that matches each definition. Some terms will not be used.

a. advertising
b. affiliate marketing programs
c. AIDA
d. banner ads
e. click-through rate (CTR)
f. cookie
g. cost per thousand (CPM)
h. impressions
i. integrated marketing-communication strategy
j. pop-up ads
k. promotional mix
l. search engines
m. sponsorship
n. top of the search

____ 1. Sites listed at the beginning of search engine results

____ 2. Examine databases for requested information and then provide links to that information

____ 3. Includes advertising, personal selling, sales promotions, and hypermedia

____ 4. A short code that resides in the user's browser and tells a site who is visiting

____ 5. Integrates a company's brand into the editorial content of a web page

____ 6. Brings together multiple media to reach desired goals

____ 7. Include content sites that provide links to commerce sites

____ 8. Promotional placement in a medium

____ 9. Automatically load and display content as a web site is brought up

____10. Percentage of people who click through to another site

____11. The number of views an online ad receives

____12. Ads on a web site that act like placement ads in print media

____13. The traditional payment measure used by advertisers

Circle the best answer.

14. Which of the following is *not* a performance-based payment option?
    a. cost per thousand (CPM)
    b. cost per action (CPA)
    c. cost per lead (CPL)
    d. cost per click (CPC)

15. A site is most likely to end up at the "top of the search" when the site
    a. has a large number of links from other sites.
    b. routinely receives a large number of hits.
    c. belongs to a company that pays the search site for a top position.
    d. includes a large number of keywords.

THINK CRITICALLY

16. An integrated marketing-communication strategy uses multiple media to reach goals. Write a strategy indicating how a movie theater could use traditional media and hypermedia to reach its communication goals.

17. Refer to Activity 16. On poster board, develop a promotional mix and AIDA matrix as shown in Figure 11.1. Explain how each of the media you have recommended reaches AIDA goals.

18. Develop a strategy for a movie theater using only hypermedia to gain the attention of its target market. List the strengths and weaknesses of this approach. Describe the role that personalization would play in this strategy.

MAKE CONNECTIONS

19. **TECHNOLOGY** Visit the Interactive Advertising Bureau web site. Make a list of the information offered by this bureau. State how this information could help you develop an interactive advertising campaign.

20. **RESEARCH** Visit the *Advertising Age* web site. Click on the Interactive News link. Read one of the interactive news articles. Outline how interactive media was used in the described promotional campaign. Specify the goals set by the business and how it measured those goals.

21. **TECHNOLOGY** Go to your favorite search engine and run a search on your favorite sport. Specify the types of sites at the top of the search results. How far down in the search results do you need to go to find a small business site? Speculate on why some businesses made it to the top of the search. Were these paid placements?

22. **TECHNOLOGY** Assume that you are working on the next-generation Internet. The future Internet will provide broadband communication to wireless devices. Speculate on how the promotional mix will change. Develop a strategy to achieve promotional goals with this new technology.

23. **MARKETING MATH** Your manager has set a promotional goal of obtaining 1,000 click-throughs to your business's web site. You know the average CTR for banner ads is 1 percent. The CTR for personalized e-mail is 25 percent. The CPM rate for banner ads is $15. The CPM rate for personalized e-mail is $250. Which strategy is more cost effective?

This part of the project will focus on your business's promotional goals.

Work with your team members to complete the following activities.

1. Identify specific promotional goals for your business. Are you looking to inform, persuade, or remind the target audience? Do you want to gain attention, interest, desire, or action? If you want action, specify the type of action you are seeking, such as opting-in or purchasing.
2. Develop a poster showing the promotional mix and AIDA matrix for your business to reach its goals. Use Figure 11.1 as a guide. Indicate the specific media you will use for each cell. For example, specify how you will use newspapers, radio, e-mail, and web advertising. In each cell, indicate the specific strategy you will use, such as design or personalization.
3. State how your business prefers to pay for its ads. Do you want payment based on CPM or performance-based measures? Specify which media will allow you to pay based on performance.

THE INCREASING POPULARITY OF POLITICAL E-MARKETING

More than 50 percent of Americans use the Internet. Politicians realize the benefits of online interaction. The Internet has served as a useful resource to win elections, raise funds, recruit volunteers, and kill legislation. Politicians use the Internet to send important information to thousands of constituents or to members of special interest groups with just one click of the mouse.

E-marketing is useful for gathering the required number of signatures on petitions to effect change. California residents, for example, can go online and fill out a form requesting that a petition be mailed to them.

California's 2003 special election to recall Governor Gray Davis presented a unique political situation. Once a petition containing enough signatures of registered voters was submitted, the recall election was approved. Almost immediately, a windfall of candidates filed the papers and paid the entry fee to run for governor. One of the more recognized names on the list of candidates was Arnold Schwarzenegger.

The recall election was approved in August. The election was scheduled for the first week in November. There was little time for candidates to campaign. This political scenario presented a good case for an e-marketing campaign. Schwarzenegger won the recall race and replaced Gray Davis as the new governor of California.

Senator Bob Dole and Senator John Kerrey used the Internet to land one-third of their volunteers for the 1996 election. Jesse Ventura was elected governor of Minnesota in 1998 with a three to four percent margin of victory. Use of the Internet and advice from business leaders helped Ventura capture the additional three to four percent he needed to win the election.

Senator John McCain knows the importance of political e-marketing. The 2000 presidential candidate raised more than $1.4 million in less than three days using the Internet. Governor Howard Dean of Vermont can attribute much of his early success in the 2004 Democratic race for President to political e-marketing. Voting over the Internet is a distinct possibility for future elections.

Think Critically

1. **Why has e-marketing become a popular means of communication for politicians?**
2. **What can political candidates do electronically on election day to encourage more citizens to vote?**
3. **What security issue would need to be tackled before online voting could be offered?**
4. **Politics can be dirty. What precautions should be taken when designing a candidate's web site?**

BUSINESS SERVICES MARKETING

One year ago, Von Maur Department Store developed a web site to sell its merchandise. Von Maur is most noted for high-quality clothing. Alterations and gift wrap are free for Von Maur credit-card customers. The Von Maur credit card is interest-free. All credit-card purchases must be paid during a four-month period at a predetermined rate based upon the amount charged.

Von Maur has just conducted a customer survey to determine the first-year success of its e-marketing efforts. The results of the survey are not as positive as management had expected.

Most customers indicated that they had to click too many links to complete a transaction. Some were concerned about inputting credit-card information to make a purchase. Customers also didn't feel that they were getting an accurate depiction of the clothing from the pictures displayed on the web site.

You have been hired to give Von Maur ideas to increase customer use of its web site. You must give management suggestions to simplify the online-purchasing process. Also, you must suggest improvements for the presentation of clothing sold online by the store.

Von Maur wants to increase its base of credit-card customers. You must create a strategy to increase the number of credit-card applications received over the Web. A promotion should be developed to encourage offline customers to visit the store's web site.

Performance Indicators Evaluated

- Understand the opportunities and challenges faced by Von Maur Department Store.
- Explain the importance of a department store selling its merchandise both online and offline.
- Explain the importance of maintaining high-quality customer service when conducting e-commerce.
- Describe the information to be included on Von Maur's web site.
- Explain why consumers are reluctant to make purchases over the Internet and how to overcome this hesitancy.
- Describe how customers will get a better depiction of Von Maur's clothing on the Internet.

Go to the DECA web site for more detailed information.

1. Why is e-commerce a good venue to help Von Maur reach its goals?
2. What special promotion could be offered to encourage Von Maur customers to use their credit cards for online purchases?
3. Why is customer service a big issue in Von Maur's case?
4. How can Internet customers be assured that they are getting the level of service given to in-store customers?

www.deca.org/publications/HS_Guide/guidetoc.html

CHAPTER 12
DEVELOPING AN E-COMMERCE BUSINESS

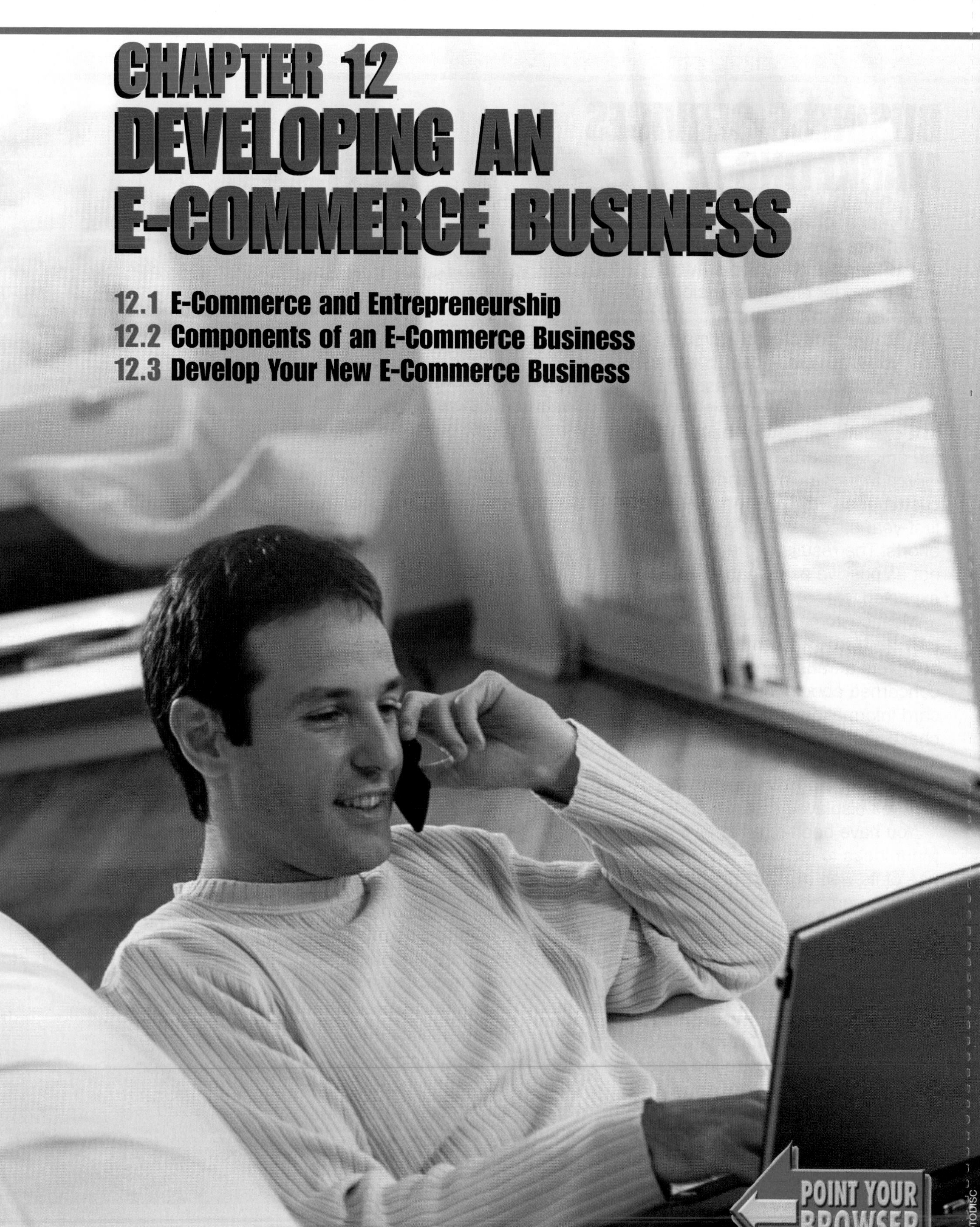

LOCAL TO WORLDWIDE DELIVERY

The American Messenger Company opened in Seattle in 1907. It offered delivery services from department stores to customers. It also offered messenger services to businesses and the general public. Messenger services could be found in most towns and cities in the late 1800s and early 1900s, but few exist today. You can still make deliveries using the American Messenger Company. However, you will know it by the name it took in 1919—United Parcel Service (UPS).

Most small businesses never achieve the growth or success of UPS. Throughout its history, UPS followed a careful plan of expanding and changing to meet customer needs. It has been at the forefront of technology used to collect millions of packages and quickly distribute them to their final destinations.

Today, UPS employs over 350,000 people worldwide. Employees distribute 3.5 billion packages annually in 200 countries using 152,000 trucks and 250 airplanes. The company has a sophisticated worldwide computer network connected by fiber optics and satellites. Each delivery person accesses the network through a DIAD, or delivery information acquisition device. The company and customer can track a package from pickup to final delivery.

Parcel distribution is a competitive business. Companies must be fast, efficient, and constantly focused on customer service.

THINK CRITICALLY

1. What are some reasons that UPS has succeeded for almost a century?
2. What future changes in parcel delivery and technology do you predict will affect UPS's success?

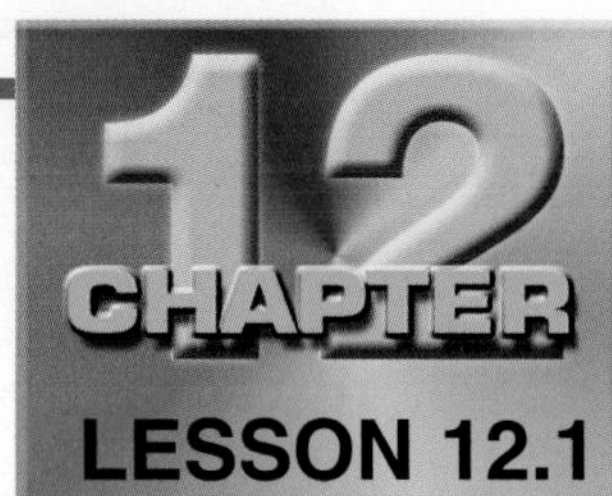

E-COMMERCE AND ENTREPRENEURSHIP

Describe success factors for an e-commerce business.

Identify e-commerce entrepreneurship opportunities.

LOGGING ON

In only a decade, the Internet has become an important resource for individuals and businesses. Up to 20 percent of people in the United States view the Internet as the most essential medium in their lives. Of 12- to 34-year-olds, 46 percent rate the Internet as most essential. Over a third of those surveyed describe it as the most "cool and exciting" medium and give it a higher rating than television.

Broadband and wireless connections, streaming media, and handheld Internet devices make the Web an even more useful resource. As consumers switch to these technologies, their time spent on the Internet increases. Consumers spend more money and are increasingly willing to buy subscriptions from Internet content providers.

Work with a partner. Discuss why consumers have accepted the Internet so quickly as an important medium in their lives. Assume you are considering the development of a new business. How can you turn the Internet's widespread acceptance into an advantage?

E-COMMERCE BUSINESSES

Starting a new business has never been easier and less expensive than with the use of the Internet. All that is needed is a low-cost computer with a high-speed Internet connection. Web design software and a low-cost distribution process are enough for you to open your virtual business. Start-up can be even simpler if you sell your products through an established online auction service such as eBay.

The risks of entrepreneurship are as great or greater with an e-commerce business as they are with a traditional brick-and-mortar business. While the five-year failure rate of all new businesses is nearly 50 percent, over 80 percent of the Internet businesses started in the mid-1990s no longer exist. The lesson learned is that planning and management are critical for e-commerce businesses. You can easily attract many prospective customers with the Internet. However, building a successful e-commerce company requires as much knowledge of business, marketing, and management as with a traditional company. It requires an even greater understanding of technology.

©GETTY IMAGES/PHOTODISC

MOVING TO ENTREPRENEURSHIP

An **entrepreneur** is a person who organizes, operates, and assumes the risk for a business venture. Most entrepreneurs start a business with the goal of making a profit. The challenge of personal responsibility and control of the new organization also excites them. First-time entrepreneurs usually start a business based on their personal interests or skills. These business owners are doing work they enjoy while leading the development of a new business.

Many e-commerce entrepreneurs were innovators in the use of the Internet. They were among the first to develop their own web pages, use broadband and multimedia programs, and make purchases from online companies. Starting an e-commerce business is a logical extension of being an early Internet enthusiast.

Coding and online processing errors are costing Internet businesses an average of $275 in lost sales per error. Of web sites checked, 62 percent experienced some type of problem that prevented customers from completing a purchase. The errors included blank pages, wrong pages, or incorrect items placed in the shopping cart.

SUCCESS FACTORS

There are several factors that contribute to a successful e-commerce business. The first is the entrepreneur. Second are customers who need a product or service. Third is a product or service that offers a value proposition.

1. **The Owner** A person who starts an e-commerce business must have interest, enthusiasm, and a willingness to take risks in a new business environment. The entrepreneur must be willing to commit long hours in order to plan, start, and build the business. The new business owner will need a general understanding of business operations and Internet technology. In addition, the entrepreneur should seek advice from others who have expertise in marketing, finance, law, technology, and other aspects of business operations and management. One factor that has led to many entrepreneurs' failure is the lack of willingness to seek help and expertise from others.
2. **Customer Base** To be successful, the e-commerce business must identify its target customer base. A business cannot be successful unless its products and services are sold. The new Internet enterprise must attract customers with needs that can be satisfied with the company's products and services. Customers should be regular Internet users who are comfortable purchasing online.
3. **Value Proposition** The final success factor is the company's value proposition. A **value proposition** is the complete offerings of the business, designed to meet customer needs better than other choices. Target customers may already purchase similar products and services from other businesses. In order to win them over, the new business must offer a marketing mix (product, distribution, price, and promotion) that customers see as a greater value than their current choices.

©GETTY IMAGES/PHOTODISC

What are three success factors for a new e-commerce business?

• The Owner • Customer Base

• Value Proposition

E-COMMERCE OPPORTUNITIES

Many new entrepreneurs have almost no business experience. They often do not realize the opportunities that exist. Since most people use the Internet as consumers, new entrepreneurs often think only of starting a consumer-to-consumer (C-to-C) or business-to-consumer (B-to-C) company. While there are certainly opportunities in those areas, the greatest amount of e-commerce occurs in the business-to-business (B-to-B) market. Additionally, serving as an e-commerce facilitator is a role in great demand.

Free shipping attracts customers to a business. In a survey of consumer shopping, Internet users reported that free handling and delivery was the promotion most likely to encourage them to purchase online. In fact, over half reported that they had purchased at a local retail store rather than online to avoid shipping charges. Just under 50 percent reported that they had switched from one online business to another because of high shipping and handling charges.

THINK CRITICALLY

1. **Why are many consumers willing to travel to a store to purchase a product rather than pay shipping costs to an Internet business?**
2. **Why are shipping costs such an important factor in online purchasing?**

CONSUMER-TO-CONSUMER

Selling from one consumer to another can be accomplished in three ways. The easiest way to get into e-commerce is to let established businesses help you sell your products. An *auction site* brings consumers together as buyers and sellers. Sellers add written descriptions and digital photographs of their products to the site using the technology provided by the auction company. The auction company will have specific procedures and policies for bidding, selling, and paying. The company may also help sellers ship products to buyers.

Another C-to-C option is a *shopping mall site*. Most Internet shopping malls promote the products of a number of competing businesses in a merchandise category. There are shopping mall sites for items such as children's toys, electronics, vacations, and apparel. The malls make it easy for consumers to locate and compare businesses and their offerings.

An entrepreneur can start a C-to-C business on a part-time basis by developing a *personal web site* and promoting products on the site. Orders may be received by telephone, fax, mail, or one of the inexpensive shopping cart services offered by several ISPs.

BUSINESS-TO-CONSUMER

©GETTY IMAGES/PHOTODISC

Business-to-consumer Internet businesses are similar to C-to-C businesses in that they direct efforts primarily toward final consumers. The difference is that, with a B-to-C business, the entrepreneur commits to form and operate a full-time business rather than to engage in a part-time sales activity. Most B-to-C e-commerce entrepreneurs sell products through their own business web sites. They also may promote their products through online shopping malls or other businesses' retail web sites.

BUSINESS-TO-BUSINESS

The largest volume of Internet sales occurs in business-to-business markets. However, few B-to-B businesses currently use an Internet-only strategy. It is more common that a brick-and-mortar business extends its marketing by allowing customers to purchase online. As companies become more comfortable with conducting business online, opportunities for Internet-only businesses will grow. The growth of e-commerce will make it easier to move into the B-to-B market. E-commerce allows easy access to customers at greater distances. It also requires less investment in facilities and personnel. Most B-to-B companies sell directly to their customers. There are a growing number of Internet wholesalers and manufacturers' representatives who sell and distribute the products of several B-to-B companies to other businesses.

E-COMMERCE FACILITATORS

Many specialized businesses participate in traditional distribution channels. They provide a range of services from sales and transportation to customer billing and collection. Specialized businesses have evolved because they provide services that primary businesses do not want to perform or cannot perform as efficiently as a specialist. E-commerce requires technologies and business processes that traditional companies have not used in the past. Companies often turn to e-commerce specialists to provide many of the activities needed to serve online customers. An **e-commerce facilitator** provides one or more important activities that support the e-commerce strategies of other businesses.

E-commerce facilitators can be specialized, offering server space, security, web design, and site management. Others provide traditional services such as shipping, billing, or payment processing, but they use Internet technologies to process information or to facilitate communication between buyers and sellers. The number of full-service e-commerce facilitators is growing. They may work with sellers to manage entire Internet businesses, or sellers can contract for only a few of the services offered.

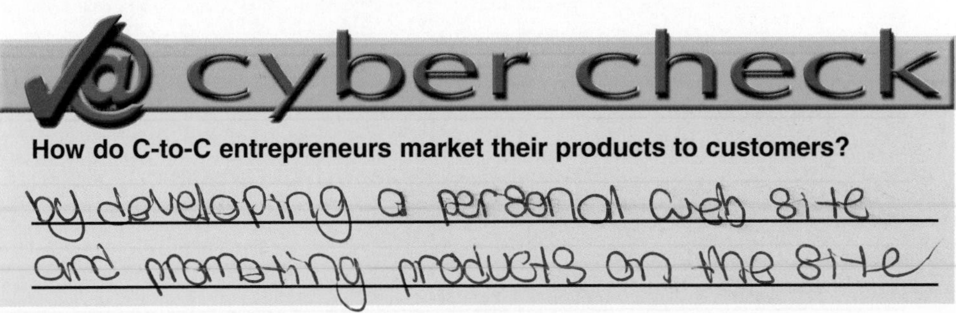

How do C-to-C entrepreneurs market their products to customers?

by developing a personal web site and promoting products on the site

LOGGING OFF

UNDERSTAND MARKETING CONCEPTS

Circle the best answer for each of the following questions.

1. The complete offerings of the business, designed to meet customer needs better than other choices, is a(n)
   a. marketing mix.
   b. value proposition.
   c. e-commerce business.
   d. product or service.
2. The largest volume of Internet sales occurs in
   a. business-to-consumer markets.
   b. e-commerce facilitator markets.
   c. consumer-to-consumer markets.
   d. business-to-business markets.

THINK CRITICALLY

Answer the following questions as completely as possible. If necessary, use a separate sheet of paper.

3. You have decided to start an e-commerce business that designs and sells customized stationery and business cards. Identify and provide detailed descriptions of C-to-C, B-to-C, and B-to-B opportunities for the new business. How would you decide which presents the best opportunity?

____

____

____

____

____

____

4. **Technology** Use the Internet to find at least three companies that could be considered e-commerce facilitators. Prepare a chart that compares the services of the businesses.

____

____

____

____

____

COMPONENTS OF AN E-COMMERCE BUSINESS

LOGGING ON

The U.S. Small Business Administration (SBA) is working with eBay to provide resources to help small businesses succeed. eBay is a logical way for the SBA to reach small businesses. Over 150,000 people are estimated to run full- or part-time businesses selling products through eBay. In addition, over 20 million eBay buyers and sellers are employed in small businesses.

The relationship will provide links from eBay to SBA information. The SBA gives guidance in the areas of financial assistance and small business management. It also supplies help in obtaining government contracts and reaching international markets. Small business owners will be able to access troubleshooting help through eBay, including direct advice from retired executives.

Work with a partner. Discuss why the SBA would want to work with eBay even though it has its own web site and online resources. How will eBay benefit from its relationship with the SBA?

Describe important business relationships.

Identify the key technology requirements for an e-commerce business.

ROLES AND RELATIONSHIPS

As an entrepreneur, you cannot operate in isolation. Many others will be a part of your success. Figure 12.1 illustrates important business relationships.

THE BUSINESS

The e-commerce business first determines the products and services that it will produce or purchase for resale. It then researches and selects its target market. It determines the companies that will be a part of its supply chain and forges relationships with those businesses. It then develops the production, marketing, management, and operations procedures needed to serve customers.

Figure 12.1
Relationships of Successful E-Commerce Businesses

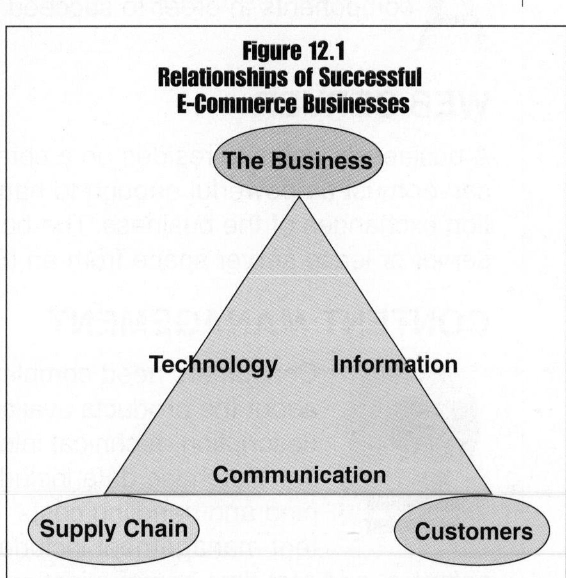

Business executives rely on the Internet for information. A recent survey revealed that 51 percent named the Web as their most important business information resource, topping newspapers, magazines, and television.

CUSTOMERS

Customers identify their needs and then seek products and services that will satisfy them. They research and analyze products, services, and businesses to determine the best choices. They purchase the products and services, and then determine if their choices provide satisfaction.

SUPPLY CHAIN

Other companies help the business meet customer needs. If the business is a manufacturer, distributors and companies that provide equipment, materials, and supplies will be parts of the chain. In e-commerce, technology and web services companies also may participate.

INFORMATION, TECHNOLOGY, AND COMMUNICATION

Seamless interaction and perpetual communication among the business, supply chain, and customers is crucial. Data-collection and information-exchange procedures must be developed. Information must be available, yet secure. Reliable technology must deliver needed services.

@cyber check

Name the participants in a successful e-commerce business.

• Customers • information, technology and comm

• supply chain • the business

E-COMMERCE TECHNOLOGY

An e-commerce business needs several important technology components in order to succeed.

WEB SERVER

A business's web site resides on a computer called a **web server**. The server must be powerful enough to handle the communication and information exchanges of the business. The business can own and manage the server or lease server space from an ISP or a web-hosting company.

CONTENT MANAGEMENT

Consumers need complete, understandable information about the products available for sale. Product data include a description, technical information, and benefits for each product. Purchase data include inventory information, price, shipping and handling costs, and taxes. The technology for content management includes relational databases, multimedia software, and real-time communication platforms to respond to customers.

SHOPPING CART

A shopping cart is a virtual location where a customer places items to be purchased. The shopping cart manages the checkout process. It completes the order, collects payment information, and obtains data needed to process and ship the order. The customer can add and delete items and change the quantity ordered. The cart shows item prices and updates the total cost of the order, including taxes and shipping, as the customer adds to it. The cart efficiently completes the order when the customer finishes shopping.

PAYMENT PROCESSING

Online payment processing involves the business, the customer, a payment-processing company, and the banks of the customer and the business. The business wants to simplify the process but ensure receipt of payment and prevent fraud. The customer wants assurance that information provided online is secure and that payment is being made to a legitimate company. The payment-processing company must confirm that payment information is valid and approve the order for processing. Funds are transferred from the customer's bank to the business's bank.

DATA WAREHOUSE

Data collected, stored, and analyzed in e-commerce businesses are product data, marketing data, customer data, and supply-chain data. Various types of data are stored in separate systems, each with its own database and software. Newer systems integrate all types of data. Data-mining software searches and analyzes the information.

ENTERPRISE APPLICATION INTEGRATION

Procedures and resources needed to operate an e-commerce business are immense. New technologies integrate systems, making activities easier, more reliable, and less expensive. Running an e-commerce business requires technical knowledge and investment in the right hardware and software. If the business doesn't want to control the system, it can hire another company to manage the e-commerce process.

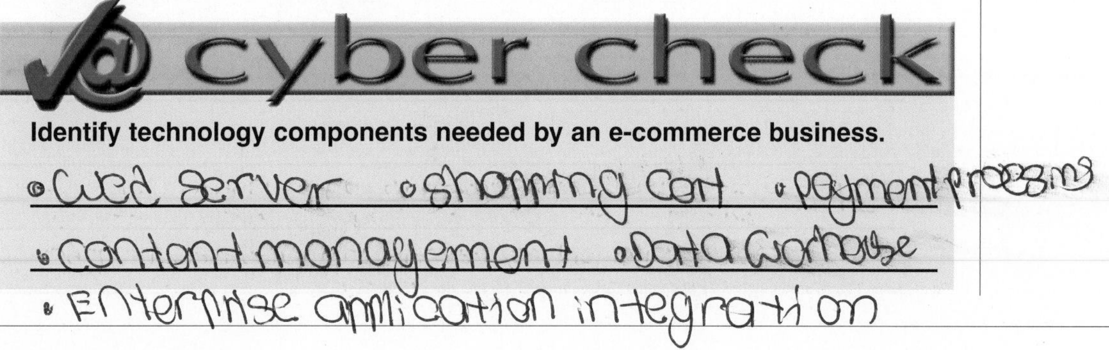

Identify technology components needed by an e-commerce business.

E-MARKETING MYTHS

Is the Internet an effective medium for formal education? Estimated spending for e-learning will grow from $10 billion in 2002 to nearly $100 billion by 2005. It is predicted that 25 percent of corporate training will be completed online in the next few years. Currently, one-third of public schools offer some type of distance learning for their students. Nearly half provide online learning for the professional development of their teachers.

THINK CRITICALLY

1. **What are the strengths and weaknesses of online learning?**
2. **What recommendations would you make to improve the quality of online educational programs?**
3. **Would you consider taking an online course in college? Why or why not?**

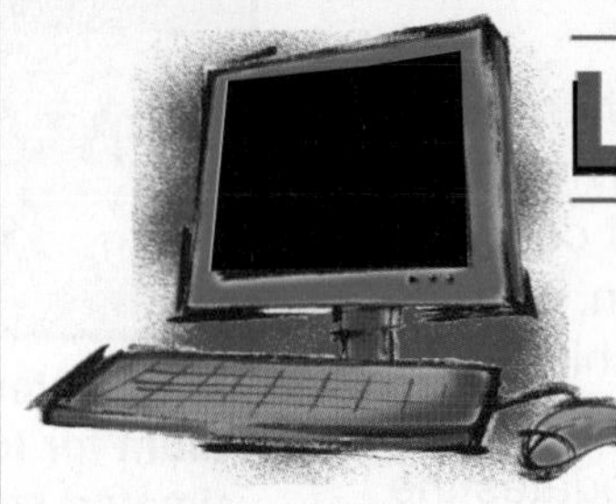

LOGGING OFF

UNDERSTAND MARKETING CONCEPTS

Circle the best answer for each of the following questions.

1. Which business would *not* be a part of a supply chain?
   a. a materials supplier
   b. a delivery company that ships products to customers
   c. a technology company that manages a company's web site
   d. a competitor

2. Online payment processing involves
   a. a payment-processing company.
   b. the customer.
   c. the business.
   d. all of the above

THINK CRITICALLY

Answer the following questions as completely as possible. If necessary, use a separate sheet of paper.

3. **Technology** Search the Internet to identify a new technology that is increasing the security of payment transactions on the Internet. Write a short report describing the technology and the benefits it offers.

4. **Marketing Math** An entrepreneur is deciding whether to own and manage a web server or pay another company to host the business's web site. Ownership would require the entrepreneur to spend $12,000 on hardware, $8,700 on software, and $83,000 a year for the salary and benefits of an employee to manage the technology. The monthly cost for another company to manage the web server would be $8,100. Compare the annual cost of each alternative. What other factors should the entrepreneur consider when making the decision? Which would you recommend choosing?

DEVELOP YOUR NEW E-COMMERCE BUSINESS

LESSON 12.3

LOGGING ON

Hewlett-Packard recently displayed a new product to enhance the online shopping experience. Called VEDA (virtual environment design automation), the product uses a visualization database that creates a 3-D online store. Customers view the front of the store on their monitors, enter the door, and take a virtual tour by moving the mouse. They can visit any department and pick up items and examine them. H-P's goal is to create a user-friendly technology that will add realism to the online shopping experience.

Work with a partner. Discuss the benefits of the 3-D shopping experience that VEDA will provide. Why would a company known for its computers and printers want to develop software to support e-commerce businesses?

Explain the steps for starting an e-commerce business.

Discuss the value of a written business plan.

STARTING AN E-COMMERCE BUSINESS

If you want to be an e-commerce entrepreneur, it is never too early to start planning. It is possible to start a business with limited resources if you are committed to the idea and plan carefully. You must be willing to invest your time to learn about business management, marketing, and e-commerce. Starting a small e-commerce business involves the steps shown in Figure 12.2.

DETERMINE YOUR PURPOSE

A web site can serve many purposes. It can provide information, offer visitor interaction with the site, or represent a fully integrated business. A *fully integrated web site*, through which a customer can complete the entire purchasing transaction online, is more complex and expensive to maintain.

STUDY YOUR CUSTOMERS

The marketing concept requires that you identify target customers and understand them in order to meet their needs. It is especially important to identify customers who are comfortable participating in e-commerce.

Figure 12.2
Establishing an E-commerce Business

1. **Determine the purpose of your business.**
2. **Study your target customers, including their needs and Internet abilities.**
3. **Plan your online business strategy.**
4. **Obtain a web server and domain name.**
5. **Develop order-processing and customer-service procedures.**
6. **Design the web site.**
7. **Advertise your online business.**
8. **Open for business.**

PLAN YOUR STRATEGY

Will you produce and market your own products, resell the products of others, or operate an online service business? A successful online business needs an effective supply chain with responsibilities assigned for all production and marketing activities. A channel captain should be identified to lead the efforts. A complete marketing mix that provides a unique value proposition must be developed.

OBTAIN YOUR BUSINESS DOMAIN

A location and a name are necessary for any company, including an e-commerce business. The physical location of an e-commerce business is the web server. People will contact your business using the *domain name*, or unique Internet address. You must decide whether you will own and maintain a web server or hire a web-hosting service. You should select and apply for a unique domain name that is easily recalled. The name should convey an appropriate image of your business. The domain name registration must be renewed yearly.

DEVELOP BUSINESS PROCEDURES

How will prospective customers acquire information, navigate the web site, and obtain help in making decisions? How will they place orders, check order status, and obtain customer service? How will orders be processed and delivered? How can customers return products if necessary? Each of these questions represents a critical business process that will affect the success or failure of your company.

DESIGN THE SITE

You may want to develop your business web site before you do other planning. However, you will not know what content to include, how to organize the site, and what technology is required until the e-commerce business is well planned. Your web site must be inviting, attractive, complete, and easy to use. Content must load rapidly, and all links must work. Information should be updated regularly. Customers should be able to easily contact the company and obtain assistance whenever they are using your web site.

VIRTUAL VIEWPOINTS

Should Girl Scouts use the Internet to sell cookies during its annual fundraising drive? Apparently, e-commerce is not yet viewed as an appropriate way for the Scouts to develop money-management, marketing, and communications skills. The National Board of Directors of Girl Scouts has a policy that prohibits members from using a personal web site or an Internet auction site to sell any products it sponsors.

You can buy Girl Scout cookies on auction sites such as eBay. Some appear to be from people who have purchased the cookies from a Girl Scout and are reselling them. Others are listings by parents who are helping their children meet sales goals.

THINK CRITICALLY

1. **What are possible reasons that Girl Scouts does not want its members to use the Internet to sell its products?**
2. **Write a short statement supporting or opposing the National Board policy.**

ADVERTISE

Prospective customers must be aware of your business before they can visit your web site. Be sure to register your business with the major search engines such as Google, Yahoo!, and Excite. Use meaningful keywords that will connect your business to appropriate customer search queries. Place advertising on other web sites where your target market makes regular visits.

OPEN FOR BUSINESS

After all of your careful planning, you are finally ready to open your new e-business. This is not a time to sit back and wait for customers. You need to ensure that technology is working, track web-site visitors, check competitor activities, and keep the site up to date. Work closely with channel members. Monitor order processing and customer service. Gather data, and use the information to update your e-business strategies. You may work harder than you ever have before. However, you will experience the pleasure of entrepreneurship as you watch your business grow and plan for its future.

Blogs (short for web logs) are publicly accessible, online, personal journals of individuals. Blogs have become a popular form of self-expression with nearly one million people maintaining active blogs on public web sites.

Why should you wait to develop your web site until much of the planning for your e-commerce business is completed?

____

____

PREPARING A BUSINESS PLAN

Starting a new e-business is complex. For the new entrepreneur, it is easy to forget important steps or fail to coordinate activities. Change occurs rapidly in all types of businesses but especially in e-commerce. It is critical to anticipate change and make necessary adjustments.

Successful entrepreneurs prepare and follow a business plan. A **business plan** is a written document that describes the nature of a business, its goals and objectives, and methods for achievement. The major parts of a business plan for an e-commerce business are outlined in Figure 12.3. Guidance in writing a business plan as well as sample plans for many types of businesses are provided on the Small Business Administration web site.

Figure 12.3
Sections of an E-commerce Business Plan

I. Description of the business
II. Business environment and competition
III. Business goals and objectives
IV. Production and operations plans
V. Technology requirements and management
VI. Marketing strategy—target market and marketing mix
VII. Supply-chain members and chain management
VIII. Three-year financial projections
IX. Financing requirements and plans
X. Supporting documents

The business plan has several purposes. It is presented to possible investors and to members of the supply chain. The business plan will help them understand the business and will build confidence in its potential. It will also serve as a short- and long-term guide for the business owner and other managers. The business plan will assist you in coordinating activities and progress checks to see if goals are being met. A business plan will make you more aware of the risks and complexities of your business. It also will make you more objective and confident in your day-to-day management responsibilities.

Identify the major sections of an e-commerce business plan.

Detemin your purpose

WORKING ONLINE

It seems that Gloria spends most of her time online, and she enjoys every minute of it. She is employed part-time as the webmaster for the Marketing Department at State University, where she is completing her undergraduate degree in business management.

Gloria volunteers at the Boys & Girls Club where she teaches after-school computer classes to students. She has formed a club for those students who have become computer enthusiasts. Gloria created a web site for the club where donated items are auctioned to raise funds. The site has raised nearly $10,000 in six months for the club.

Gloria's aunt owns and operates a decorating boutique. Gloria convinced her aunt that she needed a web site for the business. Gloria's aunt hired a consultant, Pierre LaBeau, to design the store's web site. LaBeau allowed Gloria to help with the web design. Since that project ended, LaBeau has hired Gloria to work on several other projects. She has become quite comfortable with e-commerce technology and several sophisticated software programs.

Gloria wants to work in some aspect of e-commerce after graduation. Since taking an entrepreneurship class as a part of her course work, she is interested in starting her own business. However, she recognizes the high failure rate of new businesses. Gloria is not confident she has the skills or experience needed to be a successful *entrepreneur*.

THINK CRITICALLY

1. **List the skills and personal characteristics that entrepreneurs need.**
2. **Based on the information you read, do you believe Gloria will be ready to start her own business when she graduates? Why or why not?**
3. **Given Gloria's education and experience, what types of businesses should she consider starting?**

LOGGING OFF

UNDERSTAND MARKETING CONCEPTS

Circle the best answer for each of the following questions.

1. Which of the following types of web sites is the most complex and expensive to maintain?
   a. interactive
   b. informational
   c. integrated
   d. isolated
2. A written business plan would typically be useful to all *except*
   a. customers.
   b. business managers.
   c. investors.
   d. supply-chain members.

THINK CRITICALLY

Answer the following questions as completely as possible. If necessary, use a separate sheet of paper.

3. **Research** List the resources you believe would be necessary to start a small e-commerce web site. Using the Internet and other business information sources, gather data on the cost of each resource listed. Develop a spreadsheet that lists the items and their costs. Calculate the total cost of the resources you have listed.

4. **Communication** You have decided to open a new e-commerce business. You need $20,000 to open the business and operate it for nine months until it begins to be profitable. You have an uncle who is a successful small-business owner. Write a letter to your uncle asking him to invest in your business. Provide convincing reasons why he should invest.

REVIEW

REVIEW E-COMMERCE MARKETING CONCEPTS

Write the letter of the term that matches each definition. Some terms will not be used.

- a. business plan
- b. e-commerce facilitator
- c. entrepreneur
- d. value proposition
- e. web server

____ **1.** A specialist that provides one or more important activities that support the e-commerce strategies of other businesses

____ **2.** The complete offerings of the business, designed to meet customer needs better than other choices

____ **3.** A written document that describes the nature of a business, its goals and objectives, and methods for achievement

____ **4.** A person who organizes, operates, and assumes the risk for a business venture

Circle the best answer.

5. The failure rate for new e-commerce businesses is ______ that for traditional small businesses.
   a. higher than
   b. much lower than
   c. slightly lower than
   d. exactly the same as
6. Many e-commerce entrepreneurs were the first to
   a. purchase from online companies.
   b. use the Internet.
   c. develop their own web pages.
   d. all of the above
7. A factor that has led to many entrepreneurs' failure is
   a. planning before building the web site.
   b. starting a business based on personal interests.
   c. lack of willingness to seek help and expertise from others.
   d. identification of a target customer base.
8. The first step in starting a small e-commerce business is to
   a. develop the web site.
   b. determine the purpose of the business.
   c. identify a target market and its important needs.
   d. hire an e-commerce facilitator.
9. Successful entrepreneurs
   a. prepare a business plan.
   b. obtain a low-cost loan to finance the business.
   c. involve other family members.
   d. none of the above